Female Burial Traditions of the Chalcolithic and Early Bronze Age

A pilot study based on modern excavations

Alice Rogers

BAR British Series 581

2013

Published in 2016 by
BAR Publishing, Oxford

BAR British Series 581

Female Burial Traditions of the Chalcolithic and Early Bronze Age

ISBN 978 1 4073 1111 1

BAR Publishing is the trading name of British Archaeological Reports (Oxford) Ltd.
British Archaeological Reports was first incorporated in 1974 to publish the BAR
Series, International and British. In 1992 Hadrian Books Ltd became part of the BAR
group. This volume was originally published by Archaeopress in conjunction with
British Archaeological Reports (Oxford) Ltd / Hadrian Books Ltd, the Series principal
publisher, in 2013. This present volume is published by BAR Publishing, 2016.

Printed in England

BAR
PUBLISHING

BAR titles are available from:

BAR Publishing
122 Banbury Rd, Oxford, OX2 7BP, UK
EMAIL   info@barpublishing.com
PHONE   +44 (0)1865 310431
FAX   +44 (0)1865 316916
www.barpublishing.com

CONTENTS

LIST OF FIGURES

LIST OF TABLES

PREFACE AND ACKNOWLEDGEMENTS

This work is the result of a one year MRes dissertation which was based in the Department of Archaeology, University of Reading, supervised by Professors Richard Bradley and Bob Chapman. The MRes was funded by an Arts and Humanities Research Council "Studentship" award.

Though the main body of the text is fundamentally the same as that submitted for the MRes qualification, some additions have been made in the light of new research which was not available prior to the submission date.

The major acknowledgements are to Richard Bradley and Bob Chapman, whose help and support were invaluable. I must extend additional thanks to Richard, who not only read and re-read chapter drafts prior to the submission of the dissertation, but then consented to read it all over again to help me make the text suitable for publication.

I must also extend my thanks to Cambridge Archaeological Unit, Oxford Archaeology and Wessex Archaeology who allowed me access to their unpublished excavation reports. Especial thanks are extended to Natasha Dodwell and Alistair Barclay who made me feel very welcome when I visited their units.

Finally, I must also acknowledge the help and support provided by my parents who have always encouraged me to aim high and, furthermore, consented to be my proof-readers. However, all mistakes are my own.

ABSTRACT

This study examines how females were represented in British Chalcolithic and Early Bronze Age (2500 – 1500 BC) funerary practices. Chronology relating to the burial practices is studied, from the large scale of change over time through to the small scale of individual chronology; looking to see whether the deceased's age affects their representation. In contrast to previous approaches, this study moves beyond purely looking at the grave goods and instead places greater emphasis upon other features of the burials, such as location, form and method. As a result, the methodology used in this study examines the varied forms of this period's burials, yet still considers them as a unit.

1: INTRODUCTION

The Chalcolithic period in Britain (2500 - 2250 BC; Chapter Two) marks an horizon in burial practices where there is more emphasis upon the single burials of individuals. This contrasts to the earlier Neolithic burial practices taking place within communal monuments or those which were not archaeologically visible. Although single burials had been present during the fourth millennium BC, such as at Liffs Low, Derbyshire (Loveday and Barclay 2010), it was not until 2500 BC that there was an increase in numbers. The term single burial refers to a person buried as a single, recognisable unit (though not necessarily a complete person or someone isolated from others; see below). Due to the proliferation of burial traditions associated with recognisable individuals in the archaeological record, the Chalcolithic and Early Bronze Age graves have been used to infer social aspects of the past society, such as gender representation (Sofaer Derevenski 2002).

Much of this work resulted in highly masculine interpretations of the period, the so-called 'realm of kings and warriors' (Ashbee 1960: 172). Consequently, most archaeologists are probably able to name a male burial from this period, such as the Amesbury Archer (Fitzpatrick 2002) or the Bush Barrow burial (Hoare 1812), but would struggle to name a female one.

The androcentrism of this period is apparent when considering the range of identities and roles which have been postulated for the male burials. For example, Case (1977) lists three identities formulated on the Beaker burial evidence; the 'artisan' burials which are '*sometimes* of women'; the 'arrowhead burials' which are '*never* of women'; and the 'exceptionally rich burials… *invariably* of men' (*ibid*: 81, my emphasis). Brodie (1997) illustrates this phenomenon with the example of leatherworker graves. Though there are many cases of male leatherworker burials, similar female burials have not been recognised as such. For example, the burial at Garton Slack 163 is of a supposed female who is buried with a Beaker, a bronze awl, seven flint flakes and a pebble hammer, and yet is not considered as being a leatherworker despite the similarity with the male graves.

However, even the recognition of male leatherworker graves is not without difficulties. In Barrow 154, in the landscape surrounding the Ferrybridge henge, a male was buried with a Beaker vessel, flint plano-convex knife, scraper, three barbed-and-tanged arrowheads and a dagger, 2 bone spatulae and a bone awl. Though this burial has many aspects of the leatherworker assemblage (see Chapter Four), it was instead interpreted as a warrior/ hunter grave, whereby the spatulae were postulated as being flaking tools for the production of the arrowheads (Duncan in Roberts 2005). Though it is possible that this individual was both a warrior and a

leatherworker, the emphasis in the report is on the weapon rather than craft component of the burial.

In the Chalcolithic and Early Bronze Age the males are considered to have all the social power and wealth (Harrison 1980); so much so that the defining aspects of this period, such as metallurgy, are linked to males (i.e. Burgess and Shennan 1976). Females, however, are rarely mentioned, and, when they are, it is in relation to males, in terms of wives, daughters etc. (Brück 2009).

As a result of these androcentric interpretations of Chalcolithic and Early Bronze Age burial practices, it has been suggested that it is time for its reappraisal (Brück 2009). Brück (2009) drew attention to many female burials which do not sit comfortably within their prescribed categories, and called for a re-examination of the female burial evidence. This study is a response to that call.

1.1. This research

This research provides a re-evaluation of female burial traditions by examining the evidence presented in a selection of modern, rather than antiquarian, excavations. What is meant by burial traditions is the outcomes of choices that were made regarding what to do with the deceased's body. These choices encompassed aspects such as the method of corpse disposal employed, mainly cremation or inhumation (but it is also possible to detect excarnation), the location chosen for the remains, both in the sense of the form, i.e. a round barrow, a flat grave or a henge, and also the relationship of that deposit to previous ones. Choices also involved aspects such as the construction of the burial pit itself, i.e. size, materials used or whether it was a surface deposit, and also the choice, if any, of material inclusions introduced to the grave, be they grave goods or other remains.

This type of research is applicable to the Chalcolithic and Early Bronze Age for several reasons. Firstly, this period's burial rites are more definable deposits, rather than as part of a communal tomb collection (see above). This allows interpretation of discrete burial practices which can be associated with individuals. Secondly, there is a proliferation of types of burials during this period rather than one method of disposal of the dead. This suggests that conventions governed the use of the different rites for specific situations, or groups of people.

My study only examines the female burial evidence. This approach was chosen for several reasons. Firstly, it is in reaction to the masculinist discourse permeating this period (see above). However, I also wish to move beyond the limited binary oppositions created when examining both males and females (Baker 2000). Just comparing them with each other limits the range of interpretations that can be made as it confines all males into one category and all females into another, rather than exploring variation *within* sexes.

This study's aim is to look at Chalcolithic and Early Bronze Age female burial traditions examining several aspects of their representation. It examines how females were represented to see if any patterns emerge from the evidence. This involves testing whether the perceived wisdom of this period's female burial practices is still valid on modern excavated material, such as "females not being buried in the centre of barrows" or "provided with weapons". The research also attempts to detect any representational packages which could relate to female roles, such as leatherworking. This is a response to the varied roles males are postulated as having.

The different burial traditions through time are also discussed. A chronology of the period is assembled and the burials are assigned to periods, looking to see if time has an effect on the traditions. This approach is important when considering large periods of time; the time period in this research spans a thousand years. It would be inappropriate to believe that burial traditions did not change during this time. After all, our burial traditions are different to those of AD 1000, so we should not assume they would not be as diverse in prehistoric periods.

The research also considers whether the age of the deceased affected burial representation; whether young adults were represented differently to mature adults. Considering age with burial representation is important as it has been suggested that aging changes how we are perceived (Fowler 2004). This links to ideas concerning rites of passage (see Van Gennep 1960), where at different stages in life, often age-related, people assume new identities. As a result, the age of the deceased could affect burial representation. Examining burial evidence along age divisions makes it possible to detect whether this was a feature of Chalcolithic and Early Bronze Age burial traditions.

1.2. Archaeological approaches to burials

Archaeologists have been interested in the material remains of mortuary practices since the beginning of the discipline in the nineteenth century (Nilson Stutz 2003). Originally the interest resulted purely in the excavation of burial mounds (i.e. Bateman 1848; 1861); however, early in the twentieth century archaeologists used the evidence to infer cultural groups and their movement (Binford 1972). Since then there have been several theoretical positions regarding burial evidence's potential to elucidate aspects of the past, prominently Processual and Postprocessual archaeology.

Processual archaeology developed in the late 1960s and early 1970s (Nilson Stutz 2003), and included a reaction against using burial evidence purely to define a culture and its spread. Instead, it used the burial evidence in order to determine aspects of past society, such as social structure. The burials were treated as reflections of social

differences and structure. The key figures in this movement were Saxe (1970) and Binford (1972).

The Processualists used patterns or generalisations based on cross cultural research of mortuary practices in order to elucidate social aspects from the burials of the past, such as age, sex and status. Using burials to work out the status of the deceased was one of the key features of this movement (Peebles 1971), then determining the comparative social positions of different sections of society, such as the males, females and children. The variation within burial practices was seen to be evidence of the 'social persona' of the deceased (Goodenough 1965). It was suggested that the identity represented in the burials was formed from various aspects of the social identity of the deceased. The more multifaceted the social persona represented in the burial the more complex was that past society (Binford 1972).

This approach relied heavily upon using the grave goods interred with the deceased to determine status. The grave goods were assumed to have belonged to the deceased in life (Diáz Andreu and Lucy 2005), and their quality and quantity were compared between burials to suggest the deceased's relative status (see Randsborg 1973).

However, the Processualist approach to interpreting burial evidence was criticised by the Postprocessualists. The key criticism was that the approach was simplistic and did not appreciate, or allow for, the complexity evident in burial rites. They argued that burials cannot be used as mirrors of past societies (Hodder 1980), due to the nature of ritual, the use of ideology in burials and also the relationship between the dead and the living.

They claimed that the nature of ritual, which includes burial, was designed to legitimise inequality by making it appear indisputable, even if this was not the case in life (Pader 1982). This links with the fact that burial practices are permeated with ideology. Dead bodies can be manipulated by the living to say what the living want them to express; words can literally 'be put in their mouths' (Verdery 1999: 29). The burial evidence may not represent the life of the deceased; instead it could be representing ideals, which can themselves comment upon past society. What archaeologists encounter in the burial record is not the representation by a dead person of themselves, but rather a representation created by the living; the 'dead do not bury themselves' (Parker Pearson 1993: 203).

The Postprocessualists also highlighted the difficulties of interpreting grave goods. One problem is that the meaning archaeologists assign to the artefacts encountered in burials may not have been how they were perceived in the past. This arises because objects are polysemous (Tilley 1991); an object can have more than one meaning at any time or to different people. Therefore, although we see a necklace as an item of adornment or decoration, it may not have been in the Chalcolithic and Early Bronze Age. Therefore, the status generated by the Processualists from the grave goods may not have been evident in the past. Furthermore, we cannot assume that the objects interred with the deceased were their belongings, a point expanded upon in recent archaeological discourse (see below).

Finally, the use of terms such as status and rank was questioned. What archaeologists mean when they use the term status is never defined (Chapman in press), instead there is an assumption that past status was based upon the same concepts as today; personal wealth (Babíc 2005) or ritual specialism (Woodward 2000). As such, when archaeologists assign status to past individuals it is subjective rather than a past reality. Status and prestige were probably based on different qualities in the past, with the result that archaeological discussions of status are inconclusive. This is a valid point and terms such as status and prestige will not be used in this study.

Although it may appear that Postprocessual archaeology is pessimistic in relation to the potential of interpretation from burial evidence, this is not the case. Instead it advocates caution when examining burial evidence to avoid potential pitfalls. It stresses that archaeologists need to be aware of the assumptions being made before they begin working. Even if the burials are not faithful representations of the deceased, I believe they still demonstrate *how* the society *wanted* that individual to be represented. After all, our identity is created by the society we live in.

That burial interpretations are still popular demonstrates how the Postprocessual cautionary tale has not deterred research. Instead there has been a shift in focus. Rather than using burial evidence to establish past identities and social status, the emphasis now is on understanding *how* identity was created in the past, reflected in the growing interest in the archaeology of identity and personhood (Meskell 1999). Key outcomes of this are the recognition that identities are complex; what is represented in burial evidence is not just one identity, for example sex, but instead is the intersection of different aspects, including age, gender, ethnicity etc., (similar to the Processualist approach discussed above) and also that identity is a performance (Butler 2006).

Furthermore, identity is not just related to the individual, it also relates to others; identities are constructed by peoples' relationships to other people (Whelan 1991a; Brück 2004). This is pertinent considering that it is the living who construct the deceased's representation in burials (see above). Ties with other people form a person's identity, and therefore this may also be represented in the mortuary evidence, especially as those people constructed the burial. Therefore, the examination of burial evidence must consider that identity is likely to have been formed through relationships, and these relationships may be visible in the archaeological record.

Grave goods interpretation has also developed since Processual analysis. That they may not have been the deceased's belongings has been established (Diáz Andreu and Lucy 2005) and alternative interpretations have been suggested. Firstly, the objects interred with the deceased may have been heirlooms; an idea already explored in relation to Chalcolithic and Early Bronze Age grave goods (Woodward 2002), specifically with spacer plate beads, bracers and Beaker sherds. If the objects are heirlooms then their link to the interred can be questioned, as Gillespie argues that heirlooms represent previous owners more than the current one (2001). However, the fact they were deposited with the deceased still needs consideration (Chapter Four). The inclusions of heirlooms in burials can concern relational identity; the objects linking the deceased with other people who contributed to their conceptions of self and their identity.

A second interpretation is that grave goods were gifts from mourners (King 2004). This contributes to the understanding of identity in two ways linking with the idea of relational identity. If the objects were placed in the grave by mourners, then they can symbolise the link between the deceased and other people. Alternatively, they could have been involved in constructing the burial by those close to the deceased, such as those engaged with making a shroud (Brück 2004).

It is suggested that objects can become associated with people to an extent that they become inalienable from each other (Fowler 2004). Therefore, the objects placed in a grave may be the deceased's inalienable possessions and are thus removed from circulation when the owner dies, the inalienable possession of a mourner, placed to symbolise their relationship, or an heirloom, inalienable from past owners situating the deceased in a web of relations. That personhood is formed in relation to others (*ibid*) suggests that the deceased are not individuals, but are dividual; that their identity is formed through relationships with other people. This can be evidenced through themes such as fragmentation in burials (Chapter Four).

1.3. Chalcolithic and Early Bronze Age female burials

Archaeological interpretations of female burials from this period can take many forms, including studies looking at the distribution of grave goods in relation to sex (Clarke 1970; Gerloff 1975), regional burial practices (Pierpoint 1980; Lucas 1996; Sofaer Derevenski 2002; A. Shepherd 2012), and those concerned primarily with the gender representation of the period (Gibbs 1989; Brück 2009). In all these cases the female burials are considered in comparison to male burials and sometimes sub-adult graves.

One of the first assessments of Chalcolithic and Early Bronze Age female burial traditions was Clarke's (1970) nationwide corpus of Beaker pottery. Though he looked in particular at Beaker vessels, he also considered the context of the pottery, including burials, though the emphasis is placed upon the pottery rather than the sex associations. The work examines the orientation of the burials in relation to sex, and also the positioning of the Beaker. It also considers the sex associations of the other grave goods in the burials.

One of the strengths of this study is that it attempted to examine the sex associated grave goods in relation to the chronology established by the pottery (since disproved: Needham 2005), and thus understood the importance of change over time. However, as a study of Chalcolithic and Early Bronze Age sex representation it has flaws, in particular with sex determination, as the deceased's sex was established by antiquarian reports rather than using modern anthropological techniques. This brings into question the resulting associations with grave goods. Because antiquarians often determined the deceased's sex based on the accompanying grave goods, for example daggers equal men and necklaces women (Lucy 1997), the 'strong prevailing pattern of the artefact allocation by sexes' (Clarke 1970: 264) should not come as a surprise. Using antiquarian sex determinations results in a circular argument in relation to grave good associations.

The next study of female burial representation shares some problems with Clarke's (1970) discussion of the Beaker evidence. Gerloff's (1975) study of British Early Bronze Age daggers included a re-examination of the Wessex Culture. It considered the grave goods associated with females during this period. However, it is the grave goods, rather than the biological traits of the skeleton, which were used to sex the burials; 'graves without weapons ... are held to be the graves of females' (Gerloff 1975: 197). Furthermore, only the objects associated with the burials were examined in detail. However, Gerloff does consider the chronological implications of the Wessex Culture female burials. The female burials are divided into two series, the Wilsford, or 'richly furnished' burials (*ibid*: 197), and the Aldbourne, or 'poorer' burials (*ibid*: 198), which correspond to earlier and later burial traditions. This chronological division is based upon comparisons of the grave goods with the male burials and also Continental affinities. Overall, this was a valuable study as even though it was primarily concerned with producing a typology and chronology of daggers, it still considered the female burials from this period, and then related them to the male burials and burials practices (in terms of grave good deposition) elsewhere.

Female burial traditions are also considered in regional burial studies. Yorkshire has provided the focus for several regional analyses (Tuckwell 1975; Pierpoint 1980; Lucas 1996; A. Shepherd 2012) due to the density of burials dating from the Chalcolithic and Early Bronze Age. Tuckwell (1975) examined the burial orientations of the sexes (she also considered burial orientation in north-east Scotland (A. Shepherd in Greig *et al* 1989; A. Shepherd 2012)), Pierpoint (1980) considered social patterning in the burials, such as the relationships of burials to each other, and Lucas (1996) produced a larger study of the burial traditions in general.

Since the same evidence was used for each of these studies they share the common problem of antiquarian sexing discussed above. Furthermore, chronology is also not developed in the studies. For example, Pierpoint (1980) bases his chronological divisions on the occurrence of different types of pottery within the graves.

However, it is now known that many pottery styles had overlapping currencies, and, therefore, the changes through time postulated in the study may not have been real. Nevertheless, these studies also have strengths, in that they move beyond purely using the grave goods to suggest differences between the sexes, and they consider burial construction, locations and positioning of the corpses. This produces a much more developed study of sex representation in burial traditions than focussing upon the grave goods alone, and allows for the burials without grave goods to be included in the analysis.

These previous studies of burial traditions from this period have not focussed specifically on sex representation, but have looked at artefacts or regional trends. However, Gibbs (1989) looked specifically at Chalcolithic and Early Bronze Age sex and gender representation. The study was conducted nationwide and looked at 212 male and 112 female burials. It considered several aspects of the burials; though mainly looking at the artefacts, it did consider the deceased's orientation and positioning. This was a positive study as it acknowledged that examining sex and gender representation was valid on its own, rather than as part of another topic.

However, a consideration of the period's chronology was lacking; available radiocarbon dates were disregarded and instead pottery was used to form chronological distinctions. As such, Beaker burials were separated from Food Vessels, Collared Urns and Miniature Vessels, despite the overlap between the forms (Chapter Two). In addition, the antiquarian sex determinations, though questioned, were accepted.

Sofaer Derevenski (2002) considered the relative status of males and females in her regional study of the Thames Valley burial evidence. The study focussed upon 'context' rather than grave goods, and looked at the burial methods, the burial form and the grave construction alongside the grave goods. She concluded that female representation was more varied than male representation, and that archaeologists cannot compare them in terms of status as their identities within burial traditions were constructed differently (Sofaer Derevenski 2002).

The excavations used in this study were from the last one hundred years and, therefore, information regarding sex is more likely to be correct (Chapter Two). It also looks in detail at the context of the burials rather than just the grave goods, and additionally uses available radiocarbon dates, allowing graves without the period's diagnostic artefacts to be included in the analysis. However, chronology was not used as a tool for analysis; changes over time were not examined and the period was treated as homogenous.

In addition, Brück (2009) questioned previous assumptions regarding status in relation to sex by looking at the relationship between females, death and social change. The article specifically questioned whether cremation, in comparison to inhumation, was reserved for those of lower status, assumed because it appeared more females were cremated than inhumed. This article considered evidence from across the country. The discussions were based around the current themes in archaeology of fragmentation and personhood (see above), and it was concluded that females were active in forming relations between people and kin groups, demonstrated by cremations which facilitate fragmentation and division of the remains (Brück 2009). However, the differences between the numbers of males and females being cremated or inhumed were not very convincing (figure 1.1).

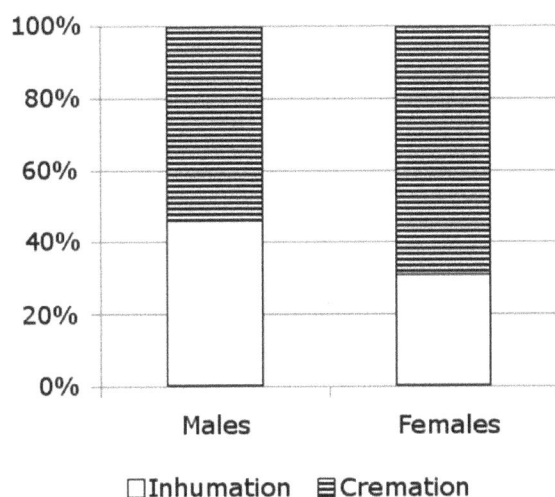

Figure 1.1: Percentage of cremation and inhumation burials by sex (adapted from Brück 2009: 4, figure 3).

There are several reasons why this is a good study of Chalcolithic and Early Bronze Age females. The first is that only excavation reports published post-1960 formed the dataset, and those used were mainly from the 1980s onwards. This provides 'confiden[ce] in the sexing' (Brück 2009: 3) and it also generates a selection of radiocarbon dates which provide a secure chronology. In fact, this article examines the burial evidence in terms of change through time, using Needham's chronological periods 1 to 4 (Needham 1996). This allowed an examination of the popularity of the different methods of burial (inhumation and cremation) over time, and demonstrated that cremation gained in popularity from 2000 BC (*ibid*: 5). Finally, it situated the results within current archaeological frameworks, demonstrating how research into sex representation in the burial record can contribute to research themes.

The most recent study examining gender representation in the British Chalcolithic and Early Bronze Age burials is A. Shepherd's 2012 paper. This draws on her earlier work looking at the burials practices of North East Scotland (A. Shepherd in Greig *et al* 1989) and East Yorkshire (Tuckwell 1975). In this paper the orientation and positioning of Beaker burials, and the vessels themselves, are examined in terms of gender divisions. In total 108 burials are included in the study, though this includes 31 which are not sexed (A. Shepherd 2012). Unfortunately,

due to the nature of the sample only around a third of the sexed burials are female, and a further problem exists in that many of these burials are sexed using the antiquarian determinations.

The study engages with chronology in order to produce a fuller interpretation of changing burial practices. In general the sample fits the pattern of male Beaker burials being placed on their left hand sides with their heads to the east, and females buried on their right sides with their heads to the west (A. Shepherd 2012). However, by engaging with chronology, A. Shepherd (2012) noted that the minority which did not fit the general pattern were those 'at either ends of the Beaker chronological spectrum' (*ibid*: 263). This illustrates the fluid nature of burial practices, and that even in areas where it seems that there are strict patterns, variation can still exist through time.

The strengths and weaknesses emerging from these previous studies informed the methodology of this research. The major weaknesses of these studies concern sexing methods and also the use of chronology. Using antiquarian results can create questions regarding the validity of sex determination and also subsequent conclusions, such as associated grave goods (see above). Only by studying burials excavated in modern times which feature anthropological sexing reports can this be avoided (Brück 2009).

The lack of chronology also created weaknesses in some studies. Accurate chronologies cannot be established using different pottery forms (Chapter Two), and thus the pottery divisions used by several studies (Pierpoint 1980; Gibbs 1989) do not reflect real time divisions. Examining change over time is rewarding, as it can demonstrate that patterns are related to time rather than sex (Chapter Four), and also how representation can change. A study is strengthened if it uses a secure chronology based upon radiocarbon dates, rather than treating a period of 1000 years as a unit.

Individual chronology is also not considered in any of these studies. Rather than examining age in conjunction with sex representation, the authors all consider "adult" as one homogenous group. This is a key problem in archaeological studies, where age research tends to focus upon childhood to address the adult-centric view of the past (Gowland 2006). This study divides adults into three categories; young adult, adult and mature, which allows an examination of the intersection between sex representation and age (*ibid;* see above).

A final weakness of the previous research is that the majority have a fairly narrow focus. Clarke (1970) focused upon Beaker burials, Gerloff (1975) is restricted to the Wessex Culture, a narrow time span and geographical area, Tuckwell/ A. Shepherd (1975; 1989; 2012), Pierpoint (1980), Lucas (1996) and Sofaer Derevenski (2002) are restricted to regions, while Brück (2009) concentrates upon the differences between cremation and inhumation rites. Only Gibbs (1989) has a broad focus, though unfortunately a small sample size. Due to the nature of the evidence, I think that a broad approach produces the best results.

However, these previous studies demonstrate that moving beyond simply examining grave goods produces a comprehensive study; many aspects are involved in sex representation. This allows for burials without grave goods to be studied. This is important as burials without grave goods make up a large proportion of the period's burial record; only 25% of the burials examined by Greenwell and 54% of those by Mortimer (Ashbee 1960) contained grave goods, as did only 63% of the burials used in this study. Clearly, to examine female burial representation a methodology needs to be developed in which all burials are considered together, regardless of whether they have grave goods (Chapter Two). It has been suggested that burials without grave goods are 'largely useless to the prehistorian' (Harrison 1980: 85), an opinion this work intends to prove wrong.

1.4. Structure of the report

This first chapter aimed to introduce the topic of study and the previous research in the area of examining female burial traditions of the Chalcolithic and Early Bronze Age. The second chapter outlines the specific aims and objectives of this research, looks in detail at its methodology, and also establishes the chronology used in the course of the analysis. The results are split between Chapter Three and Appendix Three. Chapter Four analyses and discusses the results, looking at the key themes which have emerged from the course of the work before concluding the research by suggesting future directions. Finally, attached as appendices are the dataset of female burials (Appendix One), the radiocarbon dates and justification of why burials were placed in different chronological periods (Appendix Two), and finally the results which did not directly lead into the discussions presented below (Appendix Three).

2. METHODOLOGY

2.1. Aims and objectives

The aim of this research is to provide a reanalysis of the British Chalcolithic and Early Bronze Age female burial traditions, as suggested by Brück (2009). A new look at the data is overdue as most previous studies have been conducted upon antiquarian evidence (Chapter One), rather than the new data mainly made available through commercially funded excavations. The aim of this research is divided into three sub-aims.

The first sub-aim is to see if the burial traditions reveal any patterns within the data, which could signify representational "packages" or "identities" for the females of this period. This is a direct response to the many postulated male identities of this period (Chapter One), and because it is a research method frequently employed, such as Salanova's (1998) four categories of Beaker burials; '*les sépultures à armement, les sépultures à outil, les sépultures à parure et les sépultures seulement à poterie*' (*ibid*: 316).

The next sub-aim looks to see whether the deceased's age affected burial representation. Frequently in archaeological studies of identity only one aspect, such as sex, is considered. This is despite the fact that identity is the intersection of many different traits, such as age, ethnicity, etc. (Rautman and Talalay 2000). Furthermore, when age is examined it is usually in relation to childhood (Gowland 2006), and the process and response to aging in adults is rarely considered (see Sørensen 1997, Gilchrist 2000 and Gowland 2006 for exceptions).

It is acknowledged in ethnographic research that moving through age grades can have profound effects on aspects of identity (Gowland 2006), such as different dress codes or different labour patterns. This draws upon the work looking at rites of passage (Van Gennep 1960), where at certain points in a person's life they go through transformative events, often related to age, which are designed to formally recognise changes in identity. Therefore, looking to see whether a similar phenomenon happened during the British Chalcolithic and Early Bronze Age is an important aspect of female representation. This approach also acknowledges that sex representation can be fluid (Gowland 2006), in contrast to studies which determine one representation or identity for *all* females.

Accepting sex representation as fluid also features in the research's final sub-aim; considering whether representation changed through time. The study period, 2500 – 1500 BC, spans a thousand years, and it is unlikely that burial practices remained stable during this time, especially pertinent when considering the changes happening during this period, such as monument form, construction and use and settlement practices (Bradley 2007). Therefore, this research considers if female burial

representation changed over time and how the passage of time related to the period's burial practices as a whole.

This research had several objectives designed to meet these aims. The first was the establishment of a dataset of Chalcolithic and Early Bronze Age female burials. Only burials from excavations published since 1950 which contained anthropological sex determination reports were included. This provides an up-to-date dataset and ensures that the burials included were biologically female, at least to today's standards (see below). Female burials from antiquarian excavations are not included in the study. The female burial information was then inputted into a database (see below), which provided easy access to the data and which can be made available to other members of the profession.

Once the female burials had been entered into the database, the next objective was assigning each to a chronological period (see below). This was achieved by considering previous chronologies and using the burials' diagnostic traits to determine which period they belonged to (Appendix Two). This was undertaken to specifically address the aim of looking to see whether burial representation changed over time.

The next objective was to analyse the information in the database of Chalcolithic and Early Bronze Age female burials (Chapter Three; Appendix Three). This was designed to be able to detect common aspects of the burial practices and also to examine the effects of age and time on the female representation. As part of this analysis the chi-squared test, when applicable, was used upon the data (Fletcher and Lock 2005), to see if it was statistically significant.

The final objective was comparing the results of this research with previous work conducted on the subject of sex representation and burial practices from the British Chalcolithic and Early Bronze Age. The results were then situated within current archaeological frameworks. Previous conclusions were reconsidered in respect of the new results, such as "were females buried with their heads orientated to the south?", and the new data was considered within themes such as fragmentation and personhood.

2.2. The data

In order to conduct this study a decision was made that only excavations published since 1950 would be used. This follows Brück's (2009) approach in her study of this period's male and female burial practices. It ensures a good standard of recording for each burial, including information such as locations, dimensions and stratigraphy. Additionally, only reports containing anthropological sexing of the remains were used. This ensured a sample of anthropologically determined females was created in comparison to using grave goods or orientation to determine the sex of the deceased (see Thomas 2007). By only using modern excavations data of the best quality was generated to approach the question of Chalcolithic and Early Bronze Age female burial representation, and it provided a secure group of biologically classified burials. It also resulted in a large selection of burials with associated radiocarbon dates; 88 burials in the dataset have direct radiocarbon dates (36%). This helps to place the burials into the correct period divisions.

However, in the Radley Barrow Hill monograph (Barclay and Halpin 1999), excavations prior to 1950 were re-

examined and published. These burials were included in the dataset since they had a modern anthropological report of the bones providing secure sex and age determinations.

Furthermore, females were only included in the dataset if their report contained enough information regarding the burials. In rare cases even post-1950 reports did not satisfy this condition, such as the excavation of the Bee Low cairn in Derbyshire (Marsden 1970) where information of the excavation was not sufficiently clear so the females were not included in the dataset.

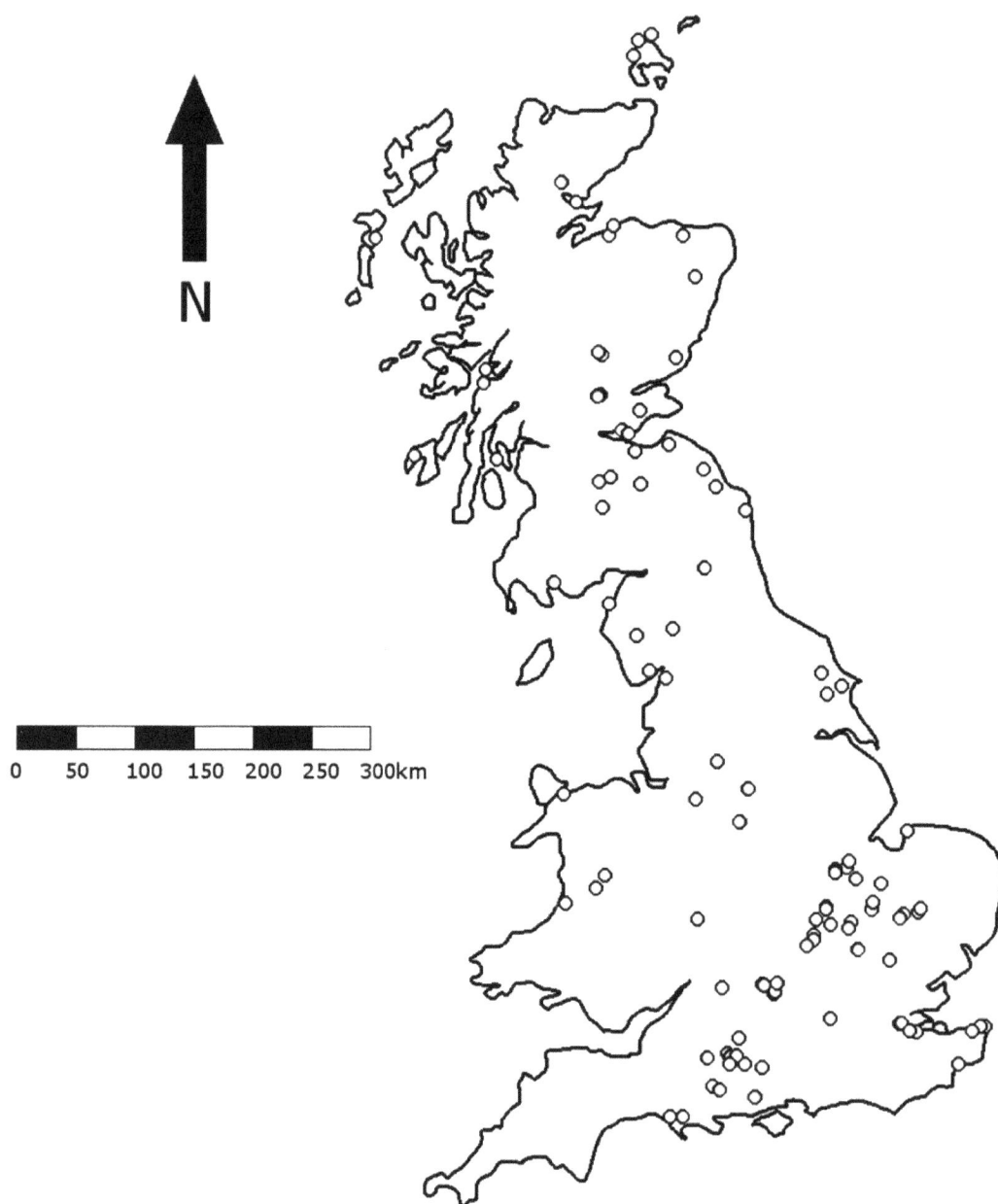

Figure 2.1: Distribution of burials in the study.

As only female burials from modern excavations were studied, the study area for this research encompasses the whole of Britain but excludes Ireland. This is not because the practices of burial between the two countries were dissimilar and thus cannot be studied together. Indeed, the study of the British and Irish evidence together has proved successful in the past (for example Bradley 2007). This decision was due instead to the availability of reports on modern Irish excavations at the time of writing. This situation has since changed with the publication of Cahill and Sikora's (2012) report on the excavations conducted by the National Museum of Ireland, and a valuable project could be conducted comparing the female burial traditions of the two countries.

Unlike antiquarian excavations where a region was intensely studied, such as the Peak District (Bateman 1848; 1861) or Wessex (Colt-Hoare 1810), modern excavations of Chalcolithic and Early Bronze Age burials tend to be a response to development, and consequently are scattered across the country. In order to develop a large sample it was prudent not to restrict the study to one geographical region. Restricting the study zone in this research would have severely limited the dataset available for use and thus the ability to detect common burial themes.

The excavations used in this study were accessed in a variety of ways. Most excavation reports were sourced from archaeology's major journals (i.e. *Proceedings of the Prehistoric Society*, *Archaeological Journal*), and smaller journals with regional foci (i.e. *Archaeologia Aeliana*). Female burials were located by looking at the anthropological reports. Major monograph series were also used (i.e. East Anglian Archaeology, Thames Valley Landscapes), finding the period's excavations then looking through the anthropological data. Chalcolithic and Early Bronze Age female burials were also accessed using the Archaeological Data Service (ADS), such as the excavation reports from the Channel Tunnel Rail Link project.

Finally, Cambridge Archaeological Unit, Oxford Archaeology and Wessex Archaeology were contacted to access unpublished material, and I thank them for allowing me to use the information prior to publication (though much of the information used in this study has since been published or is forthcoming, see the bibliography). This selection of units obviously does not represent the full output of commercial archaeological in this country, and as a result several female burials will have been missed. However, due to time constraints it was considered prudent to only contact those units where contacts were in place and those who had been engaged in recent fieldwork at burial sites of the Chalcolithic and Early Bronze Age.

The methods used to collect data were not infallible and have obviously not resulted in a definitive list of Chalcolithic and Early Bronze Age female burials published since 1950. Instead a *selection* of the available

evidence has been produced, and the results are those for this dataset alone. However, the methods generating the dataset were successful as they resulted in a database of 246 female burials (figure 2.1). This is a good number of burials to study as it created a good cross-section of the data in terms of period and practices. Furthermore, the number of female burials is good in relation to previous work done on the subject (Chapter One). For example, Gibbs (1989) only included 112 supposed females in her study, Sofaer Derevenski (2002) included 21 sexed females and Brück (2009) had 104. My sample of 246 anthropologically sexed burials is over twice the size of previous female burial datasets.

2.3. Anthropological sexing

Only anthropologically sexed burials were included for analysis in this research. Though it has been suggested that the antiquarian sex determinations were sometimes based upon the bones (Gibbs 1989: 20-21), the research conducted into deriving sex from skeletons only really began at the end of the nineteenth century (Dwight 1894; Thomson 1899; Derry 1909), and the major research, such as the use of metrical data, did not develop until well after the antiquarian sex determinations were conducted (Derry 1927; Schultz 1930; Caldwell and Moloy 1932). Therefore, antiquarian determinations should still be treated with caution.

There are several methods to biologically sex human skeletal remains. These can be divided into those considering morphological differences between the two sexes, such as shape, and those quantifying the differences metrically (Safont *et al* 2000). Studies have been conducted into using almost every bone in the body for sex determination, from the feet (İşcan 2005), through to the clavicles (Thieme and Schull 1957). However, the bones considered the most reliable are the pelvis, the skull and the major long bones (the humerus, femur, etc.) (Byers 2008). Although sex determination is easiest when all the bones are present and well preserved (a rare occurrence in archaeology), sexing can still be conducted on fragmentary remains and cremations, providing there are enough recognisable elements remaining.

The main pelvic features used for sex determination involve element shapes, such as the pelvic inlet and sciatic notch, and the presence or absence of certain traits, e.g. the preauricular sulcus (Byers 2008). A pelvis would be considered female if it had a heart-shaped pelvic inlet, a wide and shallow sciatic notch and preauricular sulcus present (*ibid*). The pelvic differences between the sexes result from the females' adaption for childbirth and how this affects locomotion (Bruzek 2002). Due to bipediality, the human pelvis was rotated forwards to allow an upright posture (Caldwell and Moloy 1932). However, due to the needs of child-bearing, the female pelvis is much wider and deeper, thus not tilted as far forwards as the male.

The skull also exhibits sexual dimorphism. The differences between male and female skulls tend to be related to size and the presence or absence of certain traits. Females have smaller mastoid processes, a small or non-existent brow ridge, and a more obtuse ramus angle (Byers 2008), resulting in female skulls tending to retain juvenile features (Keen 1950). The differences in the skull do not arise from functional differences, instead they are related to hormones and muscle attachments. Most sexually dimorphic features of the skull occur at muscle attachments sites, therefore, the greater muscle use the greater the bony element size. However, this may not necessarily relate to sex (see below). Because puberty occurs later in males it allows time for extra growth, which also results in size differences (Mays and Cox 2000).

Finally, long bones are sexually dimorphic due to size, both length and circumference; on average, females are only 92% of the size of males (Byers 2008). Therefore, male bones tend to be longer than their female counterparts. However, bone circumference is also related to muscle use, rather than just height differences (Safont *et al* 2000; see below).

There are several problems with anthropologically determining sex from skeletal remains. It has been recognised that sexual dimorphism varies between populations (Walker 2008) due to a variety of factors, such as ancestry and lifestyle. Therefore, the techniques developed by anthropologists on known sex samples only apply securely to that population; the results may not be the same if applied to a different sample. The effects of ancestry on skeletons have been recognised for a long time (Pearson 1899; Hrdlička 1920; Derry 1927).

However, recent studies have demonstrated that the differences may not entirely arise from ancestry; they could be more related to lifestyle. A study demonstrated that twentieth century American whites had more skeletal features in common with twentieth century American blacks than with nineteenth century English skeletons (Walker 2005; 2008); not what you would expect if ancestry was the main cause of variation.

Therefore, it has been suggested that lifestyle can have an effect on a population's sexual dimorphism. Many sexually dimorphic features are located at muscle attachments sites (especially on skull and long bones). Therefore, the muscle use of different populations can affect their size, and thus the sex determination. Activities which affect these attachment sites include physical labour (Safont *et al* 2000), such as hunting, or craft activities (Steen and Lane 1998; Weiss 2010). Therefore, if females were involved in more physical activities their bones could appear more masculine, and thus could be anthropologically sexed as male. An example of this occurs in the Danish Neolithic, where an individual sexed as male was determined to be female by DNA (deoxyribonucleic acid) analysis (Götherström *et al* 1997). This was important as the individual's grave goods contained a harpoon point which had previously been considered an exclusively male item.

The deceased's age also affects the accuracy of skeletal sex determination because ageing has manifestations in bony tissues. I have already mentioned how females retain more juvenile skulls, but adolescent and young adult males also feature more youthful skulls (Kjellström 2004), and thus can be mis-classified as females. Conversely, due to increased bony deposition, mature adult females can develop masculine looking skulls (Saunders and Yang 1999).

2.4. Sex versus gender

The methods anthropologists use to assign sex to human skeletal remains are firmly biological. However, there has been tension in archaeology between the notions of sex and gender and how to combine them (Sofaer 2006).

In the 1980s, feminist archaeology (Conkey and Spector 1984) argued that sex and gender were distinct from one another; sex was biological, whereas gender was culturally constructed (Whelan 1991b). Sex was then related to the skeletal remains, whereas gender was inferred from the grave goods. However, this created problems because the gender was often assigned to the grave goods using the sexed skeleton as a reference, thus conflating the two concepts together (Sofaer 2006).

It was then argued that not only is gender culturally constructed, but so is sex. Laquer (1990) demonstrated how the modern western two-sex system had only been in existence since the eighteenth century. Prior to that, it was believed that there was only one sex, but the genitalia were located on the outside (male) or inside (female) of the body. Geneticists also suggest sex categories are culturally constructed (Nordblah and Yates 1990; Fausto-Sterling 1993). They argue that biological sex is actually a scale rather than binary categories, with at least five separate sexes (Fausto-Sterling 1993). Therefore, sex is culturally constructed as we reduce the range to either male or female.

If sex is culturally constructed then the divisions made in anthropological sexing may not have been the same divisions made in the past. Therefore, we could be 'segment[ing] *their* reality using *our* conceptions' (Jacobs and Cromwell 1992: 62, authors' emphasis). This questions the applicability of using modern biological sex to classify past burials. However, we ignore sex at our peril. Without a conception of biological sex we are unable to remove our analysis from being based on our cultural conceptions of grave goods. Though sex is culturally constructed it is restrained by biology, whereas other sex/ gender determination methods have no such restraints and are entirely compelled by cultural notions of male and female.

Therefore, this research uses biological sex as a starting block for the analysis of Chalcolithic and Early Bronze Age burials. However, since we do not define people purely in terms of sex in the present, it seems wrong to do so for the past. In previous archaeological analyses of Chalcolithic and Early Bronze Age sex or gender, the division of burials into male and female was perceived as the end of the analysis (Clarke 1970; Gibbs 1989). However, we should instead be looking for variation within these classifications. By only looking at one sex we avoid simplistic binary divisions. Undertaking research in this way can reconcile the notions of sex and gender. One of the ways that female variation is approached in this research is through considering the axis of age. This involves looking at types of females, such as young adults and the mature, rather than treating them as a homogenous group.

2.5. Age

The age of the deceased can also be determined from the skeleton. This is because a skeleton changes through the life of an individual (Byers 2008). However, aging adults is more difficult than aging sub-adults; rather than looking at skeletal growth and maturation, you are instead looking at degeneration, which is more subtle (*ibid*). Despite this, areas of the skeleton can be used to determine adult age; including the pubic symphysis, the sternal rib ends and cranial sutures (*ibid*).

Since age assessment in adults is not exact, the adult age in this research has been divided into basic age ranges; young adult (aged 18 to 25 years), adult (26 to 39 years) and mature (40+ years). These age divisions are the standard ones used by many anthropologists working with archaeological human remains (see Dodwell 2010). However, more individuals can be placed in the adult age category when detailed aspects of age are missing; this is especially the case with cremations

2.6. Chronology

This research looks to see whether female burial traditions changed over time, rather than considering the thousand year period as a homogenous unit. In this work period divisions were created which reflected material culture rather than being equal time spans. To do this existing Chalcolithic and Early Bronze Age chronological schemes were examined (Needham 1996; Gerloff 2007), along with radiocarbon dates for the period's pottery traditions (Sheridan 2003a; 2004; 2007a; 2007b; Needham 2005; Brindley 2007) and the new "Wessex I" date (Needham *et al* 2010).

The term "Chalcolithic" describes the period of the first metal use at the end of the Neolithic, c. 2500 – 2250 BC, when it was much rarer than the full metalwork adoption of the Early Bronze Age, c. 2250 – 1500 BC. This follows Needham *et al*'s (2010) terminology for the period. The appropriateness of this term and its use as a chronological division is reflected in the publication of a new volume looking in detail at the possibility of a Chalcolithic period in Britain (Allen *et al* 2012).

Much new work has been done to understand the chronology of Chalcolithic and Early Bronze Age pottery styles. Radiocarbon dates have been generated by modern excavations, whereas others have been generated by

dedicated programmes of dating previously excavated material (Sheridan 2003a; 2004; 2007a; 2007b; Brindley 2007). This has resulted in an abundance of dates used to establish the chronology of the pottery classes.

However, the recent pottery dating programmes have been confined to the Scottish (Sheridan 2003a; 2004; 2007a; 2007b) and Irish evidence (Brindley 2007); the only English example being Kinnes *et al* (1991), which has been proved wrong. As a result, the chronology for Food Vessels, Collared and Cordoned Urns has been developed using the Scottish and Irish vessel dates. Nonetheless, it is thought that there was no time-lag between the pottery styles being adopted in the different countries (Sheridan 2007a; Brindley 2007). Even if there was, the resolution provided in this period's radiocarbon dates, especially around the plateau of 2100 - 1850 BC (Sheridan 2004) would not be able to detect it. Therefore, using the Irish evidence is appropriate, as it provides the most recent pottery dates, the equivalent not being available for the English or Welsh evidence.

Several studies also provide radiocarbon dating for other artefacts from this period (Needham 2005; Sheridan 2007a; Brindley 2007), such as faience, jet, daggers and bone artefacts, which also aided in establishing a chronology.

A further study used to establish a chronology for this research looked at barrow construction and how it changed through the Chalcolithic and Early Bronze Age (Garwood 2007). This examined the relative dating for various forms of barrows popular during this period, such as single-phase mounds, multiphase mounds and concentric stake circles (*ibid*).

A graph was compiled illustrating the various time spans for different aspects of burials traditions, either material culture or burial form (figure 2.2). Then, using the graph and previous divisions of the Chalcolithic and Early Bronze Age (Needham 1996; 2005; Gerloff 2007), the period divisions for this study were determined.

The first two period boundaries followed Needham's (2005) Beaker divisions; 'Beaker as circumscribed, exclusive culture, c. 2500 – 2250 cal BC' (Period One) and 'Beaker as instituted culture' c. 2250 – 1950 cal BC (Period Two) (*ibid*: 209). However, I decided the evidence suggests Period Three ended at 1700 BC, rather than 1600 BC, as this reflects the metalwork phases (Needham 1996), the S-Profile Beakers (Needham 2005), and seemed to fit with the female burial radiocarbon dates (Appendix Two). It also ensured that Period Four had a time span long enough to cope with the time periods generated by radiocarbon dating. However, as illustrated on the radiocarbon date diagram (Appendix Two), this period lasts into the Middle Bronze Age (post 1500 BC), and represents a transition stage between the Early and Middle Bronze Ages. The final three period divisions match Gerloff's (2007).

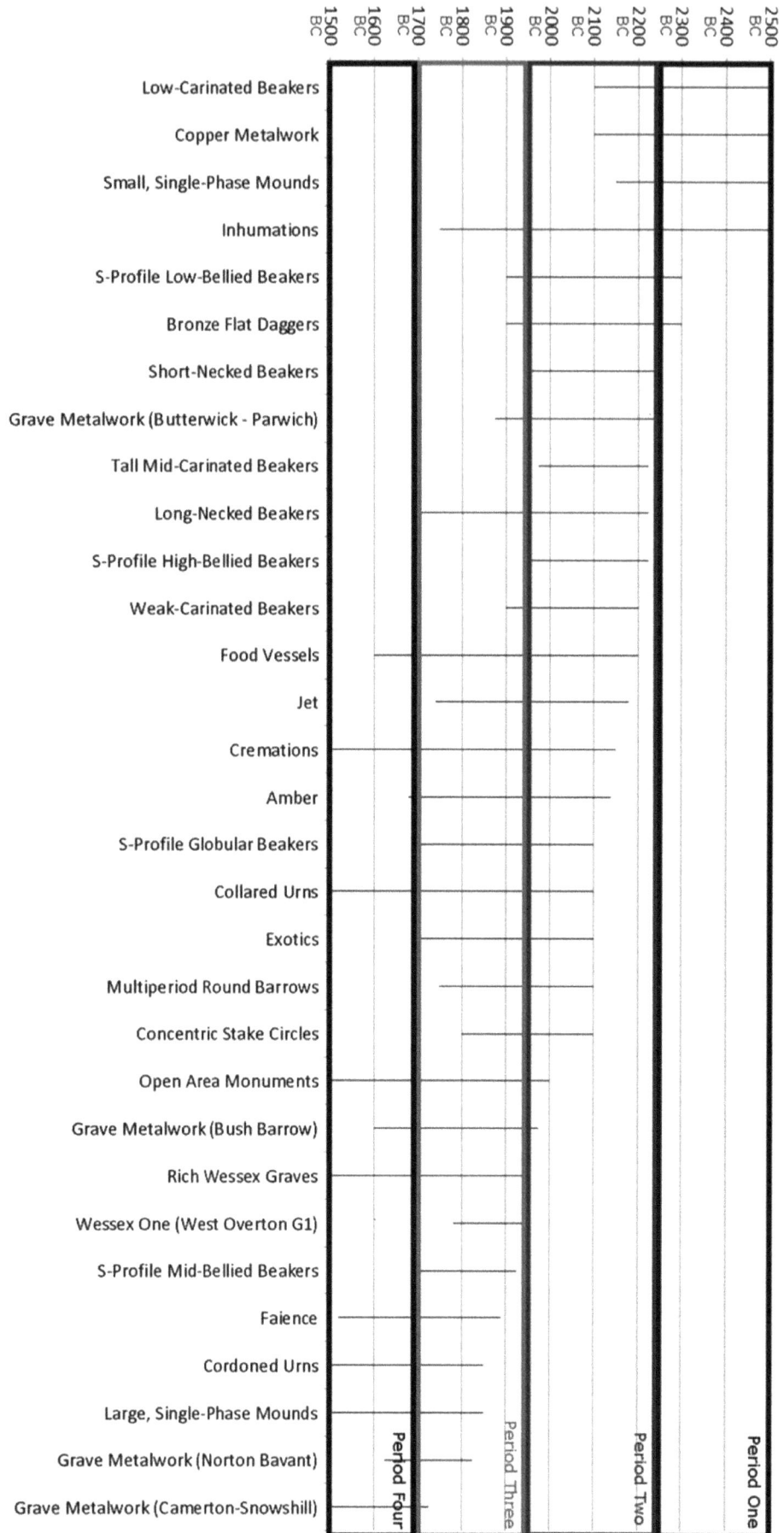

Figure 2.2: Time spans of diagnostic aspects of the Chalcolithic and Early Bronze Age, with the period divisions used in this study illustrated.

2.7. The database

In order to store the data that was collected for this research a database was created using Microsoft Access. The key feature of this database was that it had to be able to store information about a variety of burials, such as burials in barrows, flat graves, cremations in stone sockets etc., yet be able to consider all the data together. As a result, the database contained several tables linked together via a relationship function based on the unique number assigned to each burial. Therefore, each burial in the database did not have an entry in every table – only the applicable ones – but they were all linked through the Root Table. The tables used in this database were a Root, Barrow, Cairn, Flat Grave, Other Form, Inhumation, Cremation, Token Inhumation, Token Cremation and Grave Goods. These tables are explained in detail in Appendix One.

2.8. The analysis

The analysis of the burial data was conducted in a variety of ways. The major method was using Microsoft Access to generate queries. Each burial was assigned a unique identifying number which allowed searches across the different tables in the database. This allowed disparate burial types to be analysed all together. Other, qualitative analysis was also conducted using the database by looking for similar burial packages, such as the leatherworker identity postulated for several burials (Chapter Four).

Statistical analysis was conducted on some of the results to determine whether they were statistically significant. This was achieved using two versions of the chi-squared test; the 1-sample test and the chi-squared test for cross-classified data (Shennan 1997). Both these tests use the formula:

$$x^2 = \sum_{i=1}^{k} \frac{(O_i - E_i)^2}{E_i}$$

'where k is the number of categories, O_i is the observed number of cases in category i, E_i is the expected number of cases in category i' (Shennan 1997: 106).

The 1-sample test is used if there is only one category of data being analysed, for example the total number of burials in each period, whereas the second method is used if more than one category of data is being considered, such as methods of burial by the four periods.

The chi-squared test is used to determine whether the numbers in a category are expected for a dataset of a certain size and composition. A null hypothesis is formulated, often something like "inhumation burial is distributed equally across the age categories" and if the chi-squared result is greater than that expected for the significance level the null hypothesis is rejected, if it is lower it is accepted. The significance level chosen for this study was α0.050.

2.9. Limitations of the research

As with most archaeological studies this research has limitations. However, being aware of the limitations and assumptions made (Binford 1972) allows the author to mitigate them. The limitations of this research fall under three categories; the sample of burials; the dating of the burials and the analysis conducted.

The first limitation concerns the dataset collected to undertake the work. The methods used to generate the dataset would not have managed to access *all* the period's female burials. However, the number of individual burials in this research (246) provides a good representative sample of the period, and the methods used to access these excavations were not clouded by preconceived objectives, such as focusing on burials containing grave goods. Despite this, it should be stressed that although the results from this research are used to extrapolate evidence of the female burials of the Chalcolithic and Early Bronze Age in general, the results themselves are the *de facto* results only for this study's dataset. Therefore, a different dataset may produce conflicting results.

Furthermore, due to the criteria the data sources had to meet to be included in this study (published post-1950 with anthropological reports) the distribution of the burials is large. Therefore, any regional trends, which undoubtedly existed, would not be detected and could also mask general trends. Unfortunately, to have a dataset with reliable anthropological sexing this wide distribution is unavoidable, as modern excavations are often a response to developer threats. This limitation can only be addressed by concentrated Chalcolithic and Early Bronze Age excavations projects.

A final limitation of the dataset already discussed above, and thus not covered in detail here, is the limitation of anthropological sexing and aging. However, in absence of more secure methods, I believe it is best to base studies of sex and age in the burial record on anthropological determinations, rather than creating determinations based on grave goods.

Dating the burials also had limitations. Though 88 burials had direct radiocarbon dates, which were able, with either 1 or 2 sigma determinations, to place the burial in a period, it left 158 burials without direct dating. In many cases the burial had a large enough combination of diagnostic features, such as barrow construction or pottery, to be allocated to a period with a reasonable degree of certainty. However, for a few burials dating was more difficult. Rather than removing these burials from the chronological analysis they were assigned to a period to the best of my ability and the reasons for their placement are stated in Appendix Two. However, this may be the reason for the increased number of Period Three burials, as this is the period with the most diverse range of burial practices.

Another limitation concerns the nature of databases. Due to the nature of database analysis, qualitative data are reduced to numerical figures, which risks losing some of the finer nuances of the data. In many respects this cannot be avoided when looking at large quantities of data within time restrictions. However, I also considered qualitative aspects of the data by manually exploring the database and looking for similarities which were not apparent in a numerical search.

Finally, the last limitation is human error. By having several entries for each burial, information can be entered incorrectly, which could affect the analysis. However, the multiple entries for each burial also allowed the information to be cross-checked across the different tables. For example, the number of burials with grave goods in the Root Table could be checked against the number of entries in the Grave Good Table.

3: ANALYSIS

The analysis conducted for this research is presented under the following topics: burial traditions within the different forms (barrow, flat grave, other and cairn); the traditions evident in the burial methods (inhumation, cremation, token inhumation and token cremation); and finally the grave goods representation. As part of each of these topics the key themes of age representation and period patterns are also explored. However, to commence, the general overview of the dataset used in the analysis will be presented.

The following account documents the variables which resulted in patterns which have a direct bearing upon the discussions in Chapter Four. However, many more variables were also considered during the research which are included as Appendix Three. The chi-squared statistical analysis is only used if the sample size is large enough, as outlined by Fletcher and Lock (2005).

3.1. Overview

As previously mentioned, the dataset of female burials from the Chalcolithic and Early Bronze Age used in this analysis numbers 246 individuals from a total of 116 sites. These sites are distributed across the length and breadth of Britain and Appendix One lists the counties which they are from. Table 3.1 gives an overview of the density of burials within modern political country boundaries.

Country	Number of burials
England	168
Scotland	61
Wales	17

Table 3.1: Burial density in the countries included in the study area.

The difficulties of assigning sex to the burials of the past were mentioned in Chapter Two, and as a result my database includes the certainty score that the female sex was assigned to the burials (Table 3.2). It is clear that burials confidently assigned as female are the greatest in number, and by taking the female and "probably" female numbers together they make up almost 70% of the dataset. This demonstrates that there is a good level of confidence in that this dataset is of the female sex.

Sex certainty	Number of burials
Female	112
Probably female	56
Possibly female	78

Table 3.2: Assignation of sex certainty levels.

When looking at the age distributions of the females within the dataset (Table 3.3) it is obvious that the adult age category contains the majority of burials. As discussed, this is possibly the result of the difficulties in assigning anthropological age to skeletal remains (Chapter Two).

Age	Number of burials
Young adult (18 – 25 years)	70
Adult (26 – 39 years)	141
Mature (40+ years)	35

Table 3.3: Age distribution of the dataset.

Unlike the age distribution, the uneven division of burials within the four periods is probably reflective of a past reality (though acknowledging the limitations of the dating methods).

Period	Number of burials
One (2500 – 2250 BC)	9
Two (2250 – 1950 BC)	65
Three (1950 – 1700 BC)	133
Four (1700 – 1500 BC)	39

Table 3.4: Period distributions of dataset.

This is because it has been noted that from around 2000 BC, access to formal burial was widened in society (Garwood 2007), which is reflected in this dataset (Table 3.4).

Before moving on to the in-depth results of the analysis, I will give a brief overview of the number of burials provisioned with grave goods (Table 3.5).

Grave goods	154
No grave goods	92

Table 3.5: Number of burials with grave goods.

The high percentage of burials with grave goods, compared with other studies of the period (Chapter One), is a result of the items included in this study as grave goods, which is in itself the result of modern excavation techniques. Rather than only including the obvious grave goods (the necklaces, daggers and pottery), less obvious grave goods were also counted, such as animal bone and stains upon the bones.

The inclusion of these categories of grave goods makes the greatest difference in terms of the results from cremations. This is because it is only since modern excavations of cremated bone that these items could be located; indeed antiquarians often did not examine the cremated bones found within the urns at all. This is well demonstrated by the recovery of a bone toggle found in a cremation from the Hill of Tuach, Aberdeenshire, during re-examination of the nineteenth century finds in light of a new excavation (R. Bradley pers. comm.).

The presence of bone stains can indicate whether metal objects were included as part of the funerary representation of females, which had either been eroded away entirely due to the burial environment, or if the items were not included in the burial but were present during the cremation process. Recently a new technique has been developed by Chris Speed which can indicate the former presence of metal items in cremations even without staining (C. Speed pers. comm.). This then raises the interesting question of why some items were included in the final burial and why some were not (Chapter 4). Though not included in the final burial, I argue that these items were still important components of burial representation as they would have been present, and presumably visible, on the cremation pyre itself, which, not only would arguably be the biggest spectacle of the funerary process, but would also have been the moment of transformation for the representation of the deceased. The inclusion of these categories helps mitigate the differences in techniques between inhumation and cremation burial to a certain extent; though both represent the final stage in the mortuary process the cremation itself can be seen as an additional intermediate stage (as can exposure).

3.2. Burial Form

The first aspect of female burial traditions which this analysis considers is the different forms that the burials themselves took. Table 3.6 gives an outline of the numbers of burials of each form.

Barrow	116
Flat grave	86
Other	33
Cairn	11

Table 3.6: Numbers of burials within each form type.

It is clear to see that the most popular forms of burial during the Chalcolithic and Early Bronze Age were within a barrow or a flat grave. However, the different burial forms were not distributed equally among the four periods (Table 3.7). Although in Period Four the distribution of burial forms is similar to the overall average, in Periods One and Two a female is far more likely to be buried in a flat grave, whereas in Period Three there are more burials in barrows, cairns and other forms than expected, but far less flat graves. This demonstrates that the period in which a person was buried had a significant impact on the form chosen for burial.

Period	Barrow	Flat Grave	Cairn	Other Form
One	3	6	0	0
Two	24	35	3	3
Three	73	29	6	25
Four	16	16	2	5

Table 3.7: The distribution of burial types by period.

The distribution of ages among the different forms is not equal (Table 3.8). The age distribution in barrows, flat graves and other forms of burials is as expected from the dataset. However, for the cairns there are fewer young adults and more mature adults than expected.

	Barrow	Flat grave	Cairn	Other
Young adult	32	27	1	10
Adult	70	47	4	20
Mature	14	12	6	3

Table 3.8: Distribution of ages among the burial forms.

The distribution of associated monuments with the different burial forms (Table 3.9) is not equal, to a significance level of α0.001 (16.27; χ^2=20.53). This is because barrows have far more associated monuments than expected and flat graves and other forms far fewer. As part of this analysis I decided that while further barrows and cairns in the immediate area would be classed as additional monuments, associated flat graves would not be. This is because flat graves are not monumental and do not make large impacts on the landscape. Furthermore, multiple barrows can create ceremonial landscapes around monuments, such as Stonehenge and Avebury (Woodward and Woodward 1996) or in the Peak District (Rogers 2013). The difference between the results for barrows and flat graves reflect the burial forms themselves; barrows are more monumental than flat graves and thus are associated with more monuments.

	Barrow	Flat graves	Cairn	Other
Associated monuments	90	44	9	16
No associated monuments	26	42	2	17

Table 3.9: Distribution of associated monuments with burial form.

When considering how the burial cut size corresponds with the age of the deceased (Table 3.10) it seems as though the size of the cuts in cairns and other forms do not differ greatly. However, in both barrows and flat graves the adult age group seems to have the smallest graves and young adults the largest.

	Barrow	Flat grave	Cairn	Other
Young adult	$1.73m^2$	$1.21m^2$	No data	$0.33m^2$
Adult	$1.29m^2$	$0.82m^2$	$0.35m^2$	$0.53m^2$
Mature	$1.40m^2$	$1.18m^2$	$0.35m^2$	$3.15m^2*$

*Table 3.10: Average burial size by age and burial form. *One available measurement.*

For the next part of this section the individual burial forms will be analysed except the cairn burials which are discussed in Appendix Three.

Barrows

The prevalence of associated monuments with barrow burials in each period (Figure 3.1) is not equal. Instead the number of barrow burials with associated monuments increased steadily to Period Three. This is as expected since there are more monuments in the landscape as time increases. However, this trend reverses in Period Four when fewer burials in barrows are associated with other monuments. This could be illustrating change in attitudes to the past during this period.

An interesting line of inquiry concerning the female burial traditions in barrows is looking at the burial's placement within the barrows. Thirty percent of the female burials in this dataset are placed in the centre of barrows (the largest proportion of any placement). If you consider the burial placement as being central (i.e. centre or off-centre) or non-central, then 40% of female burials are central and 60% non-central. These figures demonstrate that females are located centrally within barrows more than other studies would lead us to believe (Pierpoint 1980; Mizoguchi 1992).

It is clear that the location of burial placement in barrows is closely related to the period of the burial (Figure 3.2). During the first two periods there are more females buried centrally in barrows than expected if distribution was equal, whereas in the fourth period there are more than expected non-centrally. This casts doubt on the conclusions which suggest that females are more likely to be placed non-centrally in barrows due to their sex; instead it demonstrates that the factor which makes the difference is actually the period in which the deceased was buried.

	Central	Non-central
Grave goods	37	34
No grave goods	9	36

Table 3.11: Allocation of grave goods by burial placement.

Within the barrow analysis, the only significant association between the provisions of grave goods with another feature of the burial is its relation to the burial's position within the barrow (Table 3.11). The allocation of grave goods is not distributed equally across burial placement to a significance level of $\alpha0.001$ (10.83; $\chi^2=11.86$), whereas burials in the central positions are more likely to have grave goods.

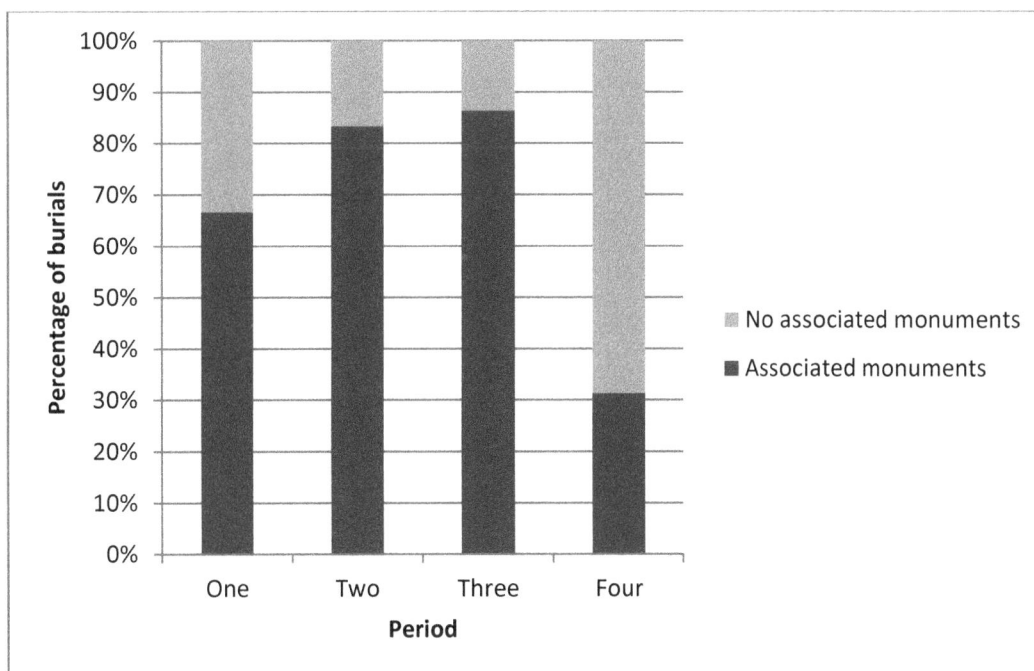

Figure 3.1: Percentage of burials with associated monuments by period.

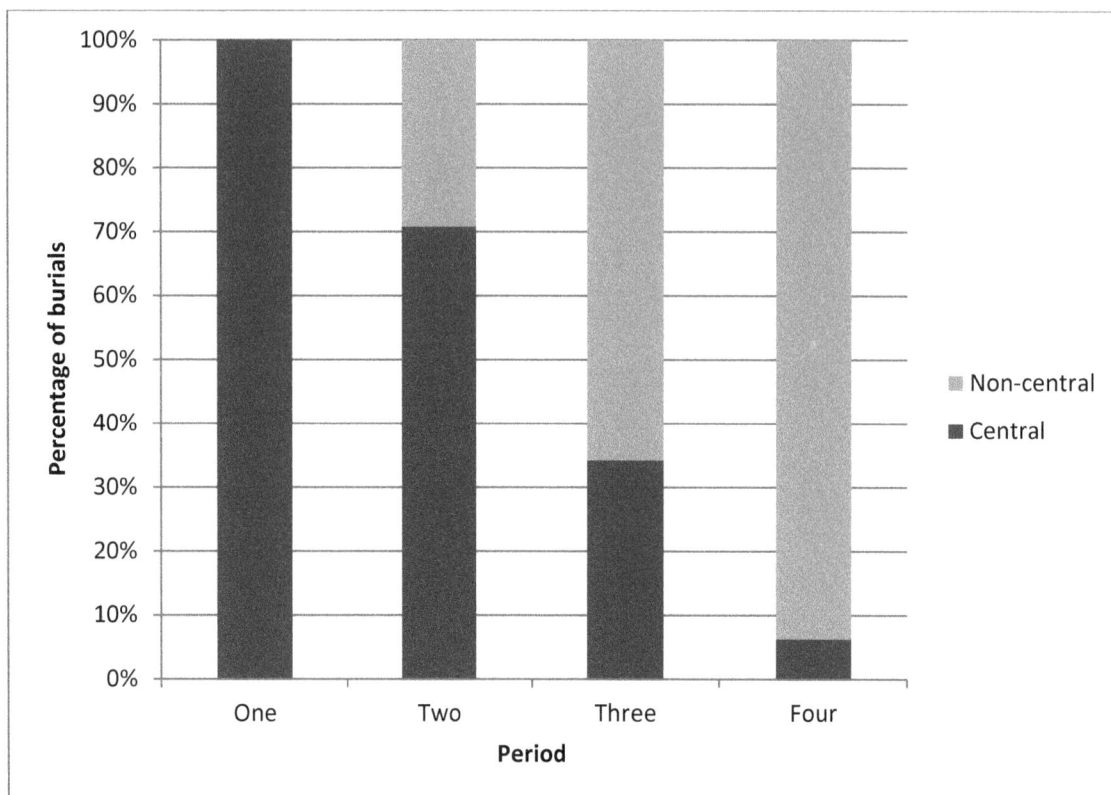

Figure 3.2: Placement of burials in barrows related to period of burial.

Flat Graves

The distribution of flat grave burials with associated monuments is not equal across the periods (Table 3.12). In general, the number of burials with associated monuments increases through time, with Period Four having the most. However, Period Two does not follow this trend as fewer burials than expected have associated monuments.

Period	Associated monuments	No associated monuments
One	3	3
Two	12	23
Three	17	12
Four	12	4

Table 3.12: Associated monument distribution in comparison with periods.

The provision of grave goods in flat grave burials depends on both the age of the deceased and also the method of burial (Table 3.13).

The null hypothesis that grave goods are distributed equally across ages is rejected at α0.050 (5.99; χ^2=6.31) significance. Though adults have the expected number of grave goods for the sample, the young adults have more than expected and mature individuals less.

The distribution of grave goods in flat graves by burial methods is also not equal. This is because token cremation burials are associated with grave goods less than expected. These two aspects of grave goods allocation (age and method) are not linked however, as, of the seven token cremations without grave goods, only one is a mature individual; the remainder are adults.

	Grave goods	No grave goods
Young adult	22	5
Adult	29	18
Mature	5	7
Inhumation	26	9
Cremation	27	12
Token inhumation	2	2
Token cremation	1	7

Table 3.13: Comparison of grave goods provision with age and method.

Other forms

Before discussing the results of the analysis conducted on the other forms of burials during the Chalcolithic and Early Bronze Age, it is prudent to describe the forms that they took (Table 3.14).

What is interesting is that sixteen of the thirty-three burials are not placed in cut features; instead they have been placed in natural features, are deposited during the construction of monuments or are surface deposits. This is in contrast to barrows and flat graves (Table 3.15).

Henge	5
Stone circle	9
Segmented ditch circle	5
Enclosure	1
Chambered tomb	1
Natural mound	6
Rock overhang	1
Hole in bed rock	5

Table 3.14: Forms of "other" burials.

In fact, the null hypothesis that the number of burials in cultural features is equally distributed across burial forms is strongly rejected at α0.001 (16.27; χ^2=66.95) significance. This is because cairns and especially other burial forms have a far greater number of the non cultural burial cuts than would be expected.

	Barrows	**Flat Graves**	**Cairns**	**Other form**
Cut feature	110	84	6	17
Natural feature	6	2	5	16

Table 3.15: Distribution of burials in cultural features across burial forms.

3.3. Burial methods

This analysis of the Chalcolithic and Early Bronze Age female burials now examines the burial methods (Table 3.16). The most popular burial method for females during this period was cremation, with almost twice as many individuals being cremated than inhumed.

Inhumation	**Cremation**	**Token inhumation**	**Token cremation**
79	139	10	18

Table 3.16: Number of burials of each method.

Looking at the period distributions for these different methods it is clear that there are changes in burial traditions during the Chalcolithic and Early Bronze Age (Table 3.17). There are more inhumations in the first two periods than expected if equally distributed, and more cremations in the fourth, with the proportions of the third period as expected. This pattern was not unanticipated and fits well with previous interpretations of the burial methods of this period (i.e. Brück 2009), where the numbers are very similar. This demonstrates that female burial traditions are not different to those of males overall.

Period	I	C	TI	TC
One	9	0	0	0
Two	32	27	4	2
Three	33	80	6	14
Four	5	32	0	2

Table 3.17: Distribution of burial methods across periods (I: Inhumation, C: Cremation, TI: Token Inhumation, TC: Token Cremation).

Like the period divisions, the different ages are distributed unequally among the different burial methods (Table 3.18).

	I	C	TI	TC
Young adult	79	37	4	2
Adult	35	87	4	15
Mature	17	15	2	1

Table 3.18: Distribution of burial methods amongst age categories (I: Inhumation, C: Cremation, TI: Token Inhumation, TC: Token Cremation).

Overall, the different methods are distributed fairly equally amongst the young adults, however, individuals in the adult age category are less likely to be buried as inhumations than expected, whereas mature individuals are more likely to be inhumed rather than cremated.

Grave goods provision between the four different burial methods is not equal (Table 3.19). When considering grave good provision across the dataset the token cremations are provisioned with grave goods far less than expected.

	Grave goods	**No grave goods**
Inhumation	52	27
Cremation	95	44
Token inhumation	4	6
Token cremation	3	15

Table 3.19: Number of burials with grave goods in each burial method.

As anticipated, the burial cuts of the greatest size are those associated with inhumation burials, both full and token. If you then consider how the sizes correspond to the age of the deceased the only pattern that emerges is that the mature individuals are consistently in the smallest graves, whilst the adults and young adults are in the larger ones. However, the difference in size between the age groups is fairly negligible, so I would not stress this pattern.

Inhumations

As part of the inhumation analysis the position of the body in the grave is considered. Several different elements make up the position of the body; the posture, the side the body is lain upon and the orientation of the head.

Burials of the Chalcolithic and Early Bronze Age are recognised as having three different postures in the grave; extended, flexed and crouched, with flexed and crouched the most common. This is reflected in the posture of the female burials in this dataset (Table 3.20). Since the number of extended burials is small it has not been included in the statistical analysis. Instead the statistical analysis looked at the distribution of the flexed and crouched positions. The null hypothesis that the distribution of burials is equal between the postures is rejected at α0.050 significance (3.84; $\chi^2=4$). Instead more burials are in a crouched position than flexed.

Flexed	24
Crouched	40
Extended	1

Table 3.20: Distribution of burial postures.

However, the age distributions do not follow this pattern (Table 3.21). Instead the null hypothesis that the distributions of the postures will be equal among the ages is rejected at α0.025 significance (7.38; $\chi^2=8.14$). This is because young adults have the opposite of what is expected; they are buried more often in the flexed rather than crouched position.

	Young adult	Adult	Mature
Flexed	11	10	3
Crouched	6	21	13

Table 3.21: Distribution of body postures among ages.

This seems to be a true pattern as, if you compare the burial postures with the period of the burials, the distribution is what is expected for the dataset (Table 3.22).

Period	One	Two	Three	Four
Flexed	4	9	9	2
Crouched	4	16	18	2

Table 3.22: Distribution of body postures among periods.

This suggests that there does seem to be a conscious decision that young adults are more appropriately buried in a flexed position than adults or mature individuals.

The orientation of the head is not distributed equally among the four cardinal directions (north, east, south, and

west) (Table 3.23). This is because more burials are orientated with heads to the south than expected.

North	17
East	13
South	27
West	12

Table 3.23: Number of burials with head to each cardinal direction.

Unlike the burial posture, the head orientation seems to be distributed equally across the age categories and the different periods (Table 3.24). The only period in which the distribution of the head orientation is not equal is Period One where more burials than expected are orientated to the south. Therefore, the only time period in which it can be stated that females are buried with their heads to the south is from 2500 – 2250 BC, whereas some authors (Gibbs 1989) suggest that this is the dominant orientation across the period.

	North	East	South	West
Young adult	6	3	6	6
Adult	5	6	16	5
Mature	6	4	5	1
Period One	1	0	6	1
Period Two	9	6	7	4
Period Three	6	6	12	6
Period Four	1	1	2	1

Table 3.24: Distribution of head orientation with ages and periods.

The side of the body a female is buried on is also a decision at the time of burial. The females in this study tend to be lain on the right or left side, with only two placed on their backs (Table 3.25). It is clear from the figures that female burials are not equally distributed on their right and left side, and that instead far more are chosen to be laid on their right.

Right	52
Left	13

Table 3.25: Numbers of burials on right or left hand sides.

This distribution is not related to the age of the deceased, the period in which they died, the orientation of the head or the provision of grave goods. Thus, the reason why some females were buried on the left hand side is beyond the scope of this study, as it appears to be unrelated to age, period, head orientation or grave good provision.

Despite the suggestion that the Chalcolithic and Early Bronze Age are typified by single burials, there are actually several burials which contain more than one individual (Table 3.26). Though these figures show that most burials are single, the dataset does include a number of multiple burials. However, the females chosen to be part of multiple burials are not selected by age or the period in which they died.

Single	66
Multiple	13

Table 3.26: Number of inhumation burials in single and multiple graves.

The demography of those interred with females in the multiple graves is also spread fairly equally across the different age categories, though adults are interred with males more than would be expected and mature individuals less.

Token Inhumations

As with the inhumation burials, the token individuals are not always the sole occupants of the graves (Table 3.27). Although it seems token inhumations of young adults are interred more frequently as single individuals this may be due to the small number in the sample. However, when there are multiple burials it appears that token inhumations of adults and mature individuals are interred with male adults and/or infants, whilst young adults are interred with other females and infants.

	Single	Multiple
Young adult	3	1
Adult	1	3
Mature	0	2

Table 3.27: Numbers of single and multiple token inhumation burials by age.

Cremations

When examining cremation deposits looking at the weights is a useful line of enquiry because in most cases the cremation rite itself was not conducted at the site of burial (although there are exceptions, such as pit pyre cremations (255: Butcher's Rise 691)). As a result the cremated remains needed to be gathered and transferred to the burial location.

The average weight of a female cremation burial from this data set was 1287.3g. When this is looked at by age (Table 3.28) it appears that mature individuals seem to have the greatest amount of bone collected from the pyre, followed by young adults, who, although less than the mature individuals, still have more than the data average.

Adults, on the other hand, have the least average cremation weight of the different age categories. The urned burials also have more cremated bone gathered for burial (Table 3.28). Unsurprisingly, the cremations which contain more than one individual also have more bone than those which appear to represent single deposits.

However, what is interesting with the average weights is that those burials which contain grave goods (either as an urn or other items) weigh less on average than those burials without (Table 3.28). If, as traditional interpretations of grave goods suggests, those with grave goods had more importance socially then we could expect more of the cremated body would be gathered for burial.

	Average weight	Number of burials
Young adults	1411.4g	20
Adults	1146.0g	59
Mature	1820g	11
Urned	1449.7g	28
Un-urned	1214.0g	62
Multiple	1922.9g	28
Single	1000.3g	62
Grave goods	1250.2g	64
No grave goods	1378.7g	26
Period One	n/a	0
Period Two	1522.9g	18
Period Three	1101.1g	54
Period Four	1610.3g	18

Table 3.28: List of average cremation weights for various burial traits.

When looking at the average period weights (Table 3.28) it appears that Periods Two and Four have the greatest amount of bone collected and three the least. However, as with all the average weight analyses, this could be a result of the numbers of each type of cremation the average was taken from. Therefore, the low result for Period Three could be a factor of the numbers involved.

Looking to see which burials featured in the dataset can be called single burials has demonstrated that not all burials from the Chalcolithic and Early Bronze Age can be termed "single" burials, that is burial of just one individual per burial context. The cremations are no exception (Table 3.29). In the case of cremations, a total of 30% of burials actually contain multiple individuals, a greater proportion than in the inhumation rite.

Seventy-four percent of the multiple cremation burials are those with only one additional individual, however, there is one burial in which it is estimated that there are seven people represented (106: North Mains, Barrow H). The most common additions to female cremations are infants, with 64% of multiple cremation deposits containing at least one. The second most common addition is an adult male, which features in around a third of the burials. Only four burials contain other adult females (311/312 and 314/315), where two females are represented in each burial.

Single	97
Multiple	42

Table 3.29: Numbers of single and multiple cremation burials.

Token cremations

The average weight of a female token cremation burial was 196.7g. As with the average weights of the full cremations by age, it is interesting to note that mature individuals seem to have the most bone collected for deposition (Table 3.30). However, the result from the mature individual was only from one burial and so may not be representative. The young adult and adult token cremations have remarkably similar weights, both smaller than the average by a slight amount. Once again, token cremations representing more than one individual include more bone than those which are believed to represent only one (Table 3.30).

In contrast to full cremations, the burials with grave goods weigh more than those without by a difference of almost 100g (Table 3.30), which is a very large difference compared to the respective averages. The results for the period averages are also different to the pattern from the full cremations (Table 3.30). For token cremation burials it appears that the weight of cremation deposits decrease through time. Once again the caveat of the number of burials these averages are taken from must be highlighted.

	Average weight	Number of burials
Young adults	186.7g	2
Adults	186.2g	12
Mature	342.8g	1
Multiple	263.0g	3
Single	180.1g	12
Grave goods	275.4g	3
No grave goods	177.0g	12
Period Two	281.2g	1
Period Three	199.5g	12
Period Four	137.5g	2

Table 3.30: List of average token cremation weights for various burial traits.

As with the other methods of burial, token cremations are also not only of single individuals. In fact, 22% of token cremations represent multiple individuals (n=4).

In the case of token cremations all multiple burials represent two individuals; one female and one other. The demography of the other individual was an equal split between adult males and infants.

3.4. Grave goods

As mentioned in Table 3.5, 154 female burials in this dataset were associated with grave goods, roughly 63% of the burials. This is a fairly high proportion, but still demonstrates the need to develop analytical methods which do not concentrate on grave goods (see above).

When considering why 154 burials were provisioned with grave goods there do not seem to be any obvious patterns. However, it seems that young adults are the most likely to be provisioned with grave goods out of the age categories (Table 3.31). To a lesser extent this was also true of the Period One burials (Table 3.31).

	Grave goods	No grave goods
Young adult	50	20
Adult	83	58
Mature	21	14
Period One	8	1
Period Two	41	24
Period Three	80	53
Period Four	25	14

Table 3.31: Distribution of burials with grave goods between ages and periods.

Though the distribution of grave good material types (i.e. ceramic, flint, metal etc.) is equal overall across the three age categories, there are a few anomalies (Figure 3.3).

The largest anomaly is that mature individuals have more burials with flint artefacts than expected, whereas young adults have less. Adults, on the other hand, have more burials with stone artefacts than expected and mature individuals less.

The burials in this dataset have up to five different material types represented by the objects in the burials (Figure 3.4). Overall it appears that young adults have fewer burials than expected containing items of four or five different material types, whereas mature individuals have more burials with items of over three different materials. Adults, however, exhibit the average pattern.

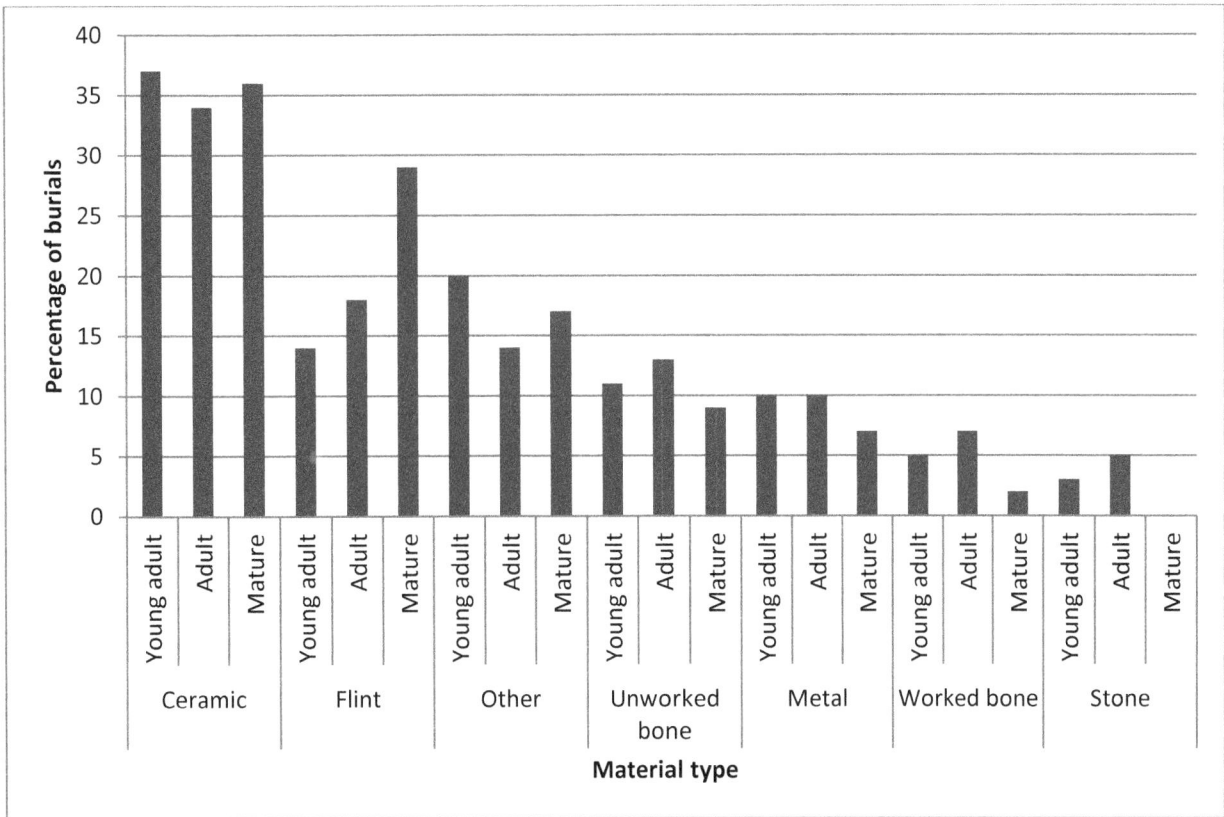

Figure 3.3: Percentage of burials with at least one grave good of the material type by age.

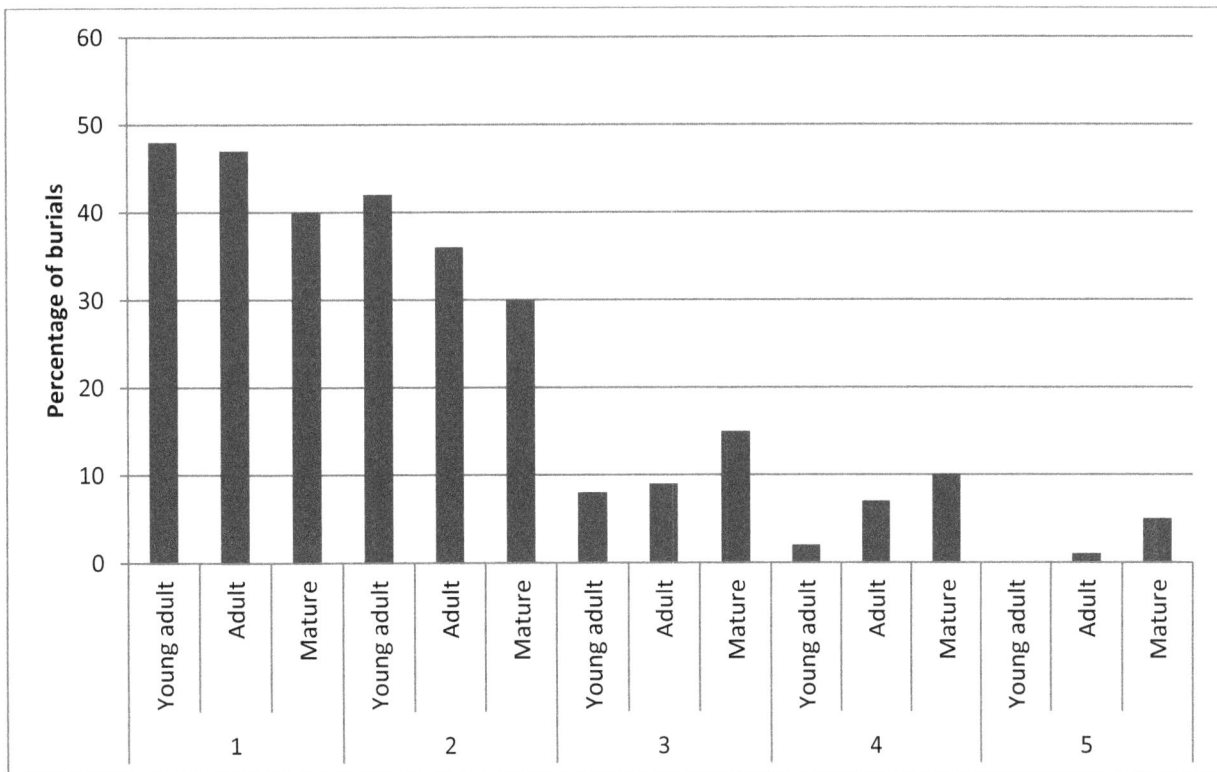

Figure 3.4: Number of burials with number of different material types by age.

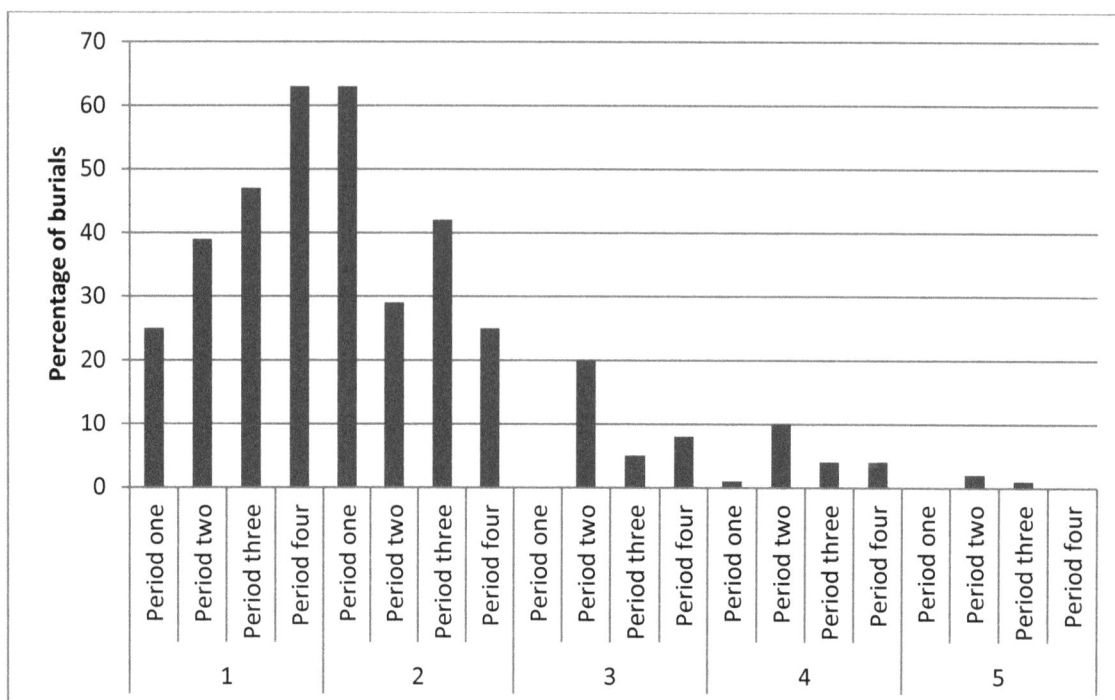

Figure 3.5: Number of burials with number of different material types by period.

When considering the number of different material types per burial by period (Figure 3.5) it appears that Period One has more burials with artefacts of two different material types than expected. Indeed, it is the only period in which there are more burials with items of two types than one. Period Two, however, has more burials with objects of three and four different material types. In contrast, Period Three has fewer burials containing artefacts of three different material types than expected. Finally, Period Four has the most burials with objects of only one material type.

Overall, Period Four is the only period in which there are more burials with grave goods of only one material type, than those with two or more. This suggests that grave good provision becomes less diverse over time in regards to the material the objects are made from (Figure 3.6).

When considering the number of grave goods in each burial two different figures are used; the number of different types and the total number of objects. This prevents burials with necklaces of 100 beads or with 10 flint flakes skewing the results (Appendix One).

The range of numbers of different types of grave goods interred in Chalcolithic and Early Bronze Age female graves extend from one to seven, with the average being two (Table 3.32).

The distribution of the number of different artefacts per burial between periods reveals some patterns (Figure 3.7). Period One has more burials than expected with both two and five different types of artefact, and consequently too few with just one. Period Two has far more burials with over five different artefacts, but less with four. The

opposite is the case with Period Three. Finally, Period Four has a greater number of burials with only one type of artefact. This echoes the pattern already discussed with grave goods made of different materials, where diversity decreases with time.

Number of different types	Number of burials
1	65
2	51
3	23
4	4
5	6
>5	5

Table 3.32: Number of burials compared to number of different types of grave good.

There are also a few departures from the expected results when looking at the distribution between the age categories (Figure 3.8). In this case it seems that young adults have fewer burials with five or more artefact types, whereas mature individuals have fewer burials with only one type, but more with five. This indicates that perhaps as age increases females get buried with a greater selection of artefacts.

The total number of grave goods within the female burials ranges from one to 213 items, with the average being eight artefacts. This large range is mainly a result of the great number of beads found in several of the graves. However, the most common number of items is just one; which accounts for 39% of all burials with grave goods (Table 3.33).

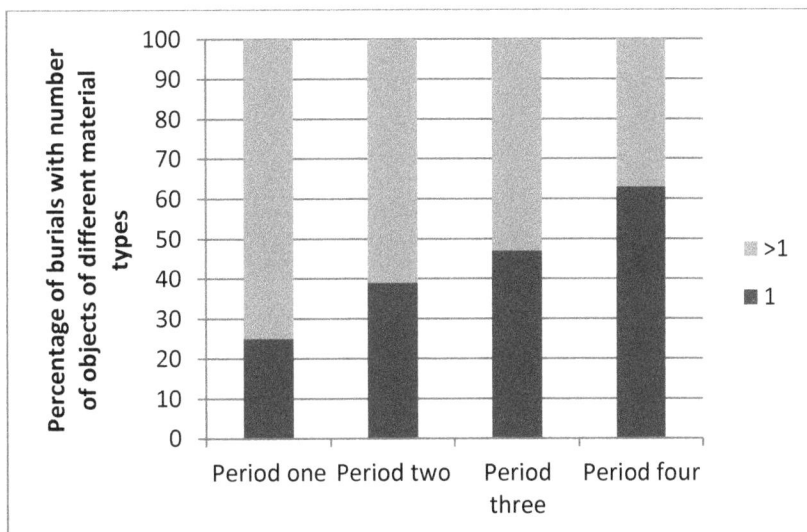

Figure 3.6: Proportion of burials by period with objects of either one or more than one material.

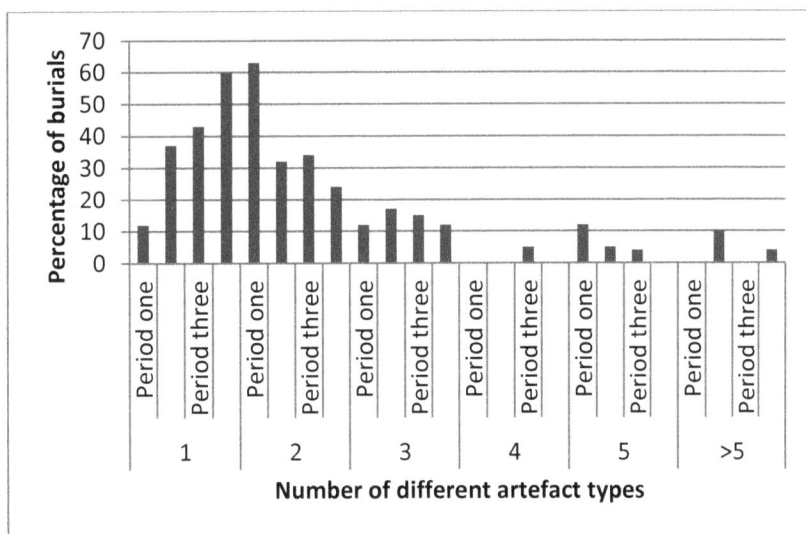

Figure 3.7: Number of different artefacts in burials by period.

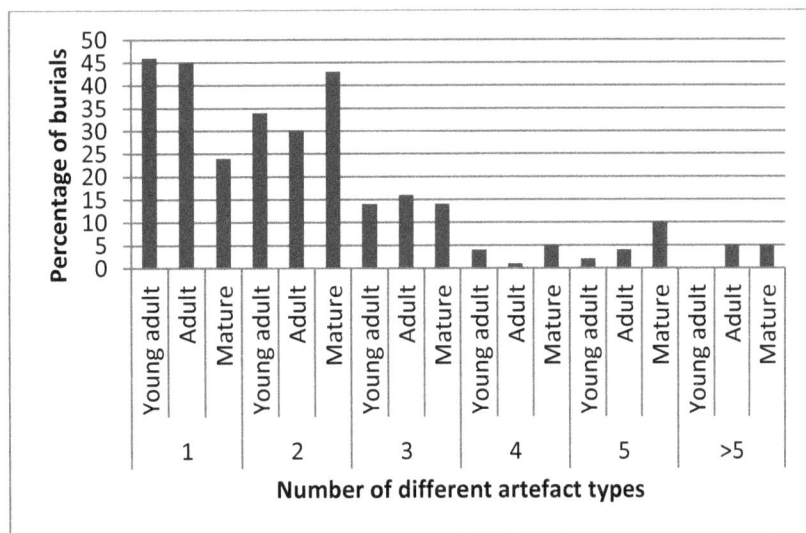

Figure 3.8: Number of different artefacts in burials by age of the deceased.

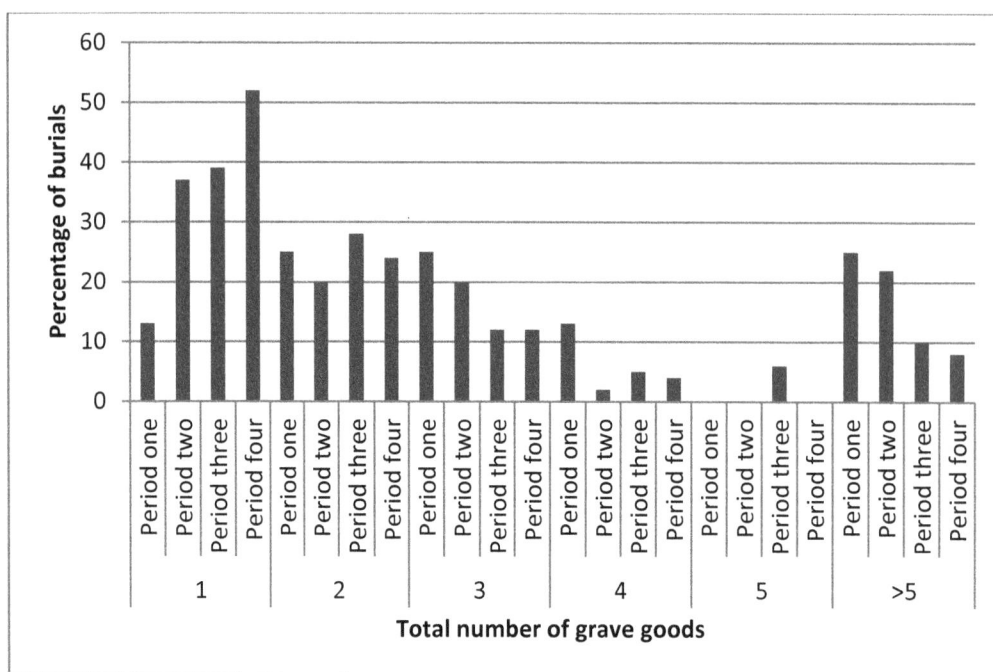

Figure 3.9: Total number of grave goods by period of the burial.

Number of grave goods	Number of burials
1	60
2	38
3	23
4	7
5	5
>5	21

Table 3.33: Number of burials compared to total number of grave goods.

As with the number of different types of grave goods in burials, the total number of grave goods was distributed equally among the different periods and ages. However, once again there were a few exceptions to the overall trend. Period One had too few burials with just one grave good and more than expected with greater than five (Figure 3.9). Period Two had fewer burials with five items, but more with greater than five. Period Three, however, had more burials with five items than expected. In contrast, Period Four had more burials with only the one item. This is continuing the trend already discussed that grave good provision becomes less diverse by 1700 BC, but seems to peak between 2250 and 1700 BC.

Although the distribution of total grave good numbers is equal overall across the age categories; the general trend, identified earlier, that mature individuals are buried with greater diversity of artefacts is continued (Figure 3.10). Mature individuals have fewer burials with just the one grave good, but more than expected with five. Young adults have more burials with four items. In contrast, adults have less than expected with three or five items.

The analysis of the grave goods interred with female burials now focuses upon looking at the different materials the items are made of; pottery, metal, stone, worked animal bone, un-worked animal bone, flint and other types. Detailed analysis of the different grave good material types is included in Appendix Three.

Pottery

Sixty percent of the female burials with grave goods contained at least one item of pottery, making it the most common artefact type included with the burials. The forms these items take fall into complete pots or sherds / incomplete examples. There are six different forms of complete pots in this study; Beakers, Food Vessels, Collared Urns, Cordoned Urns, miniature vessels (including accessory vessels and pygmy cups), and others (such as trevisker ware). The most common types of pottery found with the female burials in this dataset are Collared Urns, followed by sherds and then Beakers (Table 3.34).

Pottery type	Number of burials
Beaker	24
Food Vessel	15
Collared Urn	28
Cordoned Urn	28
Miniature Vessel	6
Other	4
Sherds/ incomplete	27

Table 3.34: Number of burials with each of the pottery types.

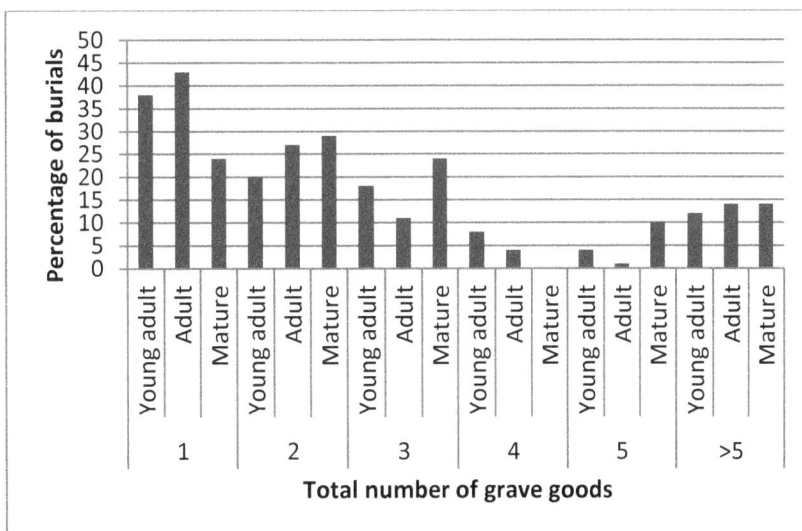

Figure 3.10: Total number of grave goods by age.

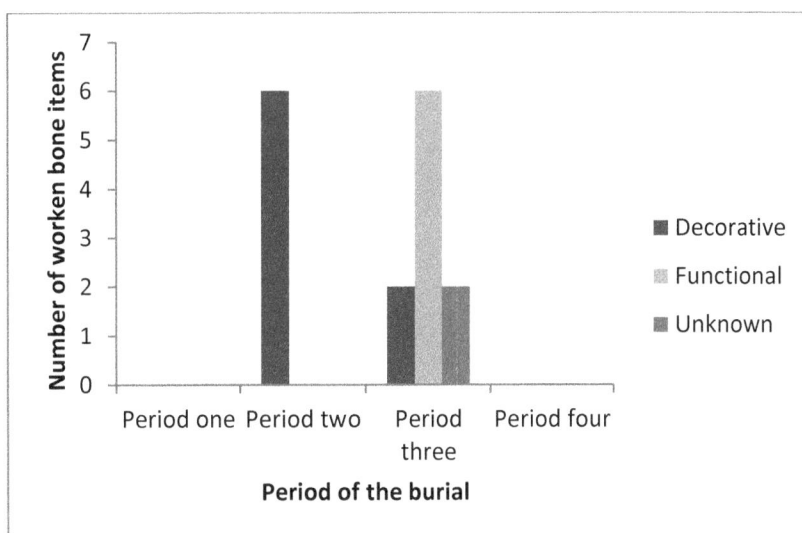

Figure 3.11: Number of worked bone item types by period of the burial.

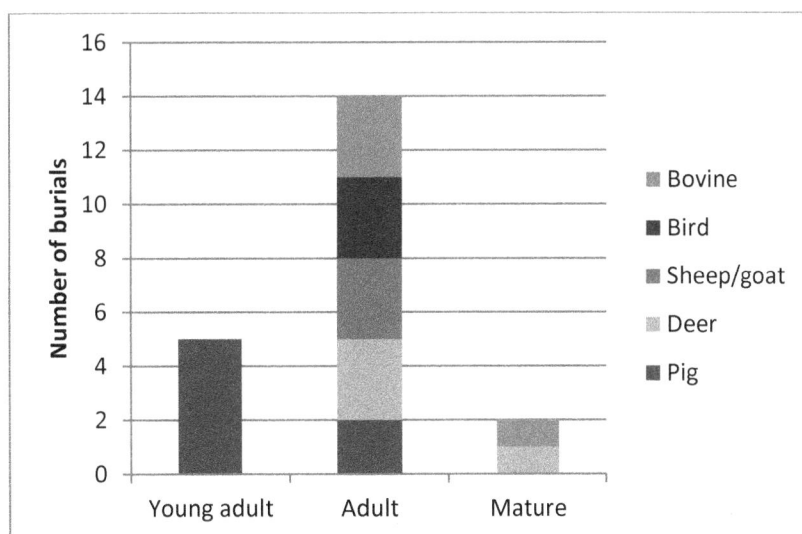

Figure 3.12: Distribution of animal species by age.

Metalwork

Of the burials in this dataset containing grave goods, 16% include at least one item of metalwork. Of the dataset as a whole this number reduces to 10%. However, this is the average number of graves which contain metalwork of the Chalcolithic and Early Bronze Age and thus demonstrates how female burials are not exceptional by the amount of metalwork in the graves. The metalwork of this period takes several forms in this dataset (Table 3.35).

Awl	17
Dagger	5
Bead	2
Cones	2
Cylinder/ rod	2
Axe	1
"Earring"	1

Table 3.35: Number of metal work items appearing in the dataset.

Awls are the most common items followed by daggers or knife-daggers. The remaining items occur either singly or twice in the burials and take the form of either "decorative" items, such as beads, "earrings" and cone button covers, or items of which the original use is unknown, such as rods or cylinders.

Worked Bone

Nine percent of female burials with grave goods contain at least one item of worked bone. These items took several forms and are divided among three categories; decorative items; functional items; and unknown (Table 3.36). Decorative items are the most numerous, but not significantly. These are composed mainly of beads, but there is also a finial, an antler plate and also a polished tusk. The functional items are pins, spatulas and points.

Decorative	Bead	5
	Finial	1
	Antler plate	1
	Polished tusk	1
Functional	Pin	4
	Point	1
	Spatula	1
Unknown	Unknown	2

Table 3.36: Numbers of the different items of worked bones by category.

Looking at the different types of worked bone artefacts (decorative, functional, and unknown), the distribution is uneven between the chronological periods (Figure 3.11). This is because Period Two only has decorative worked bone artefacts whereas Period Three tends to have

functional ones. Periods one and four have no worked bone items.

Unworked animal bone

Twenty-one percent of the female burials with grave goods contain unworked animal bone, a higher percentage than burials with worked bone. The un-worked bone probably entered the grave as a form of food offering. However, the animal bone from Kingshill North 8656 (200) is interpreted as perhaps forming a hide of leather, a "head-and-hoofs" burial. To conduct analysis on the un-worked animal bone, the bones have been divided into elements of the body; the limbs, trunk and head (Table 3.37). Clearly the most common is unidentified, then the limb bones by a slight margin.

Limbs	8
Trunk	5
Head	6
Unidentified	17
Pig	7
Deer	4
Sheep/goat	3
Bird	3
Bovine	4
Unidentified	15

Table 3.37: Number of burials with different elements and different species of animal bone.

The analysis also considers the species from which the bone was taken (Table 3.37). Once again the most common was unspecified, however, after that pig bones appear to dominate.

The animal species are not distributed equally across the age categories. This is because young adults only have pig bones in their burials, and sheep / goat and bird bones are only found in adult graves, which have the most diverse range of species (Figure 3.12).

Stone

Whetstone	2
Rubbing stone	1
Hammer-stone	1
Axe	1
Pendant	2
Stone pot lid	1
Block of limestone	1

Table 3.38: Numbers of the various stone artefacts found in female burials.

A few female graves in the dataset contain at least one item of stone (as opposed to flint; see below), amounting to 6% of the burials with grave goods (Table 3.38). The stone items in the female graves take several forms; tools such as whetstones, rubbing stones and hammer-stones; decorative items such as pendants (one of which is a perforated whetstone); and also a "weapon" in the form of a polished axe.

Flint

Thirty-two percent of female burials contain at least one item of flint, with the average number of items being two. These flint items come in many forms (Table 3.39), from tools such as scrapers and knives, to barbed-and-tanged arrowheads and finally those flint objects which have been unspecified by type. The most common flint artefact is the flake, followed by the knives or blade implements.

Knife/ blade	22
Scraper	9
Fabricator	2
Arrowhead	4
Strike-a-light	2
Flake	49
Other	5
Unspecified	11

Table 3.39: Numbers of the various flint artefacts found in the burials.

The null hypothesis that the distribution of burials with and without flint artefacts will be equal across the different age categories was rejected at α0.025 significance (7.38; χ^2=8.46). Despite the fact that adults have the expected distribution, young adults have fewer burials with flint artefacts and mature adults have more than expected (Figure 3.13). This suggests that as a female's age increases she is more likely to be associated with flint artefacts.

In the case of the period distributions of flint artefact types the distribution is not equal. Burials from Period One feature more fabricators, arrowheads and other flint items than expected, but no scrapers (Figure 3.14).

In Period Two, however, burials have more scrapers and strike-a-lights, but less arrowheads and other items; almost the opposite to Period One. Period Three, on the other hand, has a greater number of burials with knives or blades and less with flakes; Period Four has the opposite. The unequal distribution is echoed in the average number of flint items between the periods; Period One has the most at an average of 4 items, Period Two has 2, Period Three 1.6 and finally in Period Four the average is 3. However, in Period One these four items are most likely to be specialised tools, whereas in Period Four they are more likely to be flakes. This relates to the fact that by the Middle Bronze Age most flint tools had been replaced by metal ones (Ford *et al* 1984)

Other

Almost thirty percent of the female burials with grave goods contain an item classified in the "other" category. By virtue of its definition, the "other" category contains a diverse range of artefacts (Table 3.40). These have been divided into six categories; decorative, offerings, tools, grave furniture, other and unknown use items. Decorative items include beads used either as personal adornments or, in the case of burial 123 (Net Down 5L(2)) as a tie for the organic container of the cremation, pendants, buttons, studs and armlets. Cereal grains and evidence of certain types or large amounts of pollen (such as *filipendula*) have been classed as offerings. This is much in the same way as the un-worked animal bone, with cereal representing food and pollen floral tributes. Only a few items can be described as tools; iron nodules (for strike-a-light kits) and also the wooden board from burial 212 (Ravenstone) which was interpreted by the excavator as possibly forming part of a leatherworker's kit (Chapter Four). Items of grave furniture have also been included in this section mainly encompassing coffins or coffin-like structures for the remains. The leather thong from burial 289 (Long Critchel 7, 1) is also classed as furniture as it was used to arrange the corpse. Metal staining on bones and charcoal or burnt wood have been categorised as unknown, since the original item is not discernible from the remains; for example, metal staining could be a decorative bead, a functional awl or a "weapon". Finally, the pottery ball and human bone have been termed 'other' as they do not easily fit in the categories.

Decorative	Bead	904
	Pendant	4
	Armlet	1
	Stud	1
	Button	2
Offering	Cereal	2
	Pollen	2
Grave furniture	Coffin/ chamber	3
	Thong	1
Tools	Iron nodule	2
	Wooden board	1
Unknown	Stains on bone	11
	Charcoal	3
Other	Human bone	1
	Pottery ball	1

Table 3.40: Number of the various "other" artefacts found in burials.

The number of beads with each of the age categories was examined; both the number from "necklaces" or "strings" of beads (≥4) and also the total number of beads (Figure 3.15).

In both cases the adults have the number of beads expected in an equal distribution, but the young adults have less and the mature individuals far more. This could

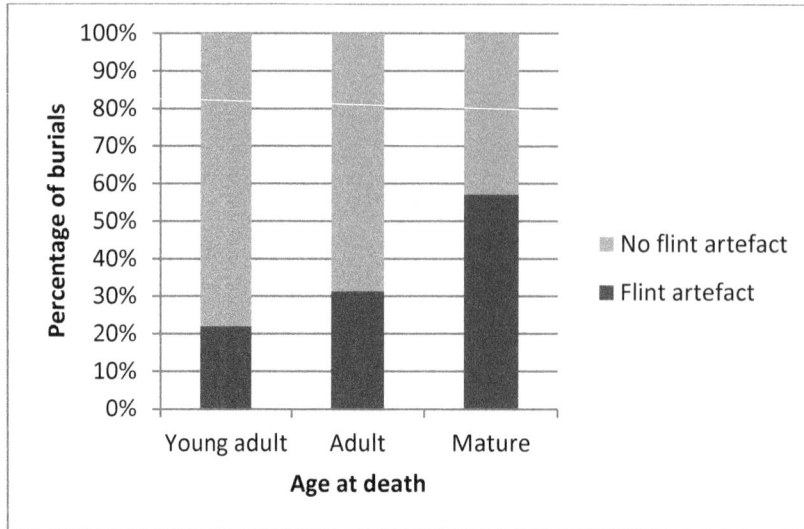

Figure 3.13: Percentage of burials with flint artefacts by age at death.

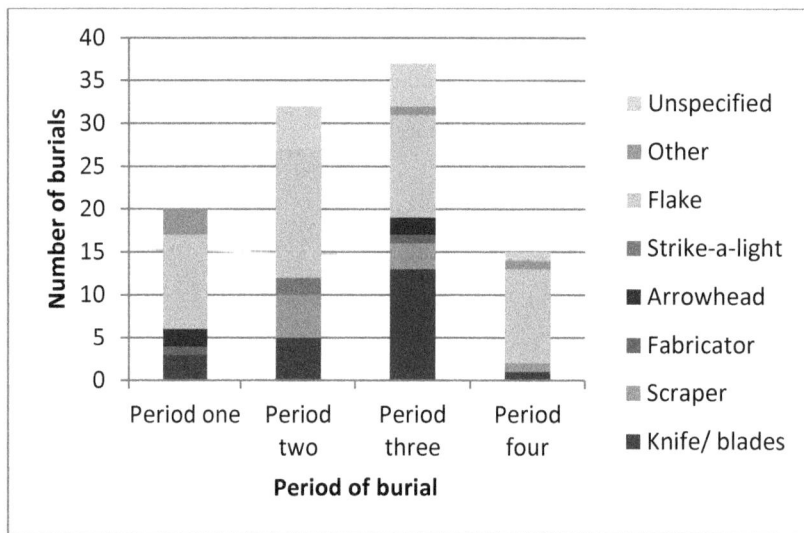

Figure 3.14: Number of burials with different flint artefacts by period.

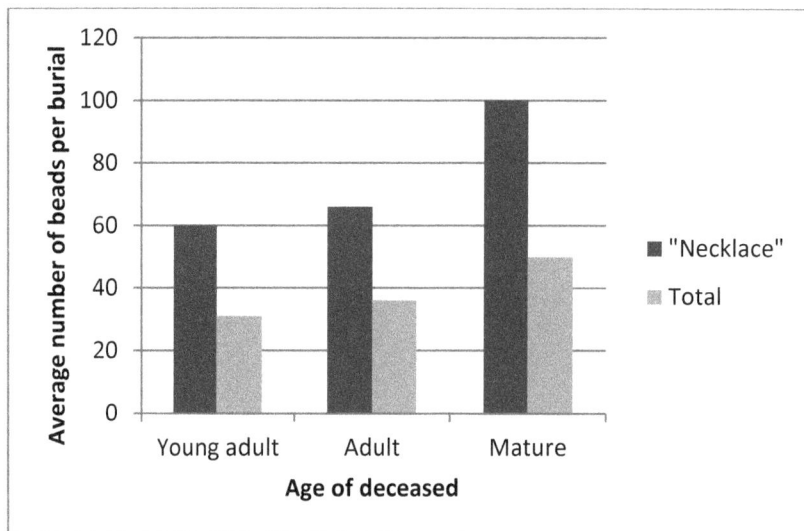

Figure 3.15: Average numbers of beads (both as "necklaces" and total) by age of deceased.

suggest that as age increases females are associated, or considered appropriate to be buried, with more beads.

3.5. Associated artefacts

It was considered during this research whether females were buried with any artefacts sets; either artefacts or types of artefacts which frequently occur together. The strongest associations of this type occur with the awls, which will be discussed below. However, the analysis was conducted on a large range of other items and types which are discussed in detail in Appendix Three.

Awls, of both bronze and copper, occur with a large number of different objects; however, the most numerous are beads (29%), flint flakes (29%), Beakers (24%) and scrapers (24%). When looking at artefact groups, awls are most likely to be found with other tools, occurring in 59% of burials, followed by decorative items and also pottery (both at 41%). It is interesting how an awl, a tool, is associated strongly with other tools and perhaps suggests a burial package for female burials (Chapter Four).

This is reflected in the associations with scrapers, which also do not occur alone in burials. Instead, scrapers are most commonly found with awls (57%) and Beakers (57%). In fact, scrapers are associated with other tools in six out of the seven burials (86%), indicating a potential female tool-kit. They also occur with pottery in 71% of burials, whereas their occurrence with decorative items is much lower, at only 29%

Due to the diversity of different items included in Chalcolithic and Early Bronze Age female burials there are not many clear associated artefacts. However, though not a significant number in comparison to the number of female burials with grave goods, there are nine different groups of artefacts. The first six concern items commonly associated with the different pottery types. Beakers have the most artefact associations (Figure 3.16), the most significant being the association of beakers, awls and scrapers.

Food Vessels have more limited associated artefacts, restricted to the flint blades and knives mentioned earlier. In fact, in this data set five burials contain the combination of a Food Vessel and either a flint knife or blade. Collared Urns are associated in burials seven times with unworked bone; almost 5% of the female burials with grave goods. In addition, there are also three Collared Urn burials which include the combination of Collared Urn, awl and bead(s).

The final two artefact groups include items common from the Beaker burials; the awls and scrapers. In fact, awls are associated with scrapers in four female burials. The clear association of awls with scrapers (and also other tools) will be discussed in more detail in Chapter Four. Although awls are commonly associated with the scrapers, they also frequently appear in burials with at least one bead. This artefact association occurs five times in the dataset. This brief discussion clearly shows that the items interred with female burials which can most likely be termed as forming grave good sets are the three major pottery types, awls, scrapers and beads.

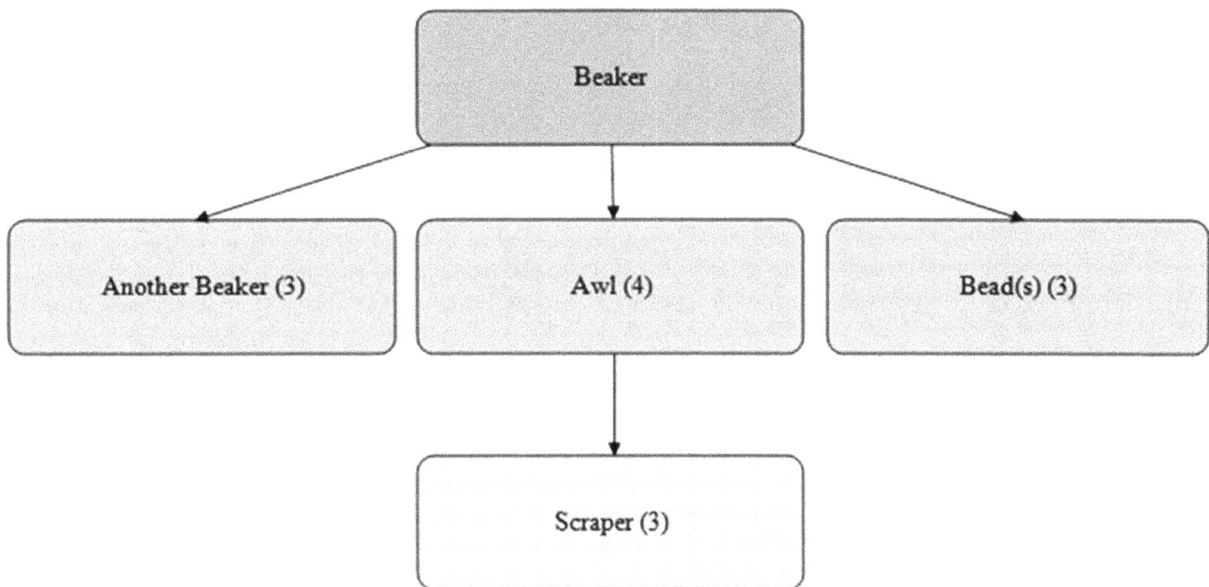

Figure 3.16: Associated artefact groups with Beaker pottery (number of burials in brackets)

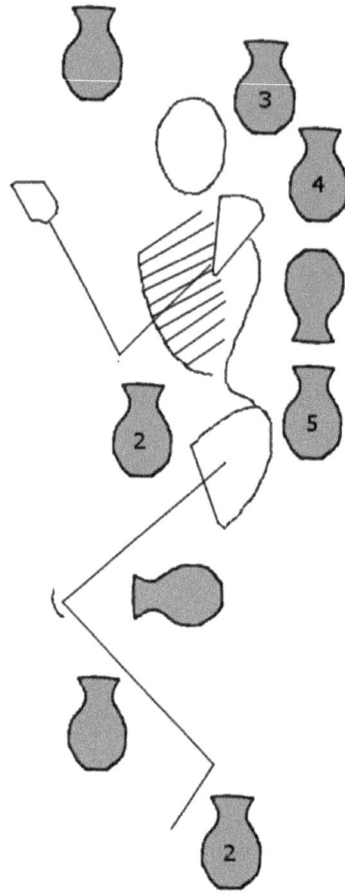

Figure 3.17: Beaker positions in relation to the body of the deceased.

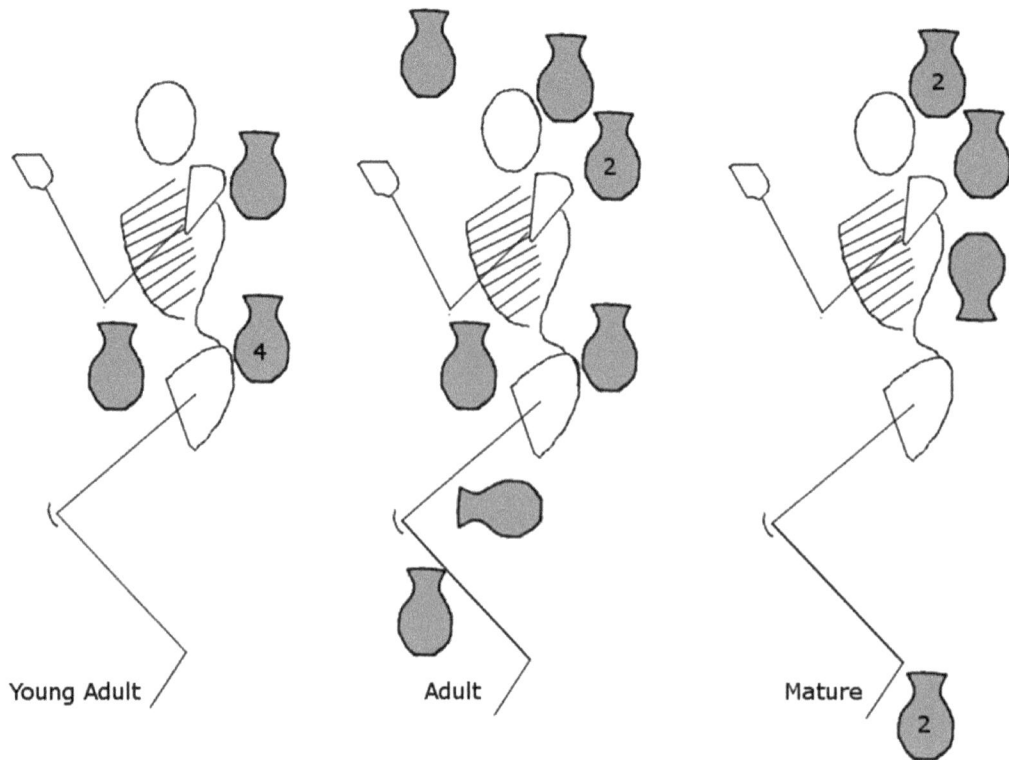

Figure 3.18: Position of beakers in relation to the body of the deceased by age.

3.6. Positions

Due to the frequency of the different artefacts in this dataset only a few could have their positions in the burials analysed. These are the beakers, flint objects, awls and beads. Beakers and flint objects are discussed below, whereas, awls and beads are discussed in Appendix Three. When looking at the position of the beakers interred with females during the Chalcolithic and Early Bronze Age no pattern is apparent (Figure 3.17), instead there are many diverse positions in which the beaker could be placed.

However, 80% of the beakers are placed behind the deceased. Furthermore, beakers are most often associated with the torso area of the body, where 60% of them are placed.

It was then asked whether the period of burial or the age of the deceased made any difference to the positioning of the beaker. The beaker's position by the deceased does not seem to be affected by period divisions either in being placed in front or behind the deceased, or the area of the body. Though beakers are equally distributed across the positions by age, a couple of points can be made (Figure 3.18). For young adults, it appears that the torso is the most appropriate place for beaker placement as all the beakers associated with young adults were placed there. It

is also interesting to note that adults appear to have a much more diverse range of positions compared to both the young adults and mature individuals, which may indicate that there were no rules for placement in relation to the adult age category.

The position of the flint artefacts have, in common with the beaker placement, a preference for being placed behind the deceased's body (71% of artefacts). Only one flint item is placed in front of the body, but three are placed directly on the body itself. Though once again there is a diverse range of positions taken by flint artefacts (Figure 3.19), there do seem to be slightly more groupings in comparison with the Beakers, in that there are concentrations of artefacts behind the head, behind the pelvis and behind the feet.

When looking at the positions of the flint artefacts in relation to period and age the distributions are equal, both in terms of in front, behind or on the body and also between the head, torso and legs. However, Period One has slightly more flints than expected placed by the head, Period Two has more by the legs and periods three and four by the torso; though not to a significant extent. For the age categories it appears that for young adults flints are more likely to be placed by the torso than for mature individuals.

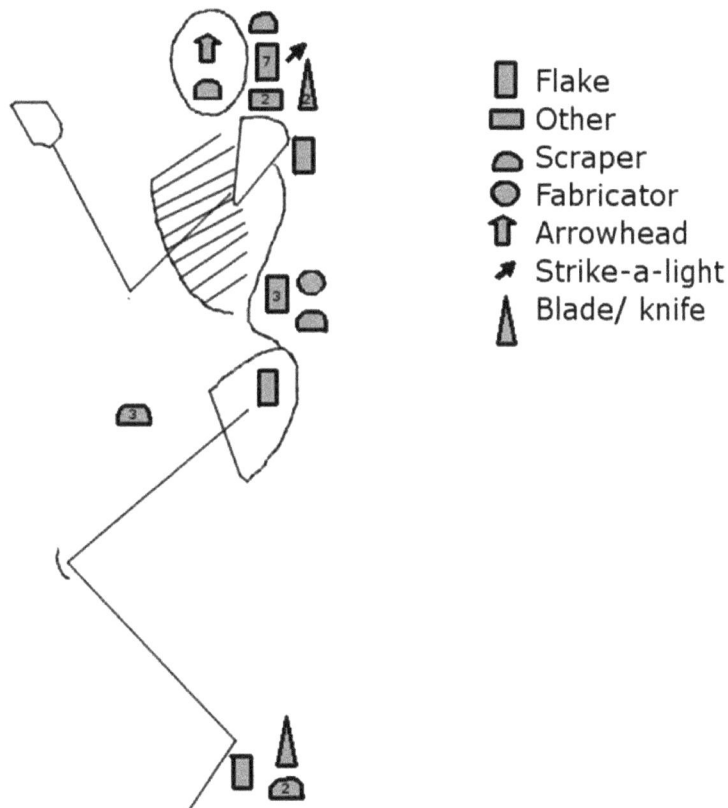

Figure 3.19: Position of flint artefacts in relation to the body of the deceased.

4: DISCUSSION

The discussions of age representation and change through time in Chalcolithic and Early Bronze Age female burials mirrors the structure of the analysis; looking at burial form, burial methods and finally grave goods. Then the discussion moves on to look at key themes within the dataset, these being fragmentation, lineage, female roles and activities and, finally, the use of grave goods.

4.1. Age

There are not many differences evident between the ages concerning burial form; the burial traditions are remarkably similar. However, young adults appear to be buried in cairns less than mature individuals and in flat graves more, although since the number of cairn burials is only eleven this may instead be a feature of the small sample size. Young adults also have the largest burial cuts in both barrows and flat graves compared to the other ages. This could result from space requirements for objects which do not survive in the archaeological record (such as piles of material or food), or the flexed position of many young adult inhumations which requires a greater cut length and width (Figure 4.1).

There are more differences between the ages relating to burial method than form. One is that adults are more likely to be cremated whereas mature individuals are more often inhumed. This may be due to the slight overrepresentation of mature individuals in period one where inhumation is the only burial method represented. However, this does not explain the prevalence of adult cremations which have the expected distribution across the periods.

One striking difference between the ages revealed during this study is that young adults are buried, to a significant extent, in the flexed rather than crouched position (Figure 4.1). This contrasts to the other ages where they are generally buried in the crouched position. The reason for this will never be immediately accessible to archaeologists. However, there are some possibilities. The flexed position results in a more open body thus displaying more to the mourners and making the deceased more visible. It is interesting to note that the sole extended female burial is also a young adult. The open body could relate to personal adornment and funerary costume being visible, or it could relate to the fact these individuals died at a young age, and the open body could prove no foul play.

Another pattern occurred in the demography of those accompanying the females in multiple burials. Though each age category is accompanied by sub-adults (< eighteen years) it appears the adult age category is more likely to be accompanied by a male rather than another female.

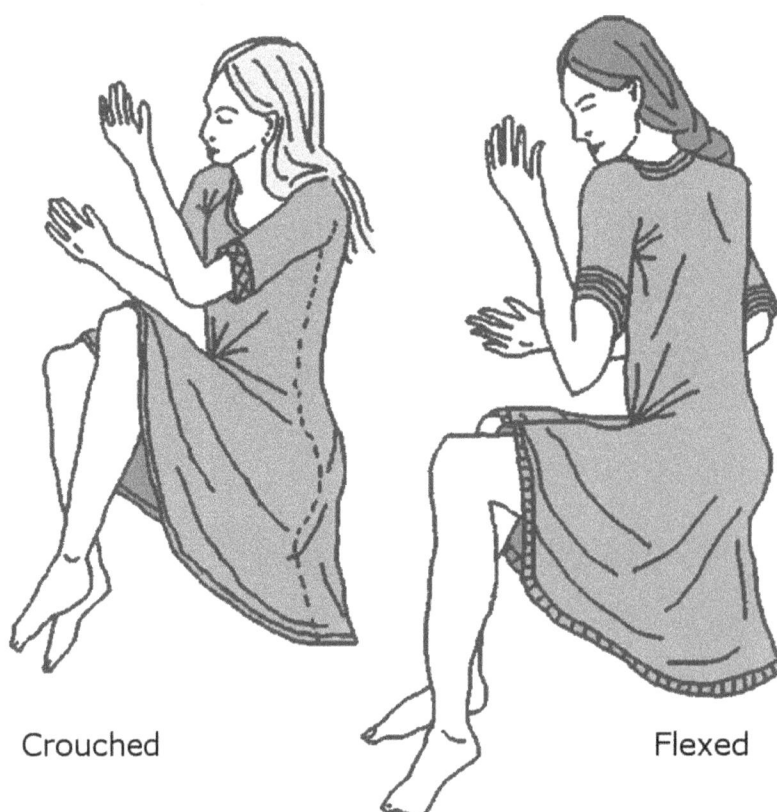

Crouched   Flexed

Figure 4.1: Illustration demonstrating different body positions of crouched and flexed burials (author's own)

In contrast, young adults and mature individuals are accompanied by both sexes more equally. We could suggest that these males represent partners of the female, though this cannot be proved.

When cremated, mature adults seem to have had more bone collected for burial in comparison to the other ages. This may contrast with Brück's (2009) argument that smaller cremation weights could represent a body being divided across kinship links; it seems logical that the older an individual is the more kinship links exist and therefore we would expect the older individuals to have the least weight.

Young adult cremation and token inhumation burials are provided with more grave goods than the other categories. For the cremations this is because young adults are more likely to be urned. For token inhumations young adults are the *only* age category to be provided with grave goods. This could indicate that only young adults are suitable for grave goods, but it may also result from the small sample size (10). However, this pattern of young adults being more likely provided with grave goods is reflected in the fact that overall the proportion of young adults with grave goods is higher than the other age categories.

Although young adults are more likely to be buried with grave goods they do not have the largest number of items, greatest variety of objects or objects made of different materials. Mature individuals, however, do have objects of several different materials, fewer burials provisioned with only a single item and more with five or more different artefacts. This suggests that as age increases a female is more likely to be buried with a greater range of artefacts and materials. This may be indicative of a greater variety of roles available for older females.

There are also trends regarding artefact types in flint objects and un-worked bone. Young adults, in this dataset, are only associated with pig bones, emphasized further by the polished pig tusk with the young adult at Deeping St Nicholas (349). This suggests an association between young adults and pigs, though the reasons are unknown.

Flint objects are included less with young adults but more with mature individuals, and, overall, adults have the largest number of flint grave goods per burial. That young adults have less flint objects could be because the flint objects in this dataset are all tools (except arrowheads, though even these can be seen as tools for hunting rather than necessarily representing interpersonal violence), and overall there is an indication that young adults are associated less with tools than adults and mature individuals.

Although mature individuals have the most burials with tools, they also have the largest number of beads per burial, suggesting no separation of functional and decorative items. Young adults, however, have the least. Once again, the evidence suggests that as age increases a

greater number of objects are placed in the burial, whether personal possessions, gifts from mourners or something else. This indicates that mature individuals were not marginalised or invisible in Chalcolithic or Early Bronze Age society, or at least represented this way in death. This may result from society's benefit in having their accumulated knowledge. This also supports the argument that the necklaces, especially composite examples (see below), were formed to represent kinship networks and relationships. The older individuals had accumulated more kinship links in their lives which were then reflected in larger strings of beads.

Finally the position of grave goods may relate to the deceased's age. The positions of beakers and flint artefacts are more diverse with adults than the other ages, especially young adults. Instead young adults have objects placed around the torso. This links with the flexed position of young adults as a flexed position increases the area available around the torso.

It appears as though the age categories which deviate from the expected patterns are young adults and mature individuals. The adult age category may be the norm with which the younger and mature individuals are contrasted, or the adult age category may not be a real one. There may be more divisions undetectable archaeologically due to the difficulties in aging bone. Alternatively, there could be a contrast between young and old females, with the division in the adult category. Whatever the reason, the fact that young and mature adults are represented differently in burial traditions indicates there was a division of females in burials due to age. Young adults could have been emphasized due to entrance to adulthood (though this may have begun during adolescence c. 12 – 18 years), and the new roles, responsibilities and potential this could have entailed (perhaps productive tasks such as food production, craft work and childbearing). The mature individuals could have been highlighted because of the low numbers (males and females) who attained that age, only 9% of this dataset. This long life could result in increased knowledge, advanced skill sets and extended networks of kith and kin.

The distinction between the female ages is similar to the distinctions between adult females of the Central European Middle Bronze Age discussed by Sørensen (1997). This regards the ornamentation of the female body in the grave, which she interprets as being related to either life-cycle stages or changing relationships with society. Though not to such a marked effect (at least in the burial evidence), it is possible that something similar is happening in the British evidence.

However, what is noticeable about different ages' burial traditions is that there is more similarity than divergence. The main contrasts appear between the grave goods, but most variables analysed showed little difference (Chapter Three; Appendix Three). This suggests that differences between females were not strongly expressed in burials.

4.2. Changes through time

This research determined whether there were changes to female burial traditions between 2500 and 1500 BC. The discussion is divided into the three areas of analysis; burial form, method and grave goods.

It is clear that there are changes in burial form through time. From 2500 – 1950 BC females are most likely to be buried in flat graves. In Period Three this changes and the most popular form is in a barrow whereas flat graves diminish in popularity. Finally, from 1700 BC, the distribution of the burial forms is equal. The change between flat graves to barrows indicates an increasing monumentalism of the burials during this period. However, it is not a simple switch between forms. Instead flat graves often provided the focus for the construction of barrows, for example, burials 180 and 181 in this database from Low Grounds, Cambridgeshire, formed the focus for a later barrow (discussed below).

The numbers of associated monuments with barrow burials form an unexpected pattern. As time passes it would be logical for burials to be associated with an increasing number of other monuments as the landscape forms a palimpsest of the traces from the past (Binford 1981). Therefore, it would be reasonable to assume that of the four periods, Period Four would have the greatest number of burials with associated monuments. However, this is not the pattern for barrow burials; instead the number of burials with associated monuments increases until Period Three, and then the numbers drop dramatically.

Overall, barrow and cairn burials have the most associated monuments, whereas flat graves and other forms have the least. This may be explained by the form of the burials themselves. Both barrows and cairns are themselves monumental; making an impact upon the landscape. Flat graves, however, do not to the same extent, even if marked. Several of the "other" burial forms are also non-monumental, for example those in gaps in bedrock, under rock overhangs or incorporated into natural mounds. The more monumental burial forms are associated with more monuments, perhaps creating monumental complexes such as those around Stonehenge (Woodward and Woodward 1996). An example from this database is Raunds, where there were a number of barrows, a henge, a long barrow and several enclosures (155–159) (Harding and Healy 2007). Altogether, 65% of female burials are associated with other monuments. This indicates that female burials were not marginalised; instead they were buried in places which had been / were still important places in the landscape.

One convincing result of this research concerns the placement of female burials in barrows. It is widely suggested that males occupy the central position in barrows, whereas females are placed around the periphery (Pierpoint 1980; Mizoguchi 1992; Lucas 1996). However, in this dataset 30% of the females are placed in the centre, increasing to 40% if off-centre positions are included. This is a large proportion suggesting that the above statement should be considered with caution. This research indicates that the location of burials within barrows is period dependent. The earlier the period of the burial, the more likely the individual will be buried centrally; in Period One 100% of the females in barrows are placed centrally, in Period Two 71%, whereas in Period Three just 34% are. By Period Four this has reduced to 6%. Obviously, these results apply only to female burials, but it would be interesting to find out if male burials followed the same pattern.

Examining the posture of inhumation burials indicates that females are generally buried in a crouched position (excepting young adults) on their right side. However, the only period where there was a domination of females being orientated to the south (one of the suggested female orientations) is during Period One when 75% of burials are in this position. This reduces to only 27% in period two compared to 35% in a north orientation. Therefore, the "typical" female orientation cited (Gibbs 1989) is only applicable for burials from the earliest part of the period studied (2500 – 2250 BC). This importance in not generalising when discussing burial traditions is emphasised in A. Shepherd's (2012) work where she emphasises the local patterns operating in Yorkshire and North-east Scotland.

It appears that a female is most likely to be provisioned with grave goods if buried in Period One, when 89% of burials had them (overall average 63%). Patterns emerge when looking at each period's average number of grave goods per burial, involving different materials, total number and number of different objects. Looking at the number of different material types per burial (i.e. items of pottery and flint, or just of flint) it appears that Period One burials are the least diverse, with 98% containing just one or two different item types. However, it is also the period with the least number of burials with only one material type. Period Four, conversely, has the most burials with just one item type; 63% of those containing grave goods. Overall, Period Two burials have the most diverse suites of artefacts, where 32% contain items of three or more different materials.

This pattern is reflected by the total number of artefacts per burial. Period One has the least burials with just one item (13%), which increases to Period Four (52%). Additionally, Period One has the most burials with more than five objects, whilst Period Four has the least. Therefore, as time progresses, the number of grave goods interred with females decreases. Period One also has the fewest burials with only one artefact type (12%), and Period Four the most (60%). Although Period One has burials with objects of few different materials, it does have the greatest number of different artefact types because several graves have distinct items of the same material, such as several different flint tools. That the earlier periods' burials have more numerous and diverse artefacts compared to the later period could be explained by the tradition of burying the dead with objects enthusiastically being adopted then gradually going out of fashion as trends change. This is demonstrated by the later Bronze Age burials where grave goods are rare (Brück 2009).

Period One features the most burials with "functional" items (i.e. flint tools, awls, pins etc.) with 63% having at least one. This decreases by Period Four where it is just 16%. This indicates that female representation changes through time; earlier in the period under study the activities undertaken by the deceased may be being represented, whereas by Period Four this is not so important. The burials with awls illustrate this. Though awls occur with burials of each period, by Period Four only a fragment of an awl is represented rather than a complete functioning item, emphasised by the accompaniment of just a flint flake rather than other parts of the leatherworker's assemblage (see below).

The trends within this dataset are as expected from burials of this period (Chapter Two), though this may be because many of the burials were dated using this framework. However, some aspects, such as burial positions in barrows, inhumation posture and grave good numbers, were not used to date the burials, so the patterns are not influenced by the dating methods . This indicates that female burials do not differ from the norm (and thus from males or infants). The most striking change through time is the number and types of grave goods per burial. This research has demonstrated that a burial from 1700 – 1500 BC is less likely to have a large range, number or

variety of grave goods, especially in comparison to earlier periods, and in this way has more in common with Middle Bronze Age burials. Furthermore, the influence of time upon the positions of the female burials in barrows and the orientation of female inhumations demonstrates how we cannot uncritically apply generalisations to the thousand year span of this period.

4.3. Fragmentation

Chapter One mentioned how fragmentation has become a popular theme in archaeology and has been applied to Chalcolithic and Early Bronze Age burial practices (Fowler 2004; Gibson 2007; Brück 2009). Fragmentation encompasses examining if / how objects can be broken into smaller units. The issue of fragmentation can be discussed in reference to the fragmentation of human remains and to the fragmentation of grave goods. Both types of fragmentation occur in this dataset.

Discussions of cremation frequently feature fragmentation in the analysis (Brück 2009) because the cremation rite itself breaks down whole bodies into fragments. Applying heat and flame to a body results in the bones splitting, cracking and warping (Byers 2008), reducing the whole body to parts. These parts can then be further disintegrated as cremated bone is more brittle than unburnt (Brickley 2007).

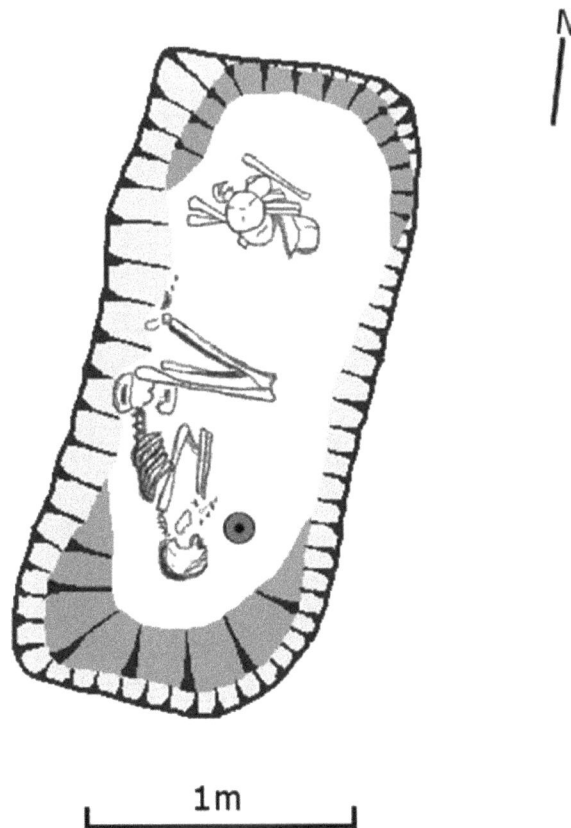

Figure 4.2: Burial 277 showing relationship between token deposit of bone and male inhumation (adapted from Bennett et al 2008: 19, fig 1/9)

Brück (2009) used this fragmentary nature of cremations to discuss differences between the sexes in relation to kinship, whereby the lower weight of female cremated bone was indicative of part of the cremation being buried elsewhere; the death of the person uniting communities as in life. However, I do not think that the bone weights within this study are significantly different, especially considering that the weights from modern crematoria range from 1001.5g to 2422.5g, with an average of 1625.9g (McKinley 1997: 136). The average weight for a female cremation (including tokens) in my dataset is 1131.5g; within the modern range. The only suggestion of deliberately reduced collection or separation of the remains is when the weight is much smaller, for example the token cremations or some of the "whole" cremations with less than 500g of bone.

However, though 'the introduction of cremation seems to suggest a total change in body ideology with a shift to it being fragmented rather than whole' (Sørensen 2010: 59), it is not that simple. There are many instances where inhumations contribute to the theme of fragmentation (Gibson 2007). Fragmentation of inhumed remains takes two forms; as "token" burials where only parts of bodies were buried, and also as "whole" burials where bones have been removed.

Token burials are those where only part of the body is formally buried (in that location). However, this can take several forms. They may be included with other burials (almost akin to grave goods), they can be arranged to look like whole inhumations or they can be placed as discrete deposits with no aim to appear whole.

The most common form token inhumations take in this study is as additions to whole inhumations, either as distinct deposits within the grave (e.g. 128, 277), or included in the backfilling (153, 154). These token burials are treated in a similar way to grave goods. A good example is burial 277 (Isle of Thanet 751), where a young adult male burial included a pile of disarticulated bone from a mature adult female and two children in the north of the burial cut (Figure 4.2).

Token burials are not restricted to females; males and infants can also be buried in token form. There are several cases in this dataset of token burials being placed with female inhumations. Burial 203 Kingshill North 1402 is a female inhumation with a juvenile femoral head and burial 298 Long Critchel 7 Grave 1 is a female inhumation buried with male hand, feet and knee bones. Because the token deposits found in inhumation burials are treated in much the same way as grave goods (by placement) they can be considered as being relics, linking people to relatives or ancestors.

Figure 4.3: Photograph illustrating the disturbance of bones from burial 163, Boscombe Down 6003 (Wessex Archaeology 2005: figure 4)

Further evidence of this occurs in complete female inhumations displaying evidence of the burial being disturbed and bones removed. There are several examples of this (burials 121, 295, 320); the best from Boscombe Down, burials 6003 (163) and 10025 (164). Burial 163 shows evidence of disturbance to the remains whilst only partially defleshed. The skull was moved to the south-west corner of the grave (Figure 4.3) and several bones were also removed (Wessex Archaeology 2005). Likewise, burial 164 was also disturbed, here the lower legs and feet were missing and the skull had been turned upside down (*ibid*). Both these burials arguably demonstrate the process of collecting bones to become token deposits or to circulate the bones among the living.

One interesting burial in this dataset is 211 from Allerwash, where the pelvis, leg and feet bones of a young adult were arranged to look like a "whole" burial in a crouched / flexed position. The pelvis and tibia were placed in the position of the head and arms, while the remaining leg bones were used for the legs (Newman and Miket 1973). Though a token burial this female was displayed as though complete and does not seem to be espousing any of the fragmentation themes, such as a dividual personhood (discussed below), it seems to be doing the opposite; maintaining a whole. However, only parts of this person were selected for deposition at this location, and the restricted selection of body parts (just the lower body) suggests that this was a deliberate gathering of remains. Presumably the remaining parts of the body were separated and treated differently. This could mean they were taken by different people; emphasising networks of relationships, or that the other parts of the person were buried elsewhere, perhaps illustrating how place can contribute to forming identities.

As cremation facilitates fragmenting the body so does the process of skeletonization. It has been suggested that without skin it becomes difficult to separate the skeleton from the material world of objects (Sofaer 2006). This allows the dead to become something akin to ancestor relics, where remains are treated more as heirlooms than as representing a person (with exceptions, see burial 211 and above). The bones from the past could be used to symbolise relationships, real or imagined, between the recent dead, and thus their family, friends or community, and the long dead. Similarities can be drawn between Chalcolithic and Early Bronze Age token inhumations and the European medieval saint relics. Additionally, there are similarities between the token inhumations and the composite necklaces discussed below; both can represent networks of relationships extending into the past.

A link to the past is made by the rearrangement of the skeletons and the removal of bones which seem to reflect the earlier Neolithic treatment of the dead (Gibson 2007). These practices were undertaken at the communal chambered tombs of the fourth millennium BC, such as Lanhill (King 1966). Perhaps a link to a past was being made through the use of token burials during this later period, but we must remember that there was a break of a thousand years between the two practices, which argues against a continuum (Healy 2012).

Therefore, the Chalcolithic and Early Bronze Age fragmentation of human remains can be seen as facilitating links to the past and expressing, or creating, social networks through time. This assumes that the token deposits are earlier in date than the complete inhumations and only a radiocarbon dating programme will elucidate this. The token bones from burial 277 did have a slightly earlier radiocarbon determination than the inhumation (Bennett *et al* 2008) and the disarticulated bones beneath the central burial in the turf mound at Raunds were over a thousand years earlier (Harding and Healy 2007). Even if the bones are contemporary, the fragmentation of remains still creates links between people and still expresses social networks, which conceivably facilitated or strengthened relationships amongst the living.

The fragmentation of human remains symbolising social networks is expressed in cremations. Brück (2009) argues that cremations, through disintegrating the body, allow a person to be split into parts. These different parts could be distributed across the deceased's social network; representing that persons' kith and kin but also reaffirming links between the living and explaining why some cremations weigh less than expected.

During the Chalcolithic and Early Bronze Age it is possible that personhood was conceived differently from our modern western "individual" (Fowler 2004). The theoretical distribution of cremated remains and the distribution of skeletal parts could be symbolising "dividual" personhood, whereby a person's identity is not self-contained, as it is conceived of today in western society, but is instead created through relationships to others. (*ibid*). Humans are not isolated, instead we are in continual contact with other people, and it is our relationships with people which form who we are (Brück 2004). People were not "*in*dividual" in the literal sense of the term, but *dividual;* they could be broken down into constituent parts, formed by relationships to other people and even places. Burial of multiple individuals symbolise this. Therefore, the Chalcolithic and Early Bronze Age so-called "single" burials are not necessarily an assertion of the individual, as they have been interpreted in the past; instead the evidence shows how the deceased were intricately linked to other people.

However, I do not believe we should use fragmentation to contrast the personhood of the past with our current conceptions as several authors do (Fowler 2004; Brück 2009). Reducing it to simply "individuals" and "dividuals" neglects many of the subtle nuances in the construction of our identity today and in prehistory. It also functions as an "us" and "them" barrier, separating us from our past. These burial practices instead say more about the importance of relationships than they do about notions of dividual identity in the Chalcolithic and Early Bronze Age.

Concepts of fragmentation can also be seen in the grave goods of the deceased, there are the "creations" produced through fragmentation, an example being the "composite" necklaces where collections of beads have been produced from several necklaces. Alternatively, objects are fragmented due to destruction, where whole objects are destroyed prior to being placed in the grave or where only part is included. Though on the surface these practices seem poles apart they both comment upon the theme of fragmentation concerning social relations.

There are many examples of potential composite necklaces in this dataset; over 50% of collections of beads contain what appear to be composite sets. These sets can be formed of beads of different materials, jet, faience etc, or can be formed from the same material but where the use-wear or style is different. An example of this latter type of composite necklace is from Northpark, Bute (350) where Sheridan (2006) determined that the 139 jet beads came from at least five necklaces by looking at the different levels of use-wear. Another composite necklace is from Radwell (327), where 111 beads are of jet, 12 are of amber, and with an amber pendant, and spacer beads of jet and amber (Hall and Woodward 1977), which has been interpreted as the remains of at least three necklaces (Woodward 2002).

It has been suggested that these necklaces were added to through inheritance of heirlooms (Woodward 2002; Sheridan 2003b), as exchange items with other communities (Needham 2011) or perhaps formed at death by mourners contributing beads (*ibid*). The beads could symbolise relationships between the people involved in the transfer of beads with the composite necklaces becoming visual metaphors for webs of relations. In some cases the beads have been demonstrated to have been old when added to the necklaces (Woodward 2000) and may have belonged to dead ancestors; perhaps symbolising links to the past (discussed above for token inhumations). Using fragmented necklaces to make a whole one could represent the relationships the wearer had, an argument Brück extends to the creation of the whole burial assemblage (2004). As with all heirlooms the moment they are removed from circulation they cease to be heirlooms. However, we must remember that the necklaces we excavate in the grave may not have been the final form owned in life; instead some of the beads may have been removed in order to feature in other composite necklaces (Needham 2011).

The other form of fragmentation in grave goods is the destruction of items placed in the grave. There are several examples of this in the dataset. The most numerous are the sherds of pottery, rather than whole vessels, included with many burials (26% of burials with pottery have sherds or incomplete vessels). These can represent large portions of the original vessel, i.e. two-thirds of an accessory vessel (114), or alternatively just one or two sherds (209, 328). Other broken objects featured in this dataset include two upper halves of jet pendants from Barns Farm cist 4 (233), and a broken whetstone at Howick Heugh (300).

It is suggested that broken items may have been placed in graves by mourners, metaphorically symbolising a broken relationship caused by death (Brück 2004), the object, perhaps once a gift from one to the other. The two pendant upper halves from burial 233 could symbolise the opposite. Since part of the pendants were retained they could be symbolising the continuing relationship even after death, not in a literal sense but a more emotive one; so something of that person is still with the other. The significance of pottery sherds has already been discussed in detail by Woodward (2002) and will not be repeated here.

However, it is important to remember that we only find broken items in some, rather than all, burials. This interpretation of the broken objects symbolising broken relationships would therefore suggest that the majority of deaths did not result in broken relationships; something which does not seem likely and perhaps casts doubt upon this interpretation.

The reason why objects placed in burials have been used as metaphors for relationships is because it is suggested that objects become intimately associated with people; they become inalienable possessions (Appadurai 1986; Fowler 2004). Especially the case when given as a gift, rather than purchased as a commodity; 'to give a gift is to give part of oneself' (Fowler 2004: 55). Therefore, the beads, sherds or pendants can represent a person and therefore express social relationships.

4.4. Lineage

Chalcolithic and Early Bronze Age kinship relationships have also been explored through the burial record. It is suggested that Chalcolithic burials represent a horizon where the earlier Neolithic ancestor veneration symbolism gave way to kinship and lineage (Garwood 1991). This was not necessarily this simple. During the Neolithic period we have examples of individual burials (such as at Liffs Low, Derbyshire (Loveday and Barclay 2010) and the burial record of the period considered in this research still provides evidence for the importance of ancestors (see above; Rogers 2013).

By looking at how barrow cemeteries develop and how they reference earlier structures aspects of lineage can be invoked (Garwood 2007). Alternatively, successive burial deposits have been explored (Petersen 1972; Mizoguchi 1993). Since this research concerns individual burials, barrow cemetery development will not be discussed. Instead, this dataset has evidence of successive burial deposits, and it is these that form the basis of the lineage discussion in the burial record.

Lineage is expressed in two ways in this dataset of female burials; it can be illustrated through multiple burials where more than one individual has been included in a grave cut, or in successive burial depositional events. Though similar, these different burial traditions represent different scales of lineage.

There are many instances in this dataset of multiple burials, for example, 30% of complete cremations include at least two individuals. Furthermore, there are several multiple inhumation burials representing at least two whole individuals. At Waterhall Farm, Grave I (284) an adult female was placed head to toe with an adult male, and, at Sithean Rosinish (134-5), two young adult females were interred in a corbelled tomb with a mature male.

These examples involve multiple interments of the same burial method. However, there are also instances where different burial methods are inserted in the same grave. At Wetwang Slack, Barrow B.G4 (269), a young adult female had a pile of cremated bones of another young adult placed over her elbow, whilst the male inhumation at Barns Farm grave 1 had three cremations interred with him. A young adult female cremation had been placed in a container over the arms (234), whilst two further deposits of cremated bone, both of juveniles, were placed above the skull and behind the back. As these cremations are placed in positions usually employed for grave goods they may therefore instead be considered as relics rather than as contemporary with the male burial.

Multiple burials within one grave could be indicating horizontal kinship more akin to family / friend relations. This suggests people deposited within the graves were contemporary; there was not a great deal of time between their deaths, if any. This contrasts to the token deposits above which suggests that defleshing had to have occurred before the elements could be removed and redeposited. Arguably, those interred in multiple burials would have known each other, and it is this sense of kinship being expressed. This relationship could be termed horizontal, and applies to close family or community associations.

Successive interments could instead be referencing a vertical lineage relationship. Successive interments refer to burials which cut through previous graves. These can involve just two burials cutting each other, such as at QEQM Hospital, Kent where an adult male was buried first and, at a later date, a female (259) was inserted above him on a different alignment, but with the heads placed next to and facing each other (Hart and Moody 2008). The grave goods were also similar, emphasizing the relationship between the two; the male had been interred with three barbed-and-tanged arrowheads and the female was also provisioned with one (*ibid*). These small successive grave sequences have much in common with the multiple burials, in that they were probably contemporary, and thus could also exhibit horizontal kinship.

However, a large number of successive burials demonstrate vertical lineage. An example of this is Wilsford cum Lake G52, where there were nine successive interments, including burial 273. The sequence seems to have been a cremation burial, a male inhumation, an infant inhumation, a young adult female inhumation (273), and, though location in the sequence is

unknown, a further adult female (not in database), another adult, and an infant, all inhumations. The whole sequence finished with two further cremations (Smith 1991). Another long sequence occurred at Ring Ditch X6 by the Devil's Quoits, Oxfordshire, where there were five successive burials. The first in the sequence was of a burial which was so disturbed by later deposits only some fill remained (and no traces of the original occupant), the second a mature male inhumation, the third a young adult female inhumation (346). Finally, two cremation deposits were cut into the top; one an infant the other an adult female (347) (Barclay *et al* 1995), demonstrating a long sequence of burials.

A final example is from Low Grounds Barrows (Evans and Tabor 2010a). This sequence is interesting for two reasons; not only are there vertical burial sequences but the location of these sequences was then marked by a barrow which had two burials directly referencing the earlier burials' locations. Furthermore, the occupants of this sequence were, excluding the infants, all females. The first interment, a young adult female inhumation (180), was followed by a mature female inhumation (181) and then the three juvenile inhumations, two in the same cut. Another young adult female inhumation (182) was buried 8m east. All these burials were sealed by Barrow 2, in which the central burial of a young adult female cremation (183) was directly above the main succession of burials and another female cremation (184) was placed above the burial 8m to the east of the central sequence (*ibid*). The burials beneath the barrow were the earliest on the site and not only provided the location for this barrow but they were arguably the focus for the entire complex. That the burials were all female demonstrates how females were not marginalised in the Chalcolithic and Early Bronze Age, but were celebrated and commemorated, providing the foundation for a monument complex.

The intercutting burials demonstrate vertical lineage due to the period of time that the burials must have taken. This is represented by the depth of the burials and also the stacking of burials. Rather than contemporary relationships, these burials have greater time depth and, although those directly above or below may have known each other, those with distance separating them probably did not. In this way these burials are possibly representing genealogies, linking the recent dead with those of the past. They are 'historical calculations of sequence and depth which refer to a mythical time of lineage creation ... concerned above all with the relative ordering of descent lines' (Garwood 1991: 15).

One of the key themes expressed in Chalcolithic and Early Bronze Age burials are relationships; the deceased's relationships with others, perhaps those known directly or from an ancestral or mythical past. This contrasts to the solitary individuals the expression "single graves" of the period suggests.

4.5. Female roles and activities

Grave goods within burials have been used to determine the occupants' roles or identities (Gibbs 1989). Though there are many problems using grave goods to determine the deceased's identity (see below) this is still a valuable exercise. Even if the identity portrayed in the burial was not that of the deceased, it is still how the living chose to represent them. The analysis of the dataset highlighted several recurring artefact groups. Recurring sets of artefacts suggest common roles or activities among the deceased and that they were represented in a particular way. The best examples in the dataset are awl burials.

Leatherworkers

Chapter One mentioned how the leatherworker identity is cited for male burials but not often for females (Brodie 1997). However, there are many examples of potential leatherworkers represented in this dataset (Table 4.1). The common items appearing in these burials are the awls, flint scrapers and other flint, bone and stone tools.

All these items have uses in leatherworking; the awls could be used on the processed hide to make leather items and could also pierce the hide to attach it to the stretching rack. Scraping tools are well attested in leatherworking (Beyries and Rots 2005) which are used to remove flesh and fat from the skin. This can also be accomplished using a knife. Blades could also be used for cutting and shaping the hide once processed. A spatula could have been used to rub in softening agents once the hide had

been stretched and pins and points could pierce the leather or join pieces together. The whetstone could have sharpened the awl, or may have been used to soften the hide. Finally, the wooden board could have been used in stretching the hide when cleaning it with the scraper, similar to the Siberian Chukchi (*ibid*).

Burial	Name	Objects
212	Ravenstone	Bronze awl, scraper, serrated flint blade, flake, wooden board, Beaker, shale button. (In cenotaph below was an antler spatula and flint fabricator).
326	Barrow Bottom, Grave 1	Bronze awl, scraper, strike-a-light, Collared Urn, 151 jet beads, bronze bead.
346	Ring Ditch X6, Burial 3	Copper awl, scraper, Beaker.
111	Doons Law	Copper awl, scraper, three flakes, Beaker, pollen.
291	Barrow Hills, 16E	Bronze awl, copper knife-dagger, necklace.
305	Roystone Grange, C	Bronze awl, plano-convex knife.
122	Rollestone, 23(1)	Handled bronze awl, whetstone.
166	Middle Barn Farm, 80078	Bone pin, bone spatula, burnt flint.
250	Barnack, 39	Three scrapers, bone point.

Table 4.1: List of possible leatherworker's burials

Figure 4.4: A woodworking awl (photo author's own)

Leatherworking would have been a valued activity in the Chalcolithic and Early Bronze Age, because many items could be produced from finished hides, including clothing, shelter, fastenings and storage, and the hides could have been exchanged. Arguably examples of the importance of leatherworking are the Chalcolithic and Early Bronze Age "head-and-hoofs" burials, one of which occurs in this dataset (300; Kingshill North, 8656), where animal bone remains suggest the presence of a hide in the burial assemblage. Well finished leathers and furs could have been exchanged with communities who could not produce the same quality of finish.

The awls themselves illustrate the importance of leatherworkers. In the Chalcolithic and Early Bronze Age awls are the first tools produced in metal. The daggers and axes found in burials often have symbolic or decorative functions rather than evidence for use as tools (see below), although some axes must have been used as tools demonstrated by the axe marks at Irish trackways (Raftery 1996). Awls, however, do show evidence of work, such as the example from Ravenstone (Allen 1981), demonstrating they were used as tools rather than as decoration or purely to demonstrate access to metallurgy, especially since their size and design does not suggest display.

There is evidence of metal awls right from the beginning of metallurgy, for example, the copper awl from Spring Road, Grave 3036 (133), is radiocarbon dated to 2460 – 2200 cal BC, 'one of the earliest copper objects from Britain' (Allen and Kamash 2008: 8). As awls were made from the earliest occurrence of metalworking it demonstrates the value of this tool. This highlights the importance of the awl and its uses. Awls and leatherworking equipment occurring in female burials of this period demonstrate their involvement in this important and skilled activity.

Gibbs (1989) also suggested female participation in leather processing. However, she suggested they were only involved in the earlier stages, whereas males were at the later stages (such as trading and exchange). However, the tools in these burials demonstrate that females were represented as involved in all stages of the process, and even the barbed-and-tanged arrowheads could have been used to hunt the animals for their hides.

However, awls and other tools, especially scrapers, may not have only been used in leatherworking. Awls can also be used in woodworking (Figure 4.4). Awls can be used to pierce wood or lay out markings to follow, whilst scrapers could whittle or shape wood. Clarke *et al* (1985) also drew attention to the fact that awls could have been used in the production of gold or jet items. This is especially interesting when we consider that this dataset has several examples of an association between awls and beads. Therefore, although these burials indicate a production activity, their interpretation as leatherworkers is not certain.

Weapon burials

One burial tradition of the Chalcolithic and Early Bronze Age which is often highlighted is the weapon or warrior burial characterised by weapons or associated objects placed with the deceased. In the Chalcolithic these would have been the barbed-and-tanged arrowheads, the metal daggers and also the archer's bracers (Mercer 2007). In the Early Bronze Age this range becomes restricted to daggers and barbed-and-tanged arrowheads, and, rarely, the bronze axe.

These burials have previously been considered to be exclusively male (i.e. Case 1977) and have given rise to the male warrior identity prevalent in this period. However, in this dataset of female burials there are nine buried with weapons (though this seems a small number it is the same as the leatherworkers above). The weapons take the form of daggers, barbed-and-tanged arrowheads, and bronze and polished stone axes (Table 4.2). The only "weapon" this dataset is missing is the bracer, which are rare even for males (in 2006 only 28 were known from burials (Woodward *et al* 2006)).

Burial	Name	Objects
170	Thomas Hardye School, 1139	Bronze knife-dagger
211	Allerwash	Bronze dagger
252	Manor Farm, 55	Bronze flat axe, bronze dagger
261	Amesbury 58(1)	Copper knife-dagger with horn hilt, iron pyrites
291	Barrow Hills, 16E	Copper knife-dagger with bronze rivets, bronze awl, necklace
148	Mousland	Polished stone axe
163	Boscombe Down, 6033	Barbed-and-tanged arrowhead, Beaker sherds, antler tine, flint blade, 6 flakes
191	Low Grounds Barrows, 1030	2 barbed-and-tanged arrowheads, 3 flake knives, 3 flakes
259	QEQM Hospital, Sk1	Barbed-and-tanged arrowhead, Beaker(?) sherds

Table 4.2: Weapon burials in dataset

Due to preconceptions excavators sometimes interpret weapon burials as male even with contrary evidence. An example of this is Manor Farm 55 (252), where a degraded inhumation was buried in a stone enclosure. All that was remaining of the skeleton were some long bones and parts of a crushed skull (Olivier 1987). The long bone lengths and diameters were considered female; however, it was suggested the skull was male, purely on the association with the bronze dagger and axe. Rather than accept it as a female burial it was suggested that more than one individual was represented. In the end the sex was determined to be inconclusive (*ibid*). If the long bone measurements had been male these problems would not have been encountered.

However, it is possible that the "weapons" found during the Chalcolithic and Early Bronze Age were not considered as such. There is very little evidence of war from the period as a whole, such as a lack of skeletons displaying evidence of violent trauma (Barber 2003; Thorpe 2006) and little evidence of defended or defensible structures (Mercer 2007). In order for warriors to exist war must also be present, as warriors are specialised users of violence (Vandkilde 2006). The barbed-and-tanged arrowheads, for example, could easily have been hunting weapons (Case 2004) and have even been found in association with animals (Mercer 2007).

Furthermore, in the majority of cases the weapons' forms actually preclude their use as such. The Chalcolithic and Early Bronze Age daggers have triangular blades and rounded points which are useless for stabbing (Mercer 2007) and many of the daggers also exhibit deliberate damage. The dagger in burial 261 (Amesbury 58(1)) had the pommel broken off and the dagger from Barrow Hills, 16E (291) had the corners of the butt snapped off. This could be ritual breakage, perhaps to remove the object's power, or symbolise death. However, in some daggers and bracers, the breaks seem old and therefore they could represent heirlooms (Woodward 2000). The bronze dagger and axe found with the burial at Manor Farm (252) could have been heirlooms, as the form of the weapons suggests a much earlier date than the radiocarbon determination (Olivier 1987). Needham (1999) also highlights the important question of when a knife becomes a "dagger", and that many of the "daggers" may have been used as knives, i.e. as tools rather than weapons.

Rather than violent functions these objects seem instead to emphasis display. They are made using rare materials, for example metal during the infancy of metallurgy, or the polished stone axe from Orkney (148) which was made from talc schist from Shetland. Furthermore, these items frequently exhibit decoration, such as rivets of different materials, decoration on the blades (the axe at Manor Farm), or decoration in terms of the hilt or sheath (the dagger in the Amesbury 58(1) burial had a horn hilt whilst the dagger at Allerwash possibly had a sheath decorated with bronze). Seeing weapons as decorative objects rather than weapons is demonstrated by the Wessex halberd pendants.

Rather than interpreting these items as weapons and warrior burials it seems prudent to consider them symbolically. The graves featuring metal daggers and axes could be symbols of metallurgy, a new and specialised knowledge and access to a limited resource. Furthermore, metallurgy is also often associated with magic (Herbert 1984), and metal weapons could symbolise danger or the ability to conquer it. Arrowheads could instead be linked with subsistence; linking back to the past when hunting was the main method to procure protein. Thus arrowheads may symbolise a person's ability to provide, linking with the bracers which have been argued to have been symbolic rather than practical (Fokkens *et al* 2008).

Tool sets and other tasks

Other activities are also indicated by the females' grave goods, such as jet working, pottery making, fire making, and general production activities. These, in addition to leatherworking, indicate that females were not represented as passive in Chalcolithic and Early Bronze Age society, just wearing necklaces displaying their male relation's wealth; instead they were symbolised as functioning members of the community, sometimes with rare or beneficial skills.

The jet working process has been described in detail by both I. Shepherd (1981; 2009) and Sheridan and Davis (2002), who discuss possible tools. To make the threading holes I. Shepherd describes how a "hollow cylindrical awl" (1981: 48) could be used. A possible example of this tool occurs in the Waterhall Farm I c-e burial (285-7), where there is a small bronze cylinder (Martin and Deviston 1975-6), which could perform this function. The possibility of jet working is supported by the small coal bead also in the grave. However, due to the burial's nature we cannot determine which female these items were associated with, or if they were even deposited together. The possibility of awls being used in jet artefact production has already been mentioned (see above).

A flint saw could have been used to cut the jet to shape (Sheridan and Davies 2002), and burial 212 (Ravenstone) included a serrated flint blade and also a v-bored shale button (Allen 1981). Once again a possible jet-working tool is associated with a jet-like object. However, this burial could also be a leatherworker's burial, highlighting the problem of assigning activities to burials since many tools are multifunctional, and also that craft-workers may have performed several different roles. Finally, to smooth the cut edges the jet items could have been '[rubbed] with solid sandstone' (I. Shepherd 1981: 49), which could have been performed by the whetstones in the dataset.

Pottery making has been suggested as a female activity (Brodie 1997). Rather than based on the burials themselves, this interpretation is formed by ethnographic analogy and the assumption that females were restricted to the domestic sphere (in contrast to males in the public). However, some ethnographic accounts demonstrate how both males and females can be involved in pottery production (Rice 1991). One of the tools from this dataset, the bone spatula from Middle Barn Farm, 80078 (166), could be used to burnish pottery. However, it could have been part of the leatherworkers' tool kit. The various pins, knives etc. could also have been used in pottery decoration.

Fire-making is the final activity or role evident in this dataset. Fire-making has traditionally been interpreted as a male role during this period (Clarke 1970; Harrison 1980), however, three females have items associated with this task included within their burials (Table 4.3).

Burial	Name	Objects
232	Barns Farm, cist 2	Strike-a-light, iron, perforated whetstone
326	Barrow Bottom, grave 1	Strike-a-light, bronze awl, scraper, Collared Urn, 151 jet beads, bronze bead.
261	Amesbury 58(1)	Iron pyrites nodule, bronze knife-dagger

Table 4.3: Burials with fire-making equipment

Rather than seeing burials with these kits as representing fire-making in a domestic sphere, it is perhaps better to see them as performing other specialised roles (otherwise many people went cold during the Chalcolithic and Early Bronze Age if we use these kits as evidence for fire making!). These could include, for example, fire-making for feasts, rituals, cremation rites, or for technical task such as kilns for pottery production or furnaces for metal-working.

Multipurpose tools are abundant in this dataset, suggesting a variety of tasks including cutting, slicing, scraping and piercing. These tools include flint knives, blades, flakes etc. An example of a general purpose toolkit is from the Centre for Gene Function, 204 (160) which incorporated eight worked flints, including a denticulate and a spurred piece (Lamdin-Whymark 2003); 'tools for a variety of tasks such as scraping … boring … cutting and whittling' (*ibid*: 191). Though these are not necessarily specialist tools; they could have been used in a variety of productive tasks.

4.6. Use of grave goods

Throughout this discussion of grave goods I have tried to avoid explicitly assuming the grave goods were the deceased's personal belongings. Instead there are other interpretations of the items; a female buried in a leatherworker's grave may never have worked leather. What is important is that someone made the decision that this representation was appropriate for that person. Even if it was not how the dead wanted to be portrayed, or if it had nothing to do with her life, it was how the living *wanted* that person represented. Therefore, grave goods still have potential to indicate aspects of society providing we accept the "mirror" may be distorted. It could be that females were never leatherworkers or made fire, but what is important is a decision was made to represent them as such.

Other caveats surrounding the use of grave goods have been alluded to through this work. It has been suggested that objects in the burials may have been placed there by mourners (King 2004), or they could have been family heirlooms (Gillespie 2001; Woodward 2002). However, the inclusion of these items in the burial still represents a decision that it was suitable to associate those items with the deceased.

Some suggest that heirlooms comment more about the past owners than they do of the person they are buried with (Gillespie 2001). However we must remember that an heirloom is no longer an heirloom when buried and taken out of circulation. Therefore, although the heirloom may represent an association with the past and previous owners, placing it in the grave links it with the deceased, perhaps even beyond past owners, as the living want it to remain with that person.

Looking at current archaeological thought concerning grave goods it is clear that we still share some beliefs with the Processualists especially regarding the use of burials to reveal aspects of past societies. Although we acknowledge that it is not as simple as the grave goods being the deceased's possessions, we still use them to comment upon society; such as social relationships and attitudes to the past and this is still a valuable exercise.

Another consideration when discussing grave goods is different material preservation capabilities. What is archaeologically visible may not be all that was placed in the burial. Items made of organic substances, such as wood, leather, feathers and food etc. may not have survived either burial or fire. If these items were placed in the burial then we would not be able to detect them. Therefore, not only could some burials with grave goods have had more, but many apparently empty graves could also have had items. Unfortunately, this problem will never be resolved; all we can do is remember we may not be seeing the complete picture.

Additional problems present themselves in cremations. This is because many grave goods found in burials show evidence of having gone through the pyre. Often not all the deceased's bones are collected for burial, therefore, it is likely that some grave goods involved in the female's representation upon the pyre were not collected for burial (McKinley 1994). Therefore, females who were cremated may have been represented with more objects than we can determine.

However, the objects placed upon the pyre could be considered vital for the burial. Two good examples of this exist in this dataset, from Middle Barn Farm (166) and 102 Findhorn (228). The cremation at Middle Barn Farm included a bone pin and spatula in the remains. Although only around 63% of the human bones were collected it is interesting that the two objects were almost complete (Ellis and Powell 2008), demonstrating how those collecting the deposit for burial considered the bone tools vital for the representation of deceased. This preferential selection would not have been related to greater visibility of the items as they would have looked very similar to the burnt human bone they were collected with. The other example is a cremation in a Cordoned Urn including 23 faience beads. A small insertion was made in the top of the grave fill where a further 2 beads (from the pyre and presumably the same necklace) were deposited (I. Shepherd & A. Shepherd 2001). This shows how pyre goods were considered vital to the deceased's representation in the grave.

The final issue concerning cremation grave goods is that some items had been thorough the pyre and some were unburnt when placed in the grave. Some even have a mixture of burnt and unburnt items (179 and 215 have both burnt and unburnt flint items). Obviously decisions were made as to which items were for the pyre and which were reserved for burial. This could relate to the fact that some of the items were worn, such as necklaces, and intimately associated with the body, whereas others were not. The cremation at Barrow Hills, barrow 2 had two burnt gold foil cones, perhaps covering buttons on the deceased's clothing on the pyre, and an unburnt bronze awl and flint flake, tools the mourners did not feel should be on the pyre. The decision could relate to ideas of public and private, what is suitable for the private burial may not be for the public pyre. Alternatively, it could be the unburnt items were gifts from mourners which was why they were unburnt and added after the cremation.

4.7. Conclusions

This work aimed to provide a re-analysis of Chalcolithic and Early Bronze Age female burials and as a result of which several new findings concerning the burial traditions have been revealed, some challenging conventional views. It appears from the dataset studied in this research that female placement in barrows seems to be related to time; that those buried in the earlier periods are more likely to be placed in the centre of barrows than those from the final period. This suggests that barrow placement was not strictly related to sex, though an examination of the male evidence is needed to confirm this. Another aspect of female burial which seems to be related to time is the orientation of the female inhumations. This work revealed that it is only from 2500 – 2250 BC that females are most likely to be arranged with their heads directed towards the south.

Another pattern revealed in the research is that the age of the deceased did influence the female burial traditions to a certain extent, specifically in contrasting the youngest and oldest age categories. The aspect of burial where this was most noticeable was in regards to the grave good provision whereby the mature adults were associated with a larger and more diverse suite of artefacts.

The artefacts buried with the females also revealed new information regarding Chalcolithic and Early Bronze Age burial representation. Females during this period were buried with an incredibly diverse suite of objects rather than a restricted range, for example only decorative items. Perhaps one of the strongest artefact groupings revealed in the dataset involved those buried with tools, with a sub-group which arguably could represent leatherworkers. These burials demonstrate that females were portrayed in death as active members of the community. Finally, this dataset also featured a number of females who had been buried with so-called "weapons". This demonstrates that we cannot assume a simple division between our modern (or rather nineteenth century) conceptions of male and female artefacts.

4.8. Future directions

The success of undertaking a re-examination of the female Chalcolithic and Early Bronze Age burial evidence has suggested that a similar study of both the male and sub-adult burials would also be rewarding. Not only would this determine whether the patterns found for the female burials, such as placement in barrows, are unique, it would also provide a thorough up-to-date understanding of the Chalcolithic and Early Bronze Age burial practices in Britain as a whole.

In conclusion, this research has demonstrated the importance of considering new archaeological excavations rather than conducting work entirely on the antiquarian investigations of the nineteenth century. Although the antiquarian evidence is a valuable resource available to archaeologists, it must be used with caution and alongside modern excavations which have reliable sex determinations, secure dating evidence and also detailed site plans. Furthermore, the conclusions drawn from the antiquarian evidence should also not be relied upon, as this research has demonstrated that in many cases the modern evidence does not support it.

Overall, this research has demonstrated how the female burial practices of the Chalcolithic and Early Bronze Age are highly complex and variable; there is no simple formula to explain them and nor should we try to look for one. Instead archaeologists need to recognize that the people in the past were just as complex as we are now, and we should not try to condense the Chalcolithic and Early Bronze Age burial evidence into generalisations and regional variations; being female was not to be part of a homogenous category.

APPENDIX 1: THE DATABASE

The following appendix concerns the database of Chalcolithic and Early Bronze Age female burials created during the course of this research. Below is a print-out from the database containing a list of all the female burials included in the dataset and their key information such as the form, method and period of the burial, the deceased's age and whether the burial included grave goods. Additionally, the reference from which the burial was taken is also included.

Due to the large body of diverse data stored in the database, a number of linking tables had to be used to store the data for each burial. These were outlined in Chapter Two and involved the Root Table, the burial form tables (Barrow, Flat Grave, Cairn, Other Form), the burial methods tables (Inhumation, Cremation, Token Inhumation, Token Cremation) and also a Grave Goods Table. The following is a detailed explanation of each type of table and the information included within them.

A1.1. Root table

The Root Table was intended to be the foundation of the database which would store the basic information about each burial. This includes the unique number assigned to each burial in order for the various components of the burial to be linked together through separate tables, the name of the burial and also the sub-name if required (which are also included in all the different tables to allow easy identification of the burials). Details regarding the location of the burial were also entered into this table, giving the nearest town, the county and also the grid reference. Basic information regarding the nature of the burial are also included in this table, such as the form that the burial takes, whether it is in a barrow, a cairn, a flat grave or something else ("other"), and the method of the deposition (inhumation, cremation, token inhumation, token cremation). This table also records whether the burial is associated with any grave goods, and also whether there is a radiocarbon date from the burial. It includes the information of the period to which the burial has been assigned (see Appendix Two), the age of the deceased, and, finally, the reference for the burial.

A1.2. Burial form tables

As mentioned above, the Root Table contains the unique reference number assigned to each burial, which can then be linked to the other tables in which the burial has an entry. Therefore, a burial will have an entry in only one of the Barrow Table, Cairn Table, Flat Grave Table, and Other Form Table, depending upon its nature.

There are several common pieces of information recorded for the burials in each of these tables, despite their different forms. Featured in each of these tables is information regarding the burial cut, recording the dimensions and the construction method (such as earth-

cut, surface deposit etc.). In the Barrow, Cairn and Other Form Tables the location of the burial is also recorded in relation to the monument or structure, for example whether it is centrally placed in the barrow or cairn, and in the Flat Grave Table the shape of the burial is also noted. Another common piece of information recorded in each of these tables is whether or not the burial has any associated monuments nearby. These can include both contemporary monuments such as other barrows, and monuments from the past, such as long barrows or causewayed enclosures.

However, the rest of the information recorded in these tables is particular to the form of the burial. Both the Barrow and Cairn Tables record the dimensions of these monuments, but the Barrow Table also includes information regarding the shape and whether or not the barrow has ditches, whereas the Cairn Table documents the construction method of the cairn. The Other Form Table, on the other hand, allows space to describe the form of the burial, for example being located in a henge. Each of the tables also includes a space for any additional notes which do not find expression in the formulated questions.

A1.3. Burial method tables

As with the four different burial form tables, each burial would only have an entry in one of the burial method tables, which are Inhumation, Cremation, Token Inhumation and Token Cremation.

First, it would be prudent to clarify why a burial would be placed in one of the token tables. An inhumation would be termed a "token" deposit rather than a full inhumation if only parts of the skeleton were represented. This would be, for example, if only the lower limb bones were included for burial. Often these feature as inclusions within the burials of complete inhumations, for example in cist 2 at Buckstone Road (128). However, they can also occur as individual burials in their own right such as at Allerwash (211), where the foot, leg bones and pelvis were arranged to look like a crouched inhumation (Newman & Miket 1973). However, a burial would only be termed a "token" if there is clear evidence that only parts of the skeleton were deposited in the first place. Incomplete skeletal representation resulting from burial conditions and decomposition would not be included in the token inhumation table, but would instead be classed as full inhumations.

A token cremation is not decided by the weight of the deposit itself. During the course of collecting the data it was clear that cremation deposits have such a wide range of weights that using a cut-off weight limit would not satisfy the distinction between a token and whole deposit. Instead I decided that it was the nature of the deposition which resulted in it being classed as either a whole or token deposit. If the cremation was in an isolated context, for example a defined pit or vessel, then it was to be considered as a whole cremation, even if not all the body was represented in the bones. A token cremation deposit was one in which there was no clear, definable context, for example, if a small amount had been placed in the gaps between the stones constructing a cairn, or if it was analogous to the other contemporary cremation deposits at the site, such as by size, nature or position.

All four tables included some of the same information for the burials. They each included the demographic data obtained from the burials, such as the age of the deceased, which was split into three choices of "young adult", "adult" and "mature". The certainty of sex was also recorded. As discussed, assigning sex to remains is difficult and therefore anthropologists often record their determinations as a range from the definitely "female", though "probably", down to "possibly". Each of the tables also has space to record any pathology evident on the bones.

The Inhumation Table also allowed for recording of the posture of the skeleton in the burial; the side the body was positioned on in the grave, the direction that the head was orientated to and also whether the burial was in a crouched, flexed or extended posture. The distinction between a crouched and flexed burial was determined to be the angle of the legs to the body; if the legs were at 90 degrees or greater to the body then it was classified as a flexed burial; if the legs were at less than 90 degrees than it was termed a crouched posture (figure 4.1; page 78). The Token Inhumation Table included a check list of the elements which were present in the burial, divided into regions of the skeleton, such as upper long bones or pelvis.

Both the Cremation and Token Cremation Tables have a field to allow for the recording of the weight of the cremation deposit and also to record whether or not the cremation was of a single individual, or if it contained more than one person. This can be determined if duplicated elements are present or if the bones have different age or sex indications. The cremation table also allows for the recording of whether or not the cremation was urned, that is being deposited *within* an urn, rather than having an urn as a separate grave good.

A1.4. Grave Goods Table

There is also a separate table for the burials which also have associated grave goods. These can range from the obvious, such as pottery vessels, daggers, flint tools and beads, to the less obvious such as burnt animal bone included in cremations or stains indicating the former presence of metal objects. It is because of the inclusion of

the less obvious grave goods that my study has such a high percentage of burials containing grave goods, 63%, compared with other studies from the period (25% of the burials examined by Greenwell, 54% of those by Mortimer (Ashbee 1960)).

Along with the standard identifying aspects of the burials as included in all other tables, the Grave Good Table also states the burial's form and also deposition method, such as barrow and inhumation, in order for a quick appraisal of the key aspects of the burial. There are then fields relating to the major materials that the grave goods of this period are made from, these being ceramics, metal, worked bone, un-worked bone, stone, flint and other. This allows for the different types of grave goods to be recorded in relevant fields.

In addition, there are two fields for the numbers of grave goods in each burial. The first of these is the total number of objects associated with the burial, with each item being counted individually, including each bead in a necklace for example. However, in order to deal with duplications of items which could skew results a second total field was also included; the total number of different types of objects. For example, a burial could be deposited with ten flint flakes. The number in the total for this burial would be ten, whereas in the number of different types it would be one.

Furthermore, there is also a field where additional notes could be made regarding the grave goods interred with the burial, in most cases this involved noting the positions of the objects, both in relation to the inhumed or cremated remains, but also in relation to the grave itself, such as whether they were found in the fill of the grave.

A1.5. The database

The following is the print out from the Root Table listing the key information for the burials used in this research.

Abbreviations used:

Type	B	Barrow
	FG	Flat Grave
	C	Cairn
	O	Other
Deposit	I	Inhumation
	C	Cremation
	TI	Token Inhumation
	TC	Token Cremation
Age	YA	Young Adult
	A	Adult
	M	Mature

Table A1.1: Female Burials of the Chalcolithic and Early Bronze Age used in this research.

UN	Name	Sub Name	County	Grid Ref	Type	Deposit	Period	Age	Grave Goods	Reference
100	Stoneyburn Farm	003	Lanarkshire	NS 9605 1957	C	C	3	A	Yes	Banks 1995
101	Stoneyburn Farm	004	Lanarkshire	NS 9605 1957	C	C	4	M	Yes	Banks 1995
102	North Mains	Henge B	Perthshire	NN 9280 1633	O	I	3	YA	Yes	Barclay 1983
103	North Mains	Henge K	Perthshire	NN 9280 1633	O	C	4	YA	Yes	Barclay 1983
104	North Mains	B A	Perthshire	NN 9262 1622	B	C	4	A	No	Barclay 1983
105	North Mains	B B	Perthshire	NN 9262 1622	B	C	3	A	Yes	Barclay 1983
106	North Mains	B D	Perthshire	NN 9262 1622	B	C	3	A	No	Barclay 1983
107	North Mains	B F	Perthshire	NN 9262 1622	B	C	4	YA	No	Barclay 1983
108	North Mains	B H	Perthshire	NN 9262 1622	B	C	3	A	No	Barclay 1983
109	North Mains	B J	Perthshire	NN 9262 1622	B	C	3	A	No	Barclay 1983
110	North Mains	B K	Perthshire	NN 9262 1622	B	C	3	A	No	Barclay 1983
111	Doons Law		Berwickshire	NT 868 516	FG	I	2	A	Yes	Clarke & Hamilton 1999
112	Eaglestone Flat	Pit 4/ Urn 1	Derbyshire	SK 2665 7406	FG	C	4	A	Yes	Barnatt 1994
113	Eaglestone Flat	Urn 3/ Pit 35	Derbyshire	SK 2665 7406	FG	C	3	M	Yes	Barnatt 1994
114	Eaglestone Flat	Urn 5/ Pit 218	Derbyshire	SK 2665 7406	FG	C	4	A	Yes	Barnatt 1994
115	Eaglestone Flat	C 273	Derbyshire	SK 2665 7406	C	C	4	M	Yes	Barnatt 1994
116	Eaglestone Flat	Pit 173	Derbyshire	SK 2665 7406	FG	TC	3	M	No	Barnatt 1994
117	Eaglestone Flat	Pit 174	Derbyshire	SK 2665 7406	FG	TC	3	A	No	Barnatt 1996
118	Eaglestone Flat	Pit 231	Derbyshire	SK 2665 7406	FG	TC	3	A	No	Barnatt 1994
119	Net Down	5J (3)	Wiltshire	SU 0900 4500	B	I	3	M	Yes	Green & Rollestone 1984
120	Net Down	5K (3)	Wiltshire	SU 0900 4500	B	I	2	YA	No	Green & Rollo-Smith 1984
121	Net Down	5K (4)	Wiltshire	SU 0900 4500	B	I	2	YA	No	Green & Rollo-Smith 1984
122	Rollestone	23 (1)	Wiltshire	SU 0900 4500	B	I	3	A	Yes	Green & Rollo-Smith 1984
123	Net Down	5L (2)	Wiltshire	SU 0900 4500	B	C	3	YA	Yes	Green & Rollo-Smith 1984
124	Net Down	5D (3)	Wiltshire	SU 0900 4500	B	C	3	A	No	Green & Rollo-Smith 1984

UN	Name	Sub Name	County	Grid Ref	Type	Deposit	Period	Age	Grave Goods	Reference
125	Net Down	5I (1)	Wiltshire	SU 0900 4500	B	C	3	A	No	Green & Rollo-Smith 1984
126	Balfarg/Balbirnie	C B(3)	Fife	NO 280030	C	TC	2	YA	No	Barclay & Russell-White 1993
127	Balfarg/ Balbirnie	Area A (9)	Fife	NO 280030	FG	TC	4	A	No	Barclay & Russell-White 1993
128	Buckstone Road	Cist 2 (2)	Midlothian	NT 248689	FG	TI	3	A	No	Close-Brooks 1972-4
129	Aberdour Road	Cist 1	Fife	NT 11738637	FG	I	3	YA	Yes	Close-Brooks et al. 1971
130	Aberdour Road	Grave 4	Fife	NT 11738637	FG	C	3	A	Yes	Close-Brooks et al. 1971
131	Aberdour Road	Grave 5	Fife	NT 11738637	FG	C	3	A	Yes	Close-Brooks et al. 1971
132	Aberdour Road	Grave 6	Fife	NT 11738637	FG	TC	3	A	No	Close-Brooks et al. 1971
133	Spring Road	Grave 3036	Oxfordshire	SU 4875 9755	FG	I	1	YA	Yes	Allen & Kamash 2008
134	Sithean Rosinish	1	Western Isles	NF 872537	B	I	3	YA	Yes	Crawford 1976-7
135	Sithean Rosinish	2	Western Isles	NF 872537	B	I	3	YA	Yes	Crawford 1976-7
136	Poor's Heath	6	Suffolk	TL 794685	B	I	3	M	No	Vatcher & Vatcher 1976
137	Poor's Heath	CR1	Suffolk	TL 794685	B	TC	3	A	No	Vatcher & Vatcher 1976
138	Poor's Heath	CR2	Suffolk	TL 794685	B	TC	3	A	No	Vatcher & Vatcher 1976
139	Balbirnie	Cist 2	Fife	NO 280030	O	C	2	A	Yes	Ritchie 1974
140	Balbirnie	Cist 3	Fife	NO 280030	O	C	2	A	Yes	Ritchie 1974
141	Balbirnie	Deposit 3	Fife	NO 280030	O	C	3	YA	No	Ritchie 1974
142	Balbirnie	Deposit 4	Fife	NO 280030	O	C	3	YA	No	Ritchie 1974
143	Balbirnie	Deposit 6	Fife	NO 280030	O	C	3	A	No	Ritchie 1974
144	Balbirnie	Deposit 7	Fife	NO 280030	O	C	3	A	No	Ritchie 1974
145	Balbirnie	Deposit 14	Fife	NO 280030	O	TC	3	YA	No	Ritchie 1974
146	Balbirnie	Deposit 18	Fife	NO 280030	O	TC	3	A	No	Ritchie 1974
147	Balbirnie	Deposit 20	Fife	NO 280030	O	TC	3	A	No	Ritchie 1974
148	Mousland		Orkney	HY 23091264	B	C	3	A	Yes	Downes 1994
149	Ferndale	004	Orkney	HY 3836 2035	B	C	3	YA	No	Duffy 2005
150	Heslerton	1L201	Yorkshire	SE 91757670	B	I	3	YA	No	Powlesland 1986
151	Heslerton	1M349	Yorkshire	SE 91757670	B	C	3	A	No	Powlesland 1986
152	Heslerton	1M117	Yorkshire	SE 91757670	B	I	3	A	No	Powlesland 1986
153	Heslerton	1R271	Yorkshire	SE 91757570	B	TI	2	A	No	Powlesland 1986
154	Heslerton	1R101	Yorkshire	SE 91757570	B	TI	3	A	No	Powlesland 1986
155	Raunds Area Project	F131	Northamptonshire	TL 000730	B	I	3	A	Yes	Harding & Healy 2007
156	Raunds Area Project	F3178	Northamptonshire	TL000730	B	C	4	YA	Yes	Harding & Healy 2007
157	Raunds Area Project	F47171	Northamptonshire	TL000730	B	C	3	A	Yes	Harding & Healy 2007

UN	Name	Sub Name	County	Grid Ref	Type	Deposit	Period	Age	Grave Goods	Reference
158	Raunds Area Project	F87541	Northamptonshire	TL 000730	O	C	3	M	No	Harding & Healy 2007
159	Raunds Area Project	F30663	Northamptonshire	TL 000730	B	C	3	YA	No	Harding & Healy 2007
160	Centre for Gene Function	204	Oxfordshire	SP 51562 07068	B	I	1	M	Yes	Boston et al 2003
161	Centre for Gene Function	137	Oxfordshire	SP 51562 07068	B	I	2	M	No	Boston et al 2003
162	Centre for Gene Function	113	Oxfordshire	SP 51562 07068	B	I	2	M	No	Boston et al 2003
163	Boscombe Down	6033	Wiltshire	416540 140420	B	I	1	A	Yes	Wessex Archaeology 56240.02
164	Boscombe Down	25225	Wiltshire	416540 140420	FG	I	2	A	Yes	Wessex Archaeology 56240.02
165	Boscombe Down	25225	Wiltshire	416540 140420	FG	C	4	M	No	Wessex Archaeology 53535.01
166	Middle Barn Farm	80078	Wiltshire	399546 - 400035	FG	C	3	A	Yes	Ellis & Powell 2008
167	Poundbury Farm	3024	Dorset	367426 090997	FG	I	2	A	No	Wessex Archaeology 60024.01; Egging Dinwiddy & Bradley 2011
168	Kingsmead Quarry		Berkshire	501636, 175480	FG	I	1	M	No	Chaffey & Brook, unpublished
169	Thomas Hardye School	1444	Dorset	SY 680 898	FG	I	2	A	No	Gardiner et al 2007
170	Thomas Hardye School	1139	Dorset	SY 680 898	B	C	3	A	Yes	Gardiner et al 2007
171	Barton Stacey	40172	Hampshire	438921 131932	FG	I	2	YA	No	De'athe, unpublished; Wessex Archaeology
172	Barton Stacey	11204	Hampshire	439193 131951	FG	C	3	YA	No	De'athe, unpublished; Wessex Archaeology
173	Barton Stacey	11203	Hampshire	439193 131951	FG	C	4	A	Yes	De'athe, unpublished: Wessex Archaeology
174	Eynesbury	2814a	Cambridgeshire	519573 259250	FG	C	3	A	Yes	Ellis 2004
175	Eynesbury	2814b	Cambridgeshire	519573 259250	FG	TC	3	A	Yes	Ellis 2004
176	Eynesbury	2820	Cambridgeshire	519573 259250	FG	C	3	A	Yes	Ellis 2004
177	Balneaves	Pit 2	Angus	NO 605 497	O	C	3	A	Yes	Russell-White et al 1992
178	Balneaves	Pit 3	Angus	NO 605 497	O	C	3	A	Yes	Russell-White et al 1992
179	Balneaves	Pit 4	Angus	NO 605 497	O	C	3	YA	Yes	Russell-White et al 1992
180	Low Grounds Barrows	Sk. 5487	Cambridgeshire	TL 3850 7400	FG	I	2	YA	Yes	Evans & Tabor 2010a; Evans 2013b
181	Low Grounds Barrows	Sk. 5486	Cambridgeshire	TL 3850 7400	FG	I	2	M	No	Evans & Tabor 2010a; Evans 2013b
182	Low Grounds Barrows	Sk. 5451	Cambridgeshire	TL 3850 7400	FG	I	2	YA	Yes	Evans & Tabor 2010a; Evans 2013b
183	Low Grounds Barrows	1063	Cambridgeshire	TL 3850 7400	B	C	3	YA	Yes	Evans & Tabor 2010a; Evans 2013b
184	Low Grounds Barrows	1053	Cambridgeshire	TL 3850 7400	B	C	3	A	Yes	Evans & Tabor 2010a; Evans 2013b

UN	Name	Sub Name	County	Grid Ref	Type	Deposit	Period	Age	Grave Goods	Reference
185	Low Grounds Barrows	1087	Cambridgeshire	TL 3850 7400	B	C	3	M	Yes	Evans & Tabor 2010a; Evans 2013b
186	Low Grounds Barrows	1098	Cambridgeshire	TL 3850 7400	B	C	3	M	No	Evans & Tabor 2010a; Evans 2013b
187	Low Grounds Barrows	1122	Cambridgeshire	TL 3850 7400	B	C	2	A	Yes	Evans & Tabor 2010a; Evans 2013b
188	Low Grounds Barrows	1111	Cambridgeshire	TL 3850 7400	B	C	3	M	Yes	Evans & Tabor 2010a; Evans 2013b
189	Low Grounds Barrows	1116	Cambridgeshire	TL 3850 7400	B	C	3	A	Yes	Evans & Tabor 2010a; Evans 2013b
190	Low Grounds Barrows	1123	Cambridgeshire	TL 3850 7400	B	C	3	A	No	Evans & Tabor 2010a; Evans 2013b
191	Low Grounds Barrows	1030	Cambridgeshire	TL 3850 7400	B	C	3	A	Yes	Evans & Tabor 2010a; Evans 2013b
192	Tandderwen	C 1	Vale of Clwyd	SJ 0815 6613	B	C	3	A	Yes	Brassil et al 1991
193	Tandderwen	C 3	Vale of Clwyd	SJ 0815 6613	B	C	3	YA	No	Brassil et al 1991
194	Tandderwen	C 4	Vale of Clwyd	SJ 0815 6613	B	C	3	YA	Yes	Brassil et al 1991
195	Tandderwen	C 6	Vale of Clwyd	SJ 0815 6613	FG	C	3	YA	Yes	Brassil et al 1991
196	Tandderwen	C 8	Vale of Clwyd	SJ 0815 6613	FG	C	4	YA	Yes	Brassil et al 1991
197	Abbey Mains Farm	1	East Lothian	NT 536 751	FG	I	2	YA	Yes	Lawson et al 2002
198	Cloburn Quarry	067	Lanarkshire	NS 947 414	C	C	3	M	No	Lelong & Pollard 1998
199	Cloburn Quarry	068	Lanarkshire	NS 947 414	C	C	3	A	Yes	Lelong & Pollard 1998
200	Kingshill North	8656	Gloustershire	SP 0365 0250	B	I	1	A	Yes	Biddulph et al 2010
201	Kingshill North	1402	Gloustershire	SP 0365 0250	FG	I	2	M	Yes	Biddulph et al 2010
202	Benderloch		Argyll	NM 9051 3835	FG	C	4	YA	Yes	MacGregor 1998
203	Darnaway		Moray	NH 994 555	FG	I	2	M	Yes	Maclagan Wedderburn 1974-75
204	Sketewan	Cist 3	Perth & Kinross	NN 9475 5282	FG	C	2	A	No	Mercer & Midgley 1997
205	Sketewan	Cist 5	Perth & Kinross	NN 9475 5282	FG	C	2	A	No	Mercer & Midgley 1997
206	Sketewan	Cist 6	Perth & Kinross	NN 9475 5282	FG	TC	2	A	No	Mercer & Midgley 1997
207	Sketewan	Cist 7	Perth & Kinross	NN 9475 5282	FG	C	2	A	No	Mercer & Midgley 1997
208	Sketewan	Cist 1	Perth & Kinross	NN 9475 5282	FG	C	2	YA	Yes	Mercer & Midgley 1997
209	Horsburgh Castle Farm		Peebleshire	NT 28993902	FG	C	2	A	Yes	Petersen et al 1972-4
210	Dridaig Cottage		Highland	NH 714 845	FG	I	4	A	Yes	Ralston 1996
211	Allerwash		Northumberland	NY 871 673	FG	TI	2	YA	Yes	Newman & Miket 1973
212	Ravenstone		Buckinghamshire	SP8535 4895	B	I	2	A	Yes	Allen 1981
213	Roxton	B4	Bedfordshire	TL 157 535	B	C	2	A	Yes	Taylor & Woodward 1985
214	Kentraw		Islay	NR 2671 6293	FG	I	3	YA	Yes	Ritchie 1987

UN	Name	Sub Name	County	Grid Ref	Type	Deposit	Period	Age	Grave Goods	Reference
215	Kiltry Knock		Aberdeenshire	NJ 6653 5652	FG	C	4	A	Yes	Shepherd & Cowie 1976-7
216	Northumberland Bottom		Kent	562536 171753	FG	I	2	A	Yes	Askew 2006 (CTRL)
217	Saltwood Tunnel		Kent	615345 136940	FG	I	2	A	No	Riddler & Trevarthen 2006 CTRL
218	Whitehill Road		Kent	565413 172456	B	I	4	YA	Yes	Bull 2006
219	Hardendale Nap	23	Cumbria	NY 5814 1401	C	TI	3	M	No	Williams & Howard-Davies 2004
220	Hardendale Nap	14	Cumbria	NY 5814 1401	C	C	3	A	Yes	Williams & Howard-Davies 2004
221	Hardendale Nap	29	Cumbria	NY 5814 1401	C	TI	3	A	No	Williams & Howard-Davies 2004
222	Carneddau	C 1, cist 5	Powys	SN 9899 9979	C	C	2	M	Yes	Gibson 1993
223	Carneddau	C 1, cist 1	Powys	SN 9899 9979	C	C	2	M	Yes	Gibson 1993
224	Carneddau	21	Powys	SN 9899 9979	FG	C	2	A	Yes	Gibson 1993
225	Butcher's Rise	691	Cambridgeshire	TL 356 719	B	C	3	YA	Yes	Evans & Knight 1998
226	Butcher's Rise	718	Cambridgeshire	TL 356 719	B	C	3	A	No	Evans & Knight 1998
227	Bradley Fen	F.1279	Cambridgeshire	TL 235 978	FG	C	4	A	Yes	Gibson & Knight 2006
228	102 Findhorn		Moray	NJ 0397 6443	FG	C	3	YA	Yes	Shepherd & Shepherd 2001
229	O'Connell Ridge East	F. 2011	Cambridgeshire	53885 274026	B	C	3	A	Yes	Evans & Tabor 2010b; Evans 2013b
231	Barns Farm	Cist 1	Fife	NT 178 842	FG	C	2	YA	No	Watkins 1982
232	Barns Farm	Cist 2	Fife	NT 178 842	FG	I	2	A	Yes	Watkins 1982
233	Barns Farm	Cist 4	Fife	NT 178 842	FG	I	3	A	Yes	Watkins 1982
234	Barns Farm	Grave 1	Fife	NT 178 842	FG	C	2	YA	Yes	Watkins 1982
235	Ewanrigg	14	Cumbria	NY 035 353	FG	I	2	YA	Yes	Bewley et al 1992
236	Ewanrigg	18	Cumbria	NY 035 353	FG	C	2	A	Yes	Bewley et al 1992
237	Ewanrigg	28	Cumbria	NY 035 353	FG	C	2	A	No	Bewley et al 1992
238	Ewanrigg	29	Cumbria	NY 035 353	FG	C	2	A	No	Bewley et al 1992
239	Ewanrigg	42	Cumbria	NY 035 353	FG	C	2	A	No	Bewley et al 1992
240	Ewanrigg	55	Cumbria	NY 035 353	FG	C	2	YA	Yes	Bewley et al 1992
241	Trelystan	I: 4	Powys	SJ 2774 0700	B	C	2	YA	Yes	Britnell 1982
242	Trelystan	I: 7	Powys	SJ 2774 0700	B	C	3	M	Yes	Britnell 1982
244	Trelystan	II: 2	Powys	SJ 2774 0700	B	C	3	M	Yes	Britnell 1982
245	Trelystan	II: 4	Powys	SJ 2774 0700	B	C	4	A	No	Britnell 1982
246	Warren Farm	C1	Buckinghamshire	SP 8033 4074	B	C	3	YA	Yes	Green 1974
248	Little Pond Ground	PB	Buckinghamshire	SP 8012 4053	B	I	2	M	Yes	Green 1974
249	Barnack	6	Cambridgeshire	TF 050 069	B	I	3	YA	No	Donaldson 1977
250	Barnack	39	Cambridgeshire	TF 050 069	B	I	3	A	Yes	Donaldson 1977
251	Barnack	68	Cambridgeshire	TF 050 069	B	I	3	A	No	Donaldson 1977

UN	Name	Sub Name	County	Grid Ref	Type	Deposit	Period	Age	Grave Goods	Reference
252	Manor Farm	55	North Lancashire	352111 472824	O	I	4	A	Yes	Olivier 1987
253	Camp Ground	F 273	Cambridgeshire	537698 278185	FG	I	3	YA	No	Regan et al 2004; Evans 2013a
254	Dalineun	C1	Argyll	NM 879267	O	C	2	A	Yes	Ritchie 1971-2
255	Queenafjold		Orkney	HY 265249	B	C	4	A	Yes	Ritchie & Ritchie 1974
257	Grandtully	Pit 36	Perthshire	NN 922 533	FG	C	4	YA	Yes	Simpson & Coles 1990
258	Beauforts	BNF 04	Kent	TR 3991 6921	B	I	2	M	Yes	Hart & Moody 2008
259	QEQM Hospital	SK1	Kent	TR3599 6938	FG	I	1	A	Yes	Hart & Moody 2008
260	Hill Road	A	Kent	TQ 7245 6445	O	C	4	A	Yes	Cruse & Harrison 1983; Cruse 2007
261	Amesbury 58	1	Wiltshire	SU 1733 4226	B	C	3	A	Yes	Ashbee 1985
262	Amesbury 61	C3	Wiltshire	SU 1783 4276	B	C	3	A	No	Ashbee 1985
263	Amesbury 61	I1	Wiltshire	SU 1783 4276	B	I	3	YA	No	Ashbee 1985
264	Milton Libourne 1	NW grave	Wiltshire	SU 1993 5790	B	C	3	YA	Yes	Ashbee 1986
265	Milton Lilbourne 5		Wiltshire	SU 2007 5789	B	C	3	A	Yes	Ashbee 1986
266	Rudston LXII	Burial 2	Yorkshire	TA 098 658	B	I	3	A	No	Pacitto 1972
267	Rudston LXII	Burial 3	Yorkshire	TA 098 658	B	I	3	A	No	Pacitto 1972
268	Wetwang Slack	B A, G1	Yorkshire	496185 458058	B	I	2	A	No	Dent 1979
269	Wetwang Slack	B B, G4	Yorkshire	496185 458058	B	I	2	YA	Yes	Dent 1979
270	Wetwang Slack	B B, G3	Yorkshire	496185 458058	B	C	2	A	Yes	Dent 1979
271	Wetwang Slack	I G3	Yorkshire	496185 458058	FG	I	3	A	Yes	Dent 1979
272	Wetwang Slack	I G2	Yorkshire	496185 458058	FG	C	3	YA	No	Dent 1979
273	Wilsford cum Lake G52	WD255	Wiltshire	SU 115 405	B	I	3	YA	No	Smith 1991
274	Caythorpe B 550	532	Yorkshire	509462 465583	B	I	3	A	No	Abramson 1996
275	Gayhurst Quarry B 1	4005	Buckinghamshire	SP 853 447	B	C	3	A	No	Chapman 2007
276	Gayhurst Quarry B 5	6005	Buckinghamshire	SP 853 447	B	C	4	YA	Yes	Chapman 2007
277	Isle of Thanet	751	Kent	628701 165315	FG	TI	2	M	No	Bennett et al 2008
278	Isle of Thanet	643	Kent	628701 165315	FG	I	2	A	No	Bennett et al 2008
279	Llandegai	A13	Gwynedd	SH 595 712	O	C	3	A	No	Lynch & Musson 2001
280	Llanilar	CR 4	Ceredigion	SN 625 751	FG	C	3	A	Yes	Briggs 1997
281	Llanilar	CR 5	Ceredigion	SN 625 751	FG	C	3	A	Yes	Briggs 1997; Benson et al 1982
282	Llanilar	CR 8	Ceredigion	SN 625 751	FG	C	3	YA	Yes	Briggs 1997
283	Grendon Quarry	B II, F8	Northamptonshire	SP 873 617	B	I	3	A	Yes	Gibson & McCormick 1985

UN	Name	Sub Name	County	Grid Ref	Type	Deposit	Period	Age	Grave Goods	Reference
284	Waterhall Farm	Grave I	Cambridgeshire	TL 6717 6665	O	I	3	A	No	Martin and Deviston 1975-6
285	Waterhall Farm	Grave Iie	Cambridgeshire	TL 6717 6665	O	I	3	M	Yes	Martin and Deviston 1975-6
286	Waterhall Farm	Grave Iid	Cambridgeshire	TL 6717 6665	O	I	3	M	Yes	Martin and Deviston 1975-6
287	Waterhall Farm	Grave Iic	Cambridgeshire	TL 6717 6665	O	TI	3	YA	Yes	Martin and Deviston 1975-6
288	Waterhall Farm	Grave IV	Cambridgeshire	TL 6717 6665	O	I	3	A	No	Martin and Deviston 1975-6
289	Waterhall Farm	C1	Cambridgeshire	TL 6717 6665	O	TC	3	A	No	Martin and Deviston 1975-6
290	Barrow Hills	801	Oxfordshire	SU 51289 98090	B	C	3	YA	Yes	Barclay and Halpin 1999
291	Barrow Hills	16 E	Oxfordshire	SU 5195 9841	B	C	2	A	Yes	Barclay and Halpin 1999
292	Barrow Hills	PB 4866, 4906	Oxfordshire	SU 51409 98110	FG	I	4	M	Yes	Barclay and Halpin 1999
293	Barrow Hills	PB 4866, 4970	Oxfordshire	SU 51409 98110	FG	I	3	A	Yes	Barclay and Halpin 1999
294	Barrow Hills	PB 4866, 4968	Oxfordshire	SU 51409 98110	FG	I	4	M	No	Barclay and Halpin 1999
295	Barrow Hills	RD 201, 206	Oxfordshire	SU 51440 98158	FG	TI	2	YA	Yes	Barclay and Halpin 1999
296	Barrow Hills	614	Oxfordshire	SU 51345 98085	FG	TC	4	A	No	Barclay and Halpin 1999
297	Barrow Hills	B 2	Oxfordshire	SU 5148 9822	B	C	3	A	Yes	Barclay and Halpin 1999
298	Long Critchel 7	1	Dorset	ST 9604 1160	B	I	2	A	Yes	Green et al 1982
299	Long Critchel 7	4	Dorset	ST 9604 1160	B	C	3	A	Yes	Green et al 1982
300	Howick Heugh	C1	Northumberland	NU 237 171	B	C	3	A	Yes	Jobey and Newman 1975
301	Sutton Veny	Urn burial	Wiltshire	ST 913 415	B	C	3	A	Yes	Johnston 1972/3
302	Kingston Russell 6g	C	Dorset	SY 5785 9043	B	I	2	YA	Yes	Bailey 1980 (Bailey 1971)
303	Kingston Russell 6g	A	Dorset	SY 5785 9043	B	I	2	YA	No	Bailey 1980 (Bailey 1971)
304	Kingston Russell 6n	C	Dorset	SY 5782 9048	B	C	2	YA	Yes	Bailey 1980
305	Roystone Grange	C	Derbyshire	SK 2034 4710	B	C	3	A	Yes	Barnatt 1996
306	Ystrad-Hynod	Cist	Montgomeryshire	SN 907 882	B	C	3	YA	Yes	ApSimon 1973
307	Broomend of Crichie	1075	Aberdeenshire	377926 819668	O	C	3	YA	Yes	Bradley 2011
308	Achinduich Farm	Pit 3	Sutherland	NC 5820 0092	O	C	4	A	Yes	Bradley 2011
309	Baldock Bypass	G59.2	Hertfordshire	TL 2645 3464	B	C	3	A	Yes	Phillips 2009
310	West Stow	4	Suffolk	TM 7970 7135	B	C	4	A	No	West 1990

UN	Name	Sub Name	County	Grid Ref	Type	Deposit	Period	Age	Grave Goods	Reference
311	West Stow	11a	Suffolk	TM 7970 7135	B	C	4	YA	Yes	West 1990
312	West Stow	11b	Suffolk	TM 7970 7135	B	C	4	A	Yes	West 1990
313	West Stow	23	Suffolk	TM 7970 7135	B	C	4	A	Yes	West 1990
314	West Stow	25a	Suffolk	TM 7970 7135	B	C	4	A	No	West 1990
315	West Stow	25b	Suffolk	TM 7970 7135	B	C	4	A	No	West 1990
316	West Stow	28	Suffolk	TM 7970 7135	B	C	4	A	No	West 1990
317	West Stow	31	Suffolk	TM 7970 7135	B	C	4	A	No	West 1990
318	West Stow	35	Suffolk	TM 7970 7135	B	C	4	A	No	West 1990
319	Etton	Grave 9	Cambridgeshire	TF 14450 07580	B	I	3	A	Yes	French and Pryor 2005
320	Etton	Grave 2	Cambridgeshire	TF 14450 07580	B	TI	3	YA	Yes	French and Pryor 2005
321	Stonea	Burial 1	Cambridgeshire	TL 451 931	B	C	2	A	Yes	Potter 1976
322	Holt	Site B F16	Hereford & Worcester	SO 8250 6210	B	C	3	A	Yes	Hunt et al 1986
323	Holt	Site E F4	Hereford & Worcester	SO 824 622	B	C	3	A	Yes	Hunt et al 1986
324	Elburton	551	Devon	SX 5262 5364	FG	C	4	A	No	Watts and Quinnell 2001
325	Elburton	554	Devon	SX 5262 5364	FG	C	4	A	Yes	Watts and Quinnell 2001
326	Barrow Bottom	Grave 1	Suffolk	TL 7737 6612	B	I	2	M	Yes	Martin 1976
327	Radwell	Ring ditch 1	Bedfordshire	TL 013 575	B	C	2	A	Yes	Hall and Woodward 1977
328	Lambourne No. 19	F3	Berkshire	SU 332 086	B	C	3	A	Yes	Richards 1986 -1990
329	Easton Down	CB1	Wiltshire	SU 23478 36377	FG	C	3	M	No	Ride 2001
330	Allithwaite	115	Cumbria	SD 3870 7665	O	C	3	YA	Yes	Wild 2003
331	Allithwaite	119	Cumbria	SD 3870 7665	O	C	3	A	Yes	Wild 2003
332	Allithwaite	117	Cumbria	SD 3870 7665	O	TC	3	A	No	Wild 2003
333	Allithwaite	106	Cumbria	SD 3870 7665	O	TC	3	A	Yes	Wild 2003
334	Allithwaite	108	Cumbria	SD 3870 7665	O	TC	3	A	Yes	Wild 2003
335	Exning	8	Suffolk	TL 6303 6357	FG	I	3	A	Yes	Martin and Denston 1986
336	Pilsgate		Lincolnshire	TF 049 0469	FG	I	3	A	Yes	Pryor 1974
337	Ringstead Downs		Norfolk	TF 6960 4025	FG	I	2	YA	Yes	Kinnes 1978
338	Monkton-up-Wimborne	7	Dorset	SU 016 150	B	C	3	A	Yes	French et al 2007

UN	Name	Sub Name	County	Grid Ref	Type	Deposit	Period	Age	Grave Goods	Reference
339	Monkton-up-Wimborne	2	Dorset	SU 016 150	FG	C	3	YA	Yes	French et al 2007
340	Monkton-up-Wimborne	8	Dorset	SU 016 150	B	C	3	M	Yes	French et al 2007
341	Goatscrag A	Burial 2	Northumberland	NT 977 371	O	C	4	YA	Yes	Burgess 1972
342	Woodford G13	236	Wiltshire	SU 110 366	B	I	3	A	Yes	Ashbee and Ashbee 1988
343	Newbiggingmill Quarry		Lanarkshire	NT 0355 4531	FG	I	1	M	Yes	Welfare 1976-77
344	Vicarage Field	Grave 1	Oxfordshire	SP 401 057	FG	I	1	YA	Yes	Barclay et al 2005
345	Vicarage Field	Grave 2	Oxfordshire	SP 401 157	FG	I	1	A	Yes	Barclay et al 1995
346	Ring ditch X.6	Burial 3	Oxfordshire	SP 4058 0554	B	I	2	YA	Yes	Barclay et al 1995
347	Ring ditch X.6	C 2	Oxfordshire	SP 4058 0554	B	C	2	A	No	Barclay et al 1995
349	Deeping St Nicholas	54	Lincolnshire	TF 17440 13135	B	I	3	YA	Yes	French 1994
350	Northpark	Cist 3	Bute	202016 661253	FG	I	2	YA	Yes	Sheridan pers. comm.

APPENDIX 2: DATING

cal BC

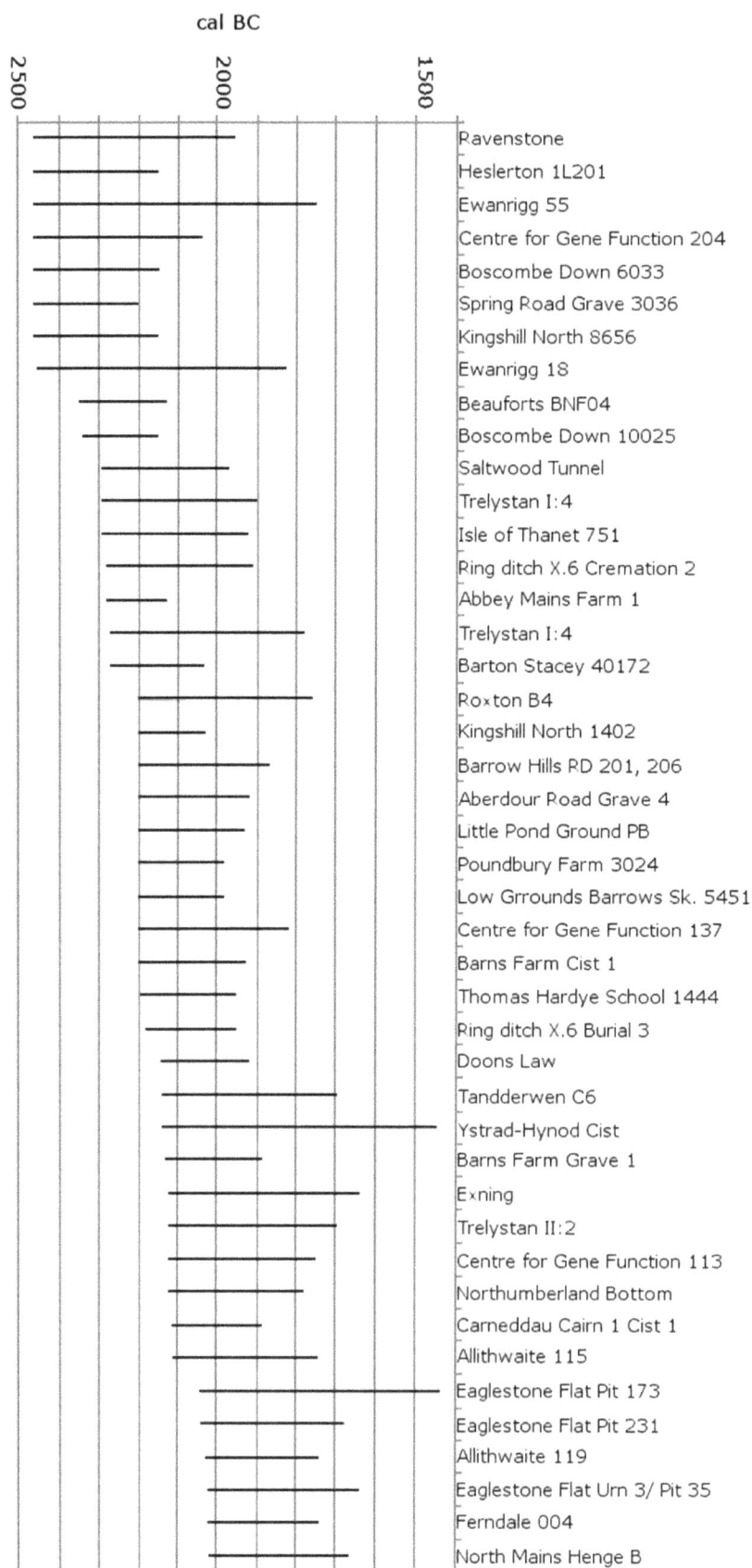

Figure A2.1: Radiocarbon dates for the Chalcolithic and Early Bronze Age female burials (at 2σ).

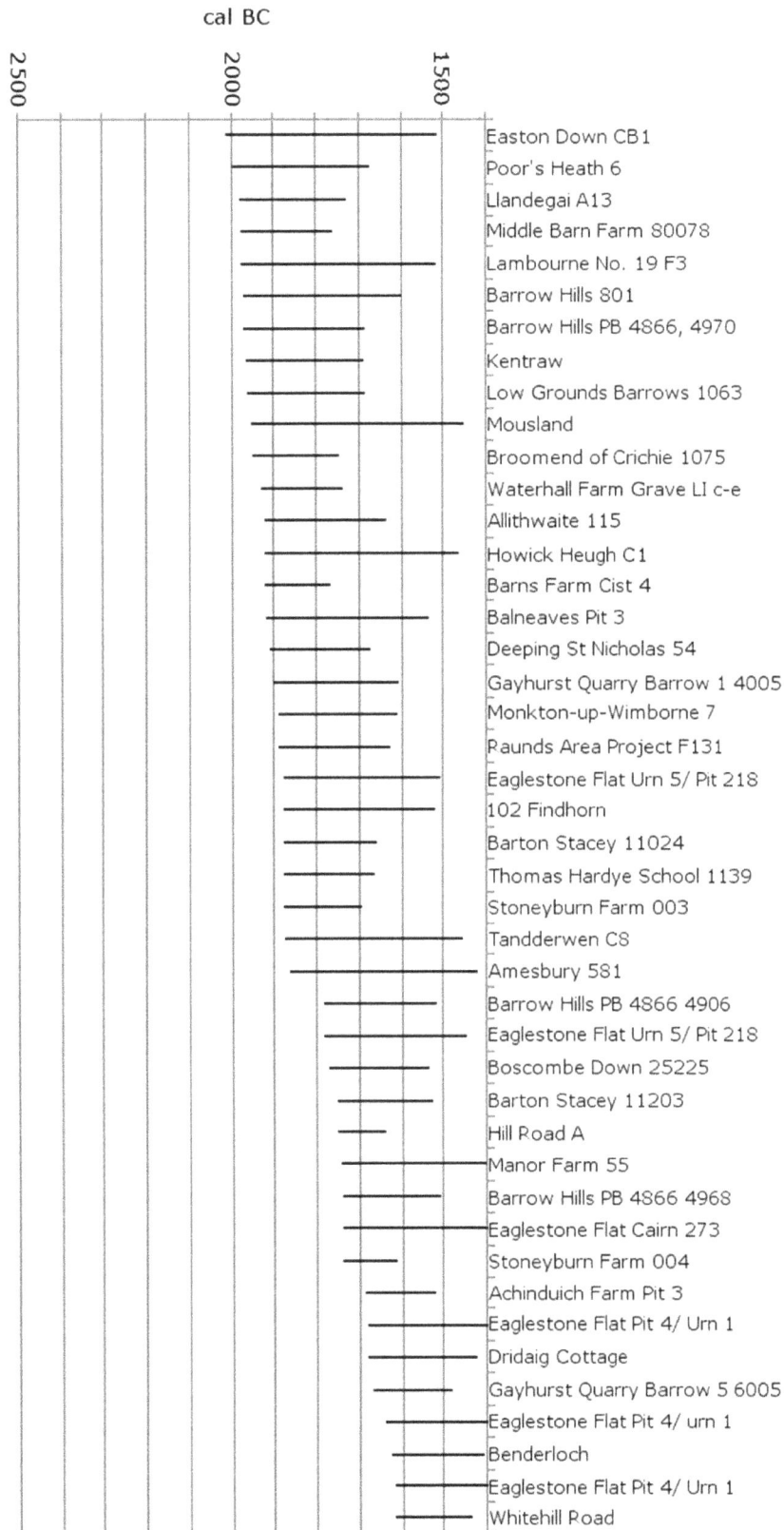

Figure A2.1 (continued): Radiocarbon dates for the Chalcolithic and Early Bronze Age female burials (at 2σ).

*Table A2.1: Dating the burials. The following table outlines the basis on which the female burials in this dataset have been assigned to the periods (outlined in Chapter Two). *Indicates the radiocarbon date was calibrated using the programme OxCal Version 4.1 (Bronk Ramsey 2009).*

UN	Name	SubName	Period	Radiocarbon Date	Reason for Period Placement
100	Stoneyburn Farm	003	3	1878 - 1695 cal BC	Radiocarbon date
101	Stoneyburn Farm	004	4	1737-1613 cal BC	Radiocarbon date
102	North Mains	Henge B	3	2016 - 1665 cal BC*	Radiocarbon date
103	North Mains	Henge K	4	c. 2016 - 1665 cal BC*	Radiocarbon date, post 102 (location, burial type), enlarged Food Vessel (later date range than Food Vessels).
104	North Mains	Barrow A	4	c. 2205 - 1744 cal BC*	Radiocarbon date, unurned cremation, could be late Period 3.
105	North Mains	Barrow B	3	c. 2205 - 1744 cal BC*	Radiocarbon date, contemporary with Food Vessels and jet necklace.
106	North Mains	Barrow D	3	c. 2205 - 1744 cal BC*	Radiocarbon date, contemporary with Food Vessels and jet necklace.
107	North Mains	Barrow F	4	c. 2205 - 1744 cal BC*	Radiocarbon date, unurned cremation, could be late Period 3.
108	North Mains	Barrow H	3	c. 2205 - 1744 cal BC*	Radiocarbon date, contemporary with Food Vessels and jet necklace.
109	North Mains	Barrow J	3	c. 2205 - 1744 cal BC*	Radiocarbon date, contemporary with Food Vessels and jet necklace.
110	North Mains	Barrow K	3	c. 2205 - 1744 cal BC*	Radiocarbon date, contemporary with Food Vessels and jet necklace.
111	Doons Law		2	2140 - 1920 cal BC	Radiocarbon date
112	Eaglestone Flat	Pit 4/ Urn 1	4	1620 - 1260 cal BC 1680 - 1328 cal BC 1640 - 1319 cal BC	Radiocarbon date
113	Eaglestone Flat	Urn 3/ Pit 35	3	2020 - 1640 cal BC	Radiocarbon date
114	Eaglestone Flat	Urn 5/ Pit 218	4	1880 - 1510 cal BC 1780 - 1450 cal BC	Radiocarbon date
115	Eaglestone Flat	Cairn 273	4	1737 - 1400 cal BC (TPQ)	Radiocarbon date, possible Bucket Urn.
116	Eaglestone Flat	Pit 173	3	2040 - 1440 cal BC	Radiocarbon date, Period 3 due to middle of radiocarbon determination and similarity to 118.
117	Eaglestone Flat	Pit 174	3		Based on radiocarbon determinations of similar features.

UN	Name	SubName	Period	Radiocarbon Date	Reason for Period Placement
118	Eaglestone Flat	Pit 231	3	2040 - 1680 cal BC	Radiocarbon date
119	Net Down	5J (3)	3		Amber, linear barrow group from Wessex.
120	Net Down	5K (3)	2		Judged contemporary with primary grave due to similar grave fills.
121	Net Down	5K (4)	2		Judged contemporary with primary grave due to similar grave fills.
122	Rollestone	23 (1)	3		Simple mound, post holes packed with Food Vessel sherds, bronze awl.
123	Net Down	5L (2)	3		Beads of shale, faience, Collared Urn sherds on mound.
124	Net Down	5D (3)	3		Concentric stake-circles, cremation.
125	Net Down	5I (1)	3		On basis of other barrows in group, but may be Period 4.
126	Balfarg/Balbirnie	Cairn B(3)	2		First interment had Food Vessel bowl and jet necklace, this burial placed in construction of cairn so contemporary.
127	Balfarg/ Balbirnie	Area A (9)	4		Bucket Urns featured in similar pits, unurned cremation.
128	Buckstone Road	Cist 2 (2)	3		Difficult to date, could have been any time from 2250 BC onwards.
129	Aberdour Road	Cist 1	3		Radiocarbon date of nearby cist with Food Vessel bowl.
130	Aberdour Road	Grave 4	3		Enlarged Food Vessel Urn.
131	Aberdour Road	Grave 5	3		Relation to others in group.
132	Aberdour Road	Grave 6	3		Relation to other in group.
133	Spring Road	Grave 3036	1	2460-2200 cal BC	Radiocarbon date
134	Sithean Rosinish	1	3		Accessory vessel in style of Collared Urn.
135	Sithean Rosinish	2	3		Accessory vessel in style of Collared Urn.
136	Poor's Heath	6	3	2000-1675 cal BC	Radiocarbon date
137	Poor's Heath	CR1	3		Multi-phase barrow and radiocarbon dates from barrow.
138	Poor's Heath	CR2	3		Multi-phase barrow and radiocarbon dates from barrow.
139	Balbirnie	Cist 2	2		Based on Food Vessel date from another cist, contemporary structures.
140	Balbirnie	Cist 3	2		Food Vessel of the bowl series.

UN	Name	SubName	Period	Radiocarbon Date	Reason for Period Placement
141	Balbirnie	Deposit 3	3		Later than 139 and 140.
142	Balbirnie	Deposit 4	3		Later than 139 and 140.
143	Balbirnie	Deposit 6	3		Later than 139 and 140.
144	Balbirnie	Deposit 7	3		Later than 139 and 140.
145	Balbirnie	Deposit 14	3		Later than 139 and 140.
146	Balbirnie	Deposit 18	3		Later than 139 and 140.
147	Balbirnie	Deposit 20	3		Later than 139 and 140.
148	Mousland		3	1951 - 1456 cal BC	Radiocarbon date
149	Ferndale	004	3	2020 - 1740 cal BC	Radiocarbon date
150	Heslerton	1L201	3		Later than 2401 – 2155 cal BC and Food Vessel burials.
151	Heslerton	1M349	3		Large multi-phase barrow, after Beaker burials.
152	Heslerton	1M117	3		Large multi-phase barrow, after Beaker burials.
153	Heslerton	1R271	2		Placed in fill of a grave containing a Beaker.
154	Heslerton	1R101	3		Placed in fill of a grave containing a Food Vessel.
155	Raunds Area Project	F131	3	1890 - 1630 cal BC	Radiocarbon date
156	Raunds Area Project	F3178	4	c. 2030 - 1490 cal BC	Radiocarbon date, stylistically late Collared Urn.
157	Raunds Area Project	F47171	3		Stage two Collared Urn
158	Raunds Area Project	F87541	3		Monument dated to 2020 – 1680 BC, deposit in backfilling of ditch.
159	Raunds Area Project	F30663	3		Monument construction 2180 – 1930 BC.
160	Centre for Gene Function	204	1	2459 - 2039 cal BC*	Radiocarbon date, 68.2% determination of 2340 – 2136 cal BC, low-carinated Beaker and single-phase barrow.
161	Centre for Gene Function	137	2	2200 1820 cal BC	Radiocarbon date
162	Centre for Gene Function	113	2	2120 - 1750 cal BC	Radiocarbon date, similar to 161.
163	Boscombe Down	6033	1	2460 - 2150 cal BC	Radiocarbon date
164	Boscombe Down	25225	2	2340 - 2150 cal BC	Radiocarbon date
165	Boscombe Down	25225	4	1770 - 1537 cal BC*	Radiocarbon date
166	Middle Barn Farm	80078	3	1975 - 1760 cal BC	Radiocarbon date (of the male inhumation)

UN	Name	SubName	Period	Radiocarbon Date	Reason for Period Placement
167	Poundbury Farm	3024	2	2200 - 1980 cal BC	Radiocarbon date
168	Kingsmead Quarry		1	2840 - 2490 cal BC	Radiocarbon date
169	Thomas Hardye School	1444	2	2190 - 1950 cal BC	Radiocarbon date
170	Thomas Hardye School	1139	3	1880 - 1670 cal BC	Radiocarbon date
171	Barton Stacey	40172	2	2270 - 2030 cal BC	Radiocarbon date
172	Barton Stacey	11204	3	1880 - 1660 cal BC	Radiocarbon date
173	Barton Stacey	11203	4	1750 - 1530 cal BC	Radiocarbon date
174	Eynesbury	2814a	3		Collared Urn style.
175	Eynesbury	2814b	3		Collared Urn style.
176	Eynesbury	2820	3		Similar to 174/5.
177	Balneaves	Pit 2	3		Radiocarbon date, Collared Urn similar to a dated example from the site (178).
178	Balneaves	Pit 3	3	1916 - 1535 cal BC*	Radiocarbon date
179	Balneaves	Pit 4	3		Radiocarbon date, Collared Urn similar to a dated example from the site (178).
180	Low Grounds Barrows	Sk. 5487	2		Long-necked Beaker with comb-zoned decoration (Southern British series), also jet and amber beads.
181	Low Grounds Barrows	Sk. 5486	2		Directly above 180 suggesting contemporary.
182	Low Grounds Barrows	Sk. 5451	2	2200 - 1980 cal BC	Radiocarbon date
183	Low Grounds Barrows	1063	3	1960 - 1690 cal BC	Radiocarbon date
184	Low Grounds Barrows	1053	3		Directly referencing 180/ 181.
185	Low Grounds Barrows	1087	3		Multi-phase barrow, associated with Collared Urn burials.
186	Low Grounds Barrows	1098	3		Multi-phase barrow, associated with Collared Urn burials.
187	Low Grounds Barrows	1122	2		Earlier phased Collared Urn.
188	Low Grounds Barrows	1111	3		Style of Collared Urn, specifically decoration on collar and neck.

UN	Name	SubName	Period	Radiocarbon Date	Reason for Period Placement
189	Low Grounds Barrows	1116	3		Date due to 188.
190	Low Grounds Barrows	1123	3		Multi-phase barrow, associated with Collared Urn burials.
191	Low Grounds Barrows	1030	3		Multi-phase barrow, associated with Collared Urn burials.
192	Tandderwen	C 1	3		Dated from 195.
193	Tandderwen	C 3	3		Dated from 195.
194	Tandderwen	C 4	3		Dated from 195.
195	Tandderwen	C 6	3	2139 - 1694 cal BC*	Radiocarbon date, 68.2% determination of 2028 – 1776 cal BC.
196	Tandderwen	C 8	4	1875 - 1459 cal BC*	Radiocarbon date
198	Cloburn Quarry	067	3	1910 - 1620 cal BC (TPQ)	Radiocarbon date, close to 199.
199	Cloburn Quarry	068	3	1910 - 1620 cal BC (TPQ)	Radiocarbon date, earlier part of site, Food Vessel accompanies cremation rather than contains it.
200	Kingshill North	8656	1	2458 -2152 cal BC	Radiocarbon date
201	Kingshill North	1402	2	2201-2030 cal BC	Radiocarbon date
202	Benderloch		4	1626 - 1408 cal BC	Radiocarbon date
203	Darnaway		2		Beaker similar to tall-mid carinated vessels.
204	Sketewan	Cist 3	2		Dated from supposed pyre site of 2040 – 1854 cal BC (78%).
205	Sketewan	Cist 5	2		Dated from supposed pyre site of 2040 – 1854 cal BC (78%).
206	Sketewan	Cist 6	2		Dated from supposed pyre site of 2040 – 1854 cal BC (78%).
207	Sketewan	Cist 7	2		Dated from supposed pyre site of 2040 – 1854 cal BC (78%).
208	Sketewan	Cist 1	2		Food Vessel bowl/ vase type, radiocarbon date from supposed pyre site of 2040 – 1854 cal BC (78%). Could overlap into Period 3.
209	Horsburgh Castle Farm		2		Flint knife with male inhumation, cremation.
210	Dridaig Cottage		4	1680 - 1430 cal BC	Radiocarbon date
211	Allerwash		2		Bronze flat-riveted dagger.

UN	Name	SubName	Period	Radiocarbon Date	Reason for Period Placement
212	Ravenstone		2	2462 - 1957 cal BC*	Radiocarbon date
213	Roxton	B4	2	2201 - 1756 cal BC*	Radiocarbon date, 68.2% determination of 2132 – 1886 cal BC, Collared Urn and post structure in barrow.
214	Kentraw		3	1964 - 1692 cal BC*	Radiocarbon date
215	Kiltry Knock		4		Enlarged Food Vessel Urn.
216	Northumberland Bottom		2	2120–1780 cal BC	Radiocarbon date, weak-carinated Beaker vessel.
217	Saltwood Tunnel		2	2290-1970 cal BC	Radiocarbon date
218	Whitehill Road		4	1620-1440 cal BC	Radiocarbon date
219	Hardendale Nap	23	3	c. 1870 - 1520 cal BC	Radiocarbon date
220	Hardendale Nap	14	3	1870 - 1520 cal BC (TAQ)	Radiocarbon date, decoration on collar and neck of Collared Urn.
221	Hardendale Nap	29	3	1870 - 1520 cal BC (TAQ)	Radiocarbon date
222	Carneddau	Cairn 1, cist 5	2		Due to 223 radiocarbon date.
223	Carneddau	Cairn 1, cist 1	2	2115 - 1885 cal BC	Radiocarbon date
224	Carneddau	21	2		Pre 222/223.
225	Butcher's Rise	691	3		Secondary to inhumation with jet, multiphase monument.
226	Butcher's Rise	718	3		Due to similarity of rites with 225 which are different to remainder of cemetery.
227	Bradley Fen	F.1279	4		Collared Urn, but could be Period 3.
228	102 Findhorn		3	1880 - 1520 cal BC	Radiocarbon date, faience and Cordoned Urn all equal across Periods 3 and 4.
229	O'Connell Ridge East	F. 2011	3	c. 1890 - 1680 cal BC	Radiocarbon date, multi-phase barrow.
231	Barns Farm	Cist 1	2	2197 - 1927 cal BC*	Radiocarbon date (of male inhumation), Food Vessel with male is bowl type.
232	Barns Farm	Cist 2	2		Due to 231, grave good assemblage sounds like Beaker assemblages.
233	Barns Farm	Cist 4	3	1920 - 1770 cal BC	Radiocarbon date
234	Barns Farm	Grave 1	2	2131 - 1886 cal BC*	Radiocarbon date
235	Ewanrigg	14	2		Based on other radiocarbon dates from the site which post-dates this burial.

UN	Name	SubName	Period	Radiocarbon Date	Reason for Period Placement
236	Ewanrigg	18	2	2450 - 1830 cal BC	Radiocarbon date, 68.2% determinations of 2205 – 1952 cal BC, Collared Urn.
237	Ewanrigg	28	2		Other dates from the site.
238	Ewanrigg	29	2		Other dates from the site.
239	Ewanrigg	42	2		Other dates from the site.
240	Ewanrigg	55	2	2460 - 1750 cal BC	Radiocarbon date, 68.2% determination of 2285 – 1921 cal BC, Collared Urn and date of 236.
241	Trelystan	I: 4	2	2271 - 1778 cal BC* 2289 - 1898 cal BC*	Radiocarbon date
242	Trelystan	I: 7	3		Later than central burial and 241, Stake-circles, multi-phase round barrow, Food Vessel. But could be Period 2.
244	Trelystan	II: 2	3	2120 - 1695 cal BC*	Radiocarbon date, multi-Period round barrow, Food Vessel and inhumation. Could have been Period 2.
245	Trelystan	II: 4	4		Multi-phase barrow, in final enlargement of mound, post Food Vessel burials.
246	Warren Farm	C1	3		From charcoal layer TPQ of 1887 – 1643 cal BC (68.2%).
248	Little Pond ground	PB	2	2200 - 1930 cal BC	Radiocarbon date
249	Barnack	6	3		Multi-phase round barrow, date of 250.
250	Barnack	39	3	1948 - 1540 cal BC*	Radiocarbon date (of male inhumation)
251	Barnack	68	3		Multi-phase round barrow, date of 250.
252	Manor Farm	55	4	1743 - 1406 cal BC*	Radiocarbon date
253	Camp Ground	F 273	3		End of inhumation practices, no grave goods.
254	Dalineun	C1	2		Beaker from tomb looks short-necked.
255	Queenafjold		4		Radiocarbon dates of other steatite pots.
257	Grandtully	Pit 36	4		Date from site of 1622 – 1406 cal BC (68%)
258	Beauforts	BNF 04	2	2350 - 2130 cal BC	Radiocarbon date, 64.3% determination of 2290 – 2190, Beaker long-neck type.
259	QEQM Hospital	SK1	1	2460 - 2200 cal BC	Radiocarbon date (of primary inhumation), similarities between two burials (position, grave goods).
260	Hill Road	A	4	1750 - 1640 cal BC	Radiocarbon date

UN	Name	SubName	Period	Radiocarbon Date	Reason for Period Placement
261	Amesbury 58	1	3	1862 - 1425 cal BC*	Radiocarbon date, knife dagger, primary in mound.
262	Amesbury 61	C3	3	2134 - 1689 cal BC*	Radiocarbon date
263	Amesbury 61	I1	3		Stake circles, other dates from barrow.
264	Milton Libourne 1	NW grave	3	1973 - 1449 cal BC*	Radiocarbon date (of SE grave), disc barrow (open monument).
265	Milton Lilbourne 5		3	1915 - 1519 cal BC*	Radiocarbon date (from branch in ditch), decoration of Collared Urn, bronze awl.
266	Rudston LXII	Burial 2	3		Inhumation, no grave goods.
267	Rudston LXII	Burial 3	3		Inhumation, no grave goods.
268	Wetwang Slack	Barrow A, G1	2		Part of primary mound, other burials from the site.
269	Wetwang Slack	Barrow B, G4	2		Copper awl, multi-phase barrow and date of 270.
270	Wetwang Slack	Barrow B, G3	2		Food Vessel of bowl type, in central area of multi-phase barrow. Could be Period 3.
271	Wetwang Slack	I G3	3	2010 - 1529 cal BC*	Radiocarbon date, Period three due to inhumation in barrow.
272	Wetwang Slack	I G2	3	2010 - 1529 cal BC* (TAQ)	Radiocarbon date, pre 271 but of the same Period as 271 cuts it.
273	Wilsford cum Lake G52	WD255	3		Inhumation, no grave goods.
274	Caythorpe Barrow 550	532	3		Inhumation, no grave goods.
275	Gayhurst Quarry Barrow 1	4005	3	1900 - 1610 cal BC	Radiocarbon date
276	Gayhurst Quarry Barrow 5	6005	4	1670 - 1485 cal BC	Radiocarbon date
277	Isle of Thanet	751	2	2289 - 1925 cal BC	Radiocarbon date
278	Isle of Thanet	643	2		Dates from site, 277 and male inhumation of 2180 – 1890 cal BC.
279	Llandegai	A13	3	1980 - 1730 cal BC	Radiocarbon date
280	Llanilar	CR 4	3		Due to Period of 282.
281	Llanilar	CR 5	3		Due to Period of 282.
282	Llanilar	CR 8	3		Decoration of Collared Urn and analogies to Irish and Scottish dated vessels.

UN	Name	SubName	Period	Radiocarbon Date	Reason for Period Placement
283	Grendon Quarry	Barrow II, F8	3		Multi-phase round barrow with stake-setting.
284	Waterhall Farm	Grave I	3		Date from 285.
285	Waterhall Farm	Grave LI e	3	1930 - 1740 cal BC	Radiocarbon date
286	Waterhall Farm	Grave LI d	3	1930 - 1740 cal BC	Radiocarbon date
287	Waterhall Farm	Grave LI c	3	1930 - 1740 cal BC	Radiocarbon date
288	Waterhall Farm	Grave IV	3		Date from 255.
289	Waterhall Farm	C1	3		Date from 255.
290	Barrow Hills	801	3	1970 - 1600 cal BC	Radiocarbon date
291	Barrow Hills	16 E	2		Copper dagger, bronze awl, jet and amber. Later addition to barrow.
292	Barrow Hills	PB 4866, 4906	4	1780 - 1520 cal BC	Radiocarbon date
293	Barrow Hills	PB 4866, 4970	3	1970 - 1690 cal BC	Radiocarbon date
294	Barrow Hills	PB 4866, 4968	4	1740 - 1510 cal BC	Radiocarbon date
295	Barrow Hills	RD 201, 206	2	2200 - 1870 cal BC	Radiocarbon date
296	Barrow Hills	614	4		Not associated with any of the monuments.
297	Barrow Hills	Barrow 2	3		Gold work like Wessex 1 (1900 – 1700 BC).
298	Long Critchel 7	1	2		Pre 299, large multiple Beaker grave.
299	Long Critchel 7	4	3		Analogies with Scottish undecorated Collared Urns, multi-Period round barrows.
300	Howick Heugh	C1	3	1921 - 1466 cal BC*	Radiocarbon date, Collared Urn suggested earlier part of radiocarbon date.
301	Sutton Veny	Urn burial	3		Due to secondary position in barrow after a Food Vessel interment.
302	Kingston Russell 6g	C	2		Beaker a cross between tall mid-carinated vessels and long-necked vessels. Shape more akin to long-necked vessel.
303	Kingston Russell 6g	A	2		Evidence of Beaker from 302.
304	Kingston Russell 6n	C	2		Other burials from site.
305	Roystone Grange	C	3		Awl described as belonging to post 2000BC.

UN	Name	SubName	Period	Radiocarbon Date	Reason for Period Placement
306	Ystrad-Hynod	Cist	3	2136 - 1450 cal BC*	Radiocarbon date, 68.2% determination of 1947 – 1541 cal BC, bronze awl
307	Broomend of Crichie	1075	3	1950 - 1750 cal BC	Radiocarbon date
308	Achinduich Farm	Pit 3	4	1690 - 1520 cal BC	Radiocarbon date
309	Baldock Bypass	G59.2	3		Decoration on rim and collar of Collared Urn, part of a barrow cemetery and primary burial.
310	West Stow	4	4		Large cremation cemetery on barrow edge.
311	West Stow	11a	4		Large cremation cemetery on barrow edge.
312	West Stow	11b	4		Large cremation cemetery on barrow edge.
313	West Stow	23	4		Large cremation cemetery on barrow edge.
314	West Stow	25a	4		Large cremation cemetery on barrow edge.
315	West Stow	25b	4		Large cremation cemetery on barrow edge.
316	West Stow	28	4		Large cremation cemetery on barrow edge.
317	West Stow	31	4		Large cremation cemetery on barrow edge.
318	West Stow	35	4		Large cremation cemetery on barrow edge.
319	Etton	Grave 9	3		Beaker is bowl shaped with lugged feet (c. 1880 – 1610 BC).
320	Etton	Grave 2	3		Cuts burial 319.
321	Stonea	Burial 1	2		Jet and amber.
322	Holt	site B F16	3		Urn shares traits with Food Vessels, multi-Period barrow, located on edge.
323	Holt	Site E F4	3		Accessory vessel and bronze bead.
324	Elburton	551	4		Flat cremation cemetery with Trevisker and Collared Urns.
325	Elburton	554	4		Flat cremation cemetery with Trevisker and Collared Urns.
326	Barrow Bottom	Grave 1	2		Inhumation accompanied by Collared Urn, bronze and jet beads and primary grave.
327	Radwell	Ring ditch 1	2		Jet, amber present in grave, centre of barrow.
328	Lambourne No. 19	F3	3	1974 - 1523 cal BC	Radiocarbon date
329	Easton Down	CB1	3	2012 - 1517 cal BC	Radiocarbon date, placed in Period 3 as middle of the determination.

UN	Name	SubName	Period	Radiocarbon Date	Reason for Period Placement
330	Allithwaite	115	3	2107 - 1747 cal BC 1922 - 1637 cal BC	Radiocarbon date
331	Allithwaite	119	3	2027 - 1741 cal BC	Radiocarbon date, 68.2% determination of 1951 – 1776 cal BC.
332	Allithwaite	117	3		Date of 330/1.
333	Allithwaite	106	3		Date of 330/1.
334	Allithwaite	108	3		Date of 330/1.
335	Exning	8	3	2120 - 1636 cal BC*	Radiocarbon date, due to inhumation and proximity to a multiple inhumation burial.
336	Pilsgate		3		Inhumation with amber, near Collared Urn and Food Vessel cremations.
337	Ringstead Downs		2		Beaker similar to short-necked vessels.
338	Monkton-up-Wimborne	7	3	1890 - 1610 cal BC	Radiocarbon date
339	Monkton-up-Wimborne	2	3		Radiocarbon date from another burial (338)
340	Monkton-up-Wimborne	8	3		Collared Urn decoration down to shoulder.
341	Goatscrag A	Burial 2	4		Enlarged Food Vessel urn.
342	Woodford G13	236	3		Inhumation, no grave goods.
343	Newbiggingmill Quarry		1		Beaker similar to low-carinated vessels.
344	Vicarage Field	Grave 1	1		Beaker similar to low-carinated vessels.
345	Vicarage Field	Grave 2	1		Beaker similar to low-carinated vessels.
346	Ring ditch X.6	Burial 3	2	2180 - 1950 cal BC	Radiocarbon date
347	Ring ditch X.6	Cremation 2	2	2280 - 1910 cal BC	Radiocarbon date
349	Deeping St Nicholas	54	3	1910 - 1675 cal BC	Radiocarbon date
350	Northpark	Cist 3	2	2135 - 1900 cal BC	Radiocarbon date

APPENDIX 3: ADDITIONAL ANALYSIS

The analysis which specifically led into the discussions and conclusions of Chapter Four were reported in Chapter Three. However, due to the large number of variables within the dataset of Chalcolithic and Early Bronze Age female burials many more analyses were undertaken. These results are presented within this appendix. Though the results did not contribute directly to the discussions concerning female burial traditions, they are interesting in their own right, and, as such, have been included here. The structure of this appendix mirrors that of Chapter Three; discussing burial forms, methods and finally grave goods.

A3.1. Burial Forms

When looking at the distribution of burial methods by burial form (Table A3.1) it appears that the distribution is not equal across the different forms.

	Inhumation	Cremation	Token inhumation	Token cremation
Barrow	38	73	3	2
Flat grave	35	39	4	8
Other	6	19	1	7
Cairn	0	8	2	1

Table A3.1: Distribution of burial method by burial form.

"Other" forms of burials have too few inhumations but too many token cremations. Similarly, cairn burials also have fewer inhumations than expected, but a greater number of token inhumation. Flat graves, alternatively, feature a greater number of inhumations than expected, but a smaller number of cremations, which indicates that inhumations are considered more appropriate for flat grave burial than cremations. Both the cairn and "other" forms of burial had greater numbers of token deposits than expected, whereas, on the whole, flat graves and barrows had less. This seems to indicate that the less common burial methods (token deposits) were associated with the less common burial forms.

	Barrow	Flat grave	Cairn	Other
Grave goods	71	56	7	20
No grave goods	45	30	4	13

Table A3.2: Distribution of grave goods among burial forms.

The distribution of grave goods among the different burial forms (Table A3.2) is as expected from the dataset. This demonstrates that grave good provision is not dependent upon the form that the burial takes; a female could be buried in a barrow or at a henge and still have the same chance of having grave goods.

When looking at the figures for the size of the average female burial from the different forms (Table A3.3), it is clear that the largest in size are those from barrows, whereas the smallest are those from cairns. This is not a result of the burial method as all the forms have larger numbers of cremations compared to other methods. This indicates the size of the burial cuts is related to the form of the burial.

	Barrow	Flat grave	Cairn	Other
Average size	1.44m^2	0.97m^2	0.35m^2	0.65m^2

Table A3.3: Average size of burials in each form.

Barrows

When looking at the barrows themselves it is clear that there are a few key points to make regarding their design. It is clear that the largest barrows seem to be a feature of Period Three, where the average diameter is 27.61m, in comparison to 15.6m in Period One, 21.04m in Period Two and 19.45m in Period Four.

If you look at the diameters in relation to the age of the burial in the barrow then there does not seem to be an obvious pattern (Table A3.4). However, it can be said that in Period Two mature adults have the largest barrows, but in Period Three adults have the largest barrows and in Period Four this changes again and young adult have the largest diameter.

Period	Young adult	Adult	Mature
One	No data	14.00m	18.8m*
Two	19.75m	19.29m	**21.31m**
Three	22.18m	**26.53m**	16.67m
Four	**20.38m**	17.86m	No data
Average	21.23m	23.69m	18.58m

*Table A3.4: Diameters of barrows relating to age of the deceased. *Sample of one.*

If you consider the placement of burials in barrows by age it is clear that, despite a superficial trend for central placement in barrows to increase with age (Table A3.5), it is not to a significant extent (χ^2: 1.94; $\alpha0.050 = 5.99$). Therefore, age does not seem to be a factor in barrow burial placement.

	Central	Non-central
Young adult	10	22
Adult	29	41
Mature	7	7

Table A3.5: Placement of burials in barrows related to age.

Grave good allocation in barrow burials is distributed equally among ages, methods and even periods. This is significant when we consider the analysis of burial placement in barrows in relation to grave good position (Table 3.K, page 44). Grave good provision thus appears to be related to the burial's position in the monument rather than to the period of the burial. Overall, grave goods are equally allocated across the burials in barrows.

Flat Graves

Like barrow burials, those in flat graves do not show a relationship between the period of the burial and the likelihood of provision with grave goods.

Cairns

Cairn burials have much in common with those buried in barrows, perhaps reflected by the similarity of the forms. This is shown by the fact that the provision of grave goods is not related to the age of the deceased, the period of the burial, nor the burial method (Table A3.6).

	Grave goods	No grave goods
Young adult	0	1
Adult	3	1
Mature	4	2
Period One	0	0
Period Two	2	1
Period Three	3	3
Period Four	2	0
Inhumation	0	0
Cremation	7	1
Token inhumation	0	2
Token cremation	0	1

Table A3.6: Comparison of grave good provision with ages, periods and also burial method.

The distribution of grave goods in cairn burials by both age and period is as expected from the dataset. However, cremation burials were furnished with grave goods more often than expected; indeed it was the only method in cairn burials which were furnished with grave goods.

Associated monuments were distributed equally across the cairn burials of different periods (Table A3.7).

Period	Associated monuments	No associated monuments
One	0	0
Two	3	0
Three	4	2
Four	2	0

Table A3.7: Associated monuments distribution in comparison with periods.

This contrasts to barrow burials and flat graves in which the period of burial does influence the likelihood of being associated with other monuments.

Other Forms

Like both barrows and cairns, the provision of grave goods in other form burials is not related to the age of the deceased, the method of burial or the period in which they were buried (Table A3.8).

	Grave goods	No grave goods
Young adult	7	3
Adult	11	9
Mature	2	1
Period One	0	0
Period Two	3	0
Period Three	12	13
Period Four	5	0
Inhumation	4	2
Cremation	13	6
Token inhumation	1	0
Token cremation	2	5

Table A3.8: Comparison of grave good provision with ages, periods and also burial method.

Finally, like the cairn burials, associated monuments were equally distributed amongst other forms of burial. However, it is notable that the Period Two burials do have a higher prevalence of associated monuments than would be expected; *all* of the burials have associated monuments (Table A3.9).

Period	Associated monuments	No associated monuments
One	0	0
Two	3	0
Three	11	14
Four	2	3

Table A3.9: Associated monuments distribution in comparison with periods.

A3.2. Burial Methods

Inhumations

The presence of grave goods with inhumation burials is not related to the age of the deceased or the period of burial. However, it is also obvious that an inhumation burial is most likely to be provisioned with grave goods during Period One (Table A3.10).

	Grave goods	No grave goods
Young adults	18	19
Adults	23	12
Mature	11	6
Period One	9	1
Period Two	19	12
Period Three	19	14
Period Four	3	2

Table A3.10: Distribution of grave goods with ages and periods.

Token Inhumations

Since token inhumation deposits represent just parts of full inhumations it seems prudent to look at the parts of the body which are selected to be included in token deposits. However, this can only be achieved looking at the deposits of young adults and adults as the mature token burials did not include information regarding the parts of the body represented.

When looking at the numbers of different elements represented in each burial (Table A3.11) it is evident that young adults seem to be represented by more elements than the adults; that more of the young adults are included in each token deposit than the adults (however, there are only four young adults and three adults represented in the table).

Element	Young adult	Adult
Cranium	3	1
Mandible	2	0
Upper long bones	2	1
Hands	1	1
Ribs	1	0
Vertebrae	2	2
Pelvis	3	1
Lower long bones	4	2
Feet	2	1

Table A3.11: Skeletal elements represented in young adult and adult token inhumations.

There seems to be an emphasis on lower limb bones in flat graves in comparison to the upper bones of the body, and also in comparison to the other forms of burial (Table A3.12). This is perhaps made more interesting when considering that there are a few burials in the dataset which seem to have a similar theme. The burial 5k(4) at

Net Down (121) was interred with the lower legs and feet cut off and removed from the grave, and burial 10025 at Boscombe Down (164) was disturbed after being buried and the lower legs and feet were removed. Finally, the emphasis on lower limb bones is emphasised by the inclusion of a juvenile femoral head with burial 1402 at Kingshill North (201).

	Barrow	Cairn	Flat Grave	Other
Head	3	0	1	2
Upper body	7	1	0	2
Lower body	4	1	6	2
Unknown	1	1	1	0

Table A3.12: Distribution of token inhumation body elements by different burial forms.

When we consider the provision of grave goods amongst the token inhumation burials and the age of the interred a clear pattern emerges (Table A3.13). Young adults have far more burials with grave goods than would be expected and adults and mature individuals have less. This is because *all* young adults have grave goods and no other age does. Again, we have to acknowledge that the number of token inhumation burials is very small.

	Grave goods	No grave goods
Young adult	4	0
Adult	0	4
Mature	0	2

Table A3.13: Distribution of grave goods with age of the deceased.

Cremations

	Urned	Un-urned
Young adult	15	22
Adult	21	66
Mature	4	11
Period One	0	0
Period Two	7	20
Period Three	21	59
Period Four	12	20

Table A3.14: Distribution of urned and un-urned cremation burials by ages and period.

Out of the 139 cremation burials included in this study, 72% were not buried in an urn (n. = 100), whereas 39 cremations were urned. This clearly shows that the dominant cremation rite was un-urned burial during this period under study. However, just because cremations were not included in ceramic containers it does not mean that they were placed loose in the ground; instead they may have been placed in organic containers which have not survived, indeed several burials in this dataset indicate evidence of this (burial numbers 105, 123, 195, 222, 234 and 170).

However, if we look at the number of urned or un-urned cremations by age or period (Table A3.14) no clear pattern emerges as the distribution is equal. The only slight point of interest is that young adults do seem to have more urned burials than expected, but not significantly so.

The number of single and multiple cremation burials (Table A3.15) are distributed equally among the different ages, burial forms and also the different periods, though there are slightly more single burials in Period Three than expected and less in Period Four. Therefore, a cremation is most likely to be multiple rather than single if it from Period Four, as 44% of the cremations from this period are of multiple individuals.

	Single	Multiple
Young adults	27	10
Adults	57	30
Mature	13	2
Period One	0	0
Period Two	17	10
Period Three	62	18
Period Four	18	14
Urned	26	14
Un-urned	71	28

Table A3.15: Distribution of single and multiple cremation burials by age, period and nature.

When looking at the figures of grave good provision (Table A3.16) it appears that there is no significant patterning amongst the ages. This does not change even when you do not classify the urn as a grave good, but as a functional item (i.e. as a container for the cremated remains). Although the pattern is not significant it still appears that young adults are slightly more likely to be provisioned with grave goods than the other age categories.

	Grave goods	No grave goods
Young adult	28	9
Adult	57	30
Mature	10	5

Table A3.16: Distribution of grave goods by age.

Token Cremations

The choice of whether an individual in a token cremation is selected for multiple burial is not dependent upon either the age of the deceased or the period in which they were buried (Table A3.17), as in both cases the distribution was as expected from the dataset.

	Single	Multiple
Young adults	2	0
Adults	11	4
Mature	1	0
Period Two	1	1
Period Three	11	3
Period Four	2	0

Table A3.17: Distribution of single and multiple burials by age and period.

There does not seem to be a pattern in the provision of grave goods with token cremations with regards to age, form or period of burial (Table A3.18).

	Grave goods	No grave goods
Young adults	0	2
Adults	0	1
Mature	0	1
Barrow	0	2
Flat grave	1	7
Cairn	0	1
Other	2	5
Period Two	0	2
Period Three	3	11
Period Four 0	0	2

Table A3.18: Distribution of grave goods by age, form of burial and period.

A3.3. Grave goods

Figure A3.1 provides a breakdown of the number of burials with at least one grave good in each of the seven different material types in this database. When looking at the diagram it is clear to see that the most common material of grave good is ceramic, and the second most common are artefacts made of flint.

Objects of the different material types are distributed equally across the time periods, as shown in Figure A3.2. However, there are a few cases in which the numbers of the different material types are not as expected for the dataset. In Period One there are too many flint items and not enough artefacts of the "other" material category. In Period Two there are too few stone and unworked bone objects in the burials, whereas in Period Four there are too many unworked bone objects but not enough worked bone. Period Three, however, does exhibit the expected pattern.

It is clear from Figure A3.3 that most burials in the dataset have objects of only one material type, i.e. one urn. Next most common are burials having items made from two different material types, such as a Beaker and a flint flake. In fact, burials with objects of only one or two different material types make up 81% of all burials with grave goods.

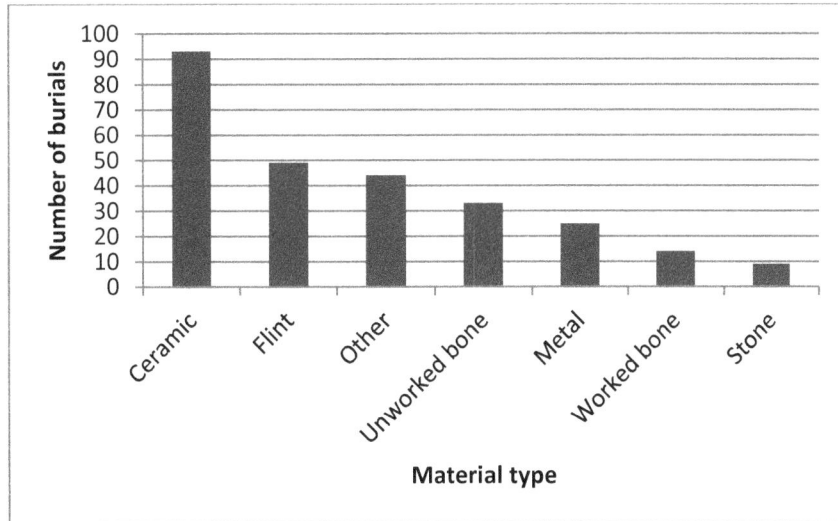

Figure A3.1: Number of burials with at least one grave good of the material type.

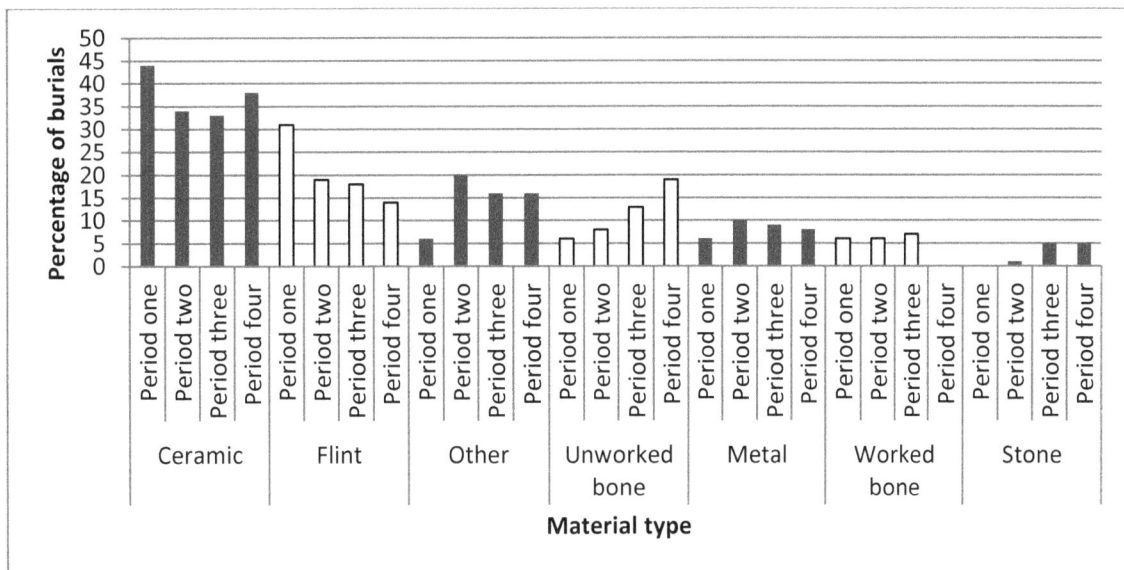

Figure A3.2: Percentage of burials with at least one grave good of the material type by period.

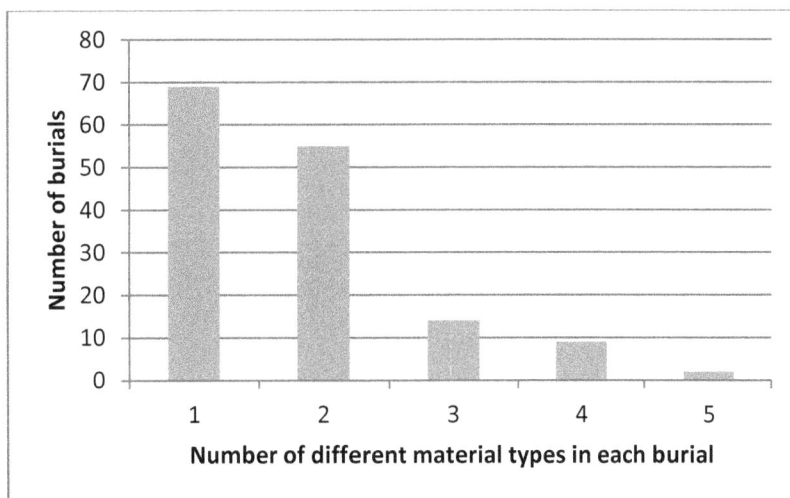

Figure A3.3: Number of burials by number of different material types.

Appendix 3: Additional Analysis

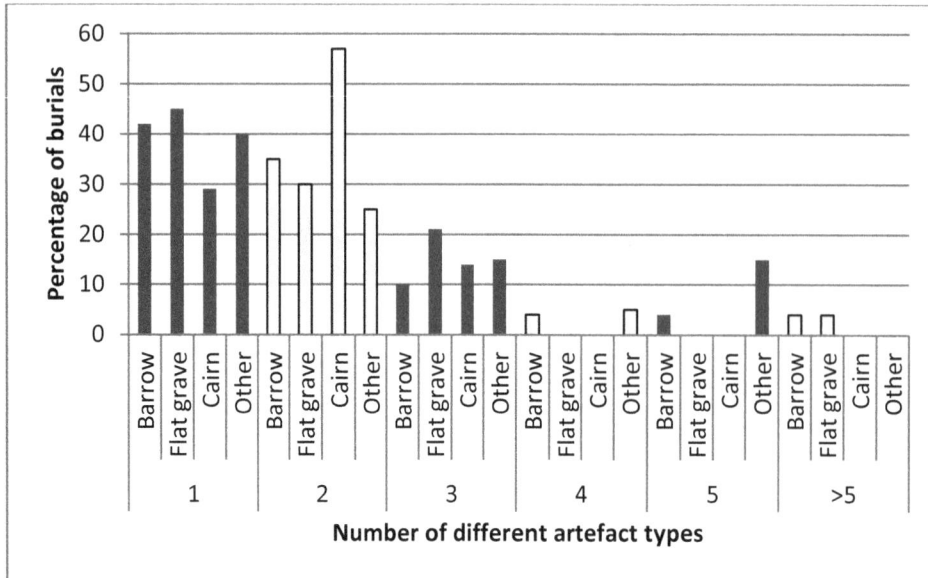

Figure A3.4: Number of different artefacts in burials by burial form.

Burial forms have some anomalous results regarding the number of different artefacts per burial (Figure A3.4). Barrows have fewer burials with three different artefacts types than we would expect if the distribution was equal, whereas cairn burials have more with two. The most divergent burial type are the flat graves, where more burials than expected have three different types, but less burials have four or five.

There are also some points of interest with the results for burial methods (Figure A3.5). Inhumation burials of both whole and token types provide the unexpected results, with inhumations having fewer burials than expected with just the one type of grave good; but more with greater than five. Similarly, token inhumation burials have more

burials than expected with five different types of grave good; this seems to indicate that inhumations are buried with a more diverse suite of artefacts than cremations, a pattern which also emerges in the total number of grave goods between the different types of burials (see below).

The number of grave goods within each burial is equal across the four different burial forms (Figure A3.6). However, barrows had fewer burials with three grave goods but more with greater than five. Flat graves have less with two and five items, but more with three and other form burials have more with five items but less than expected with greater than five.

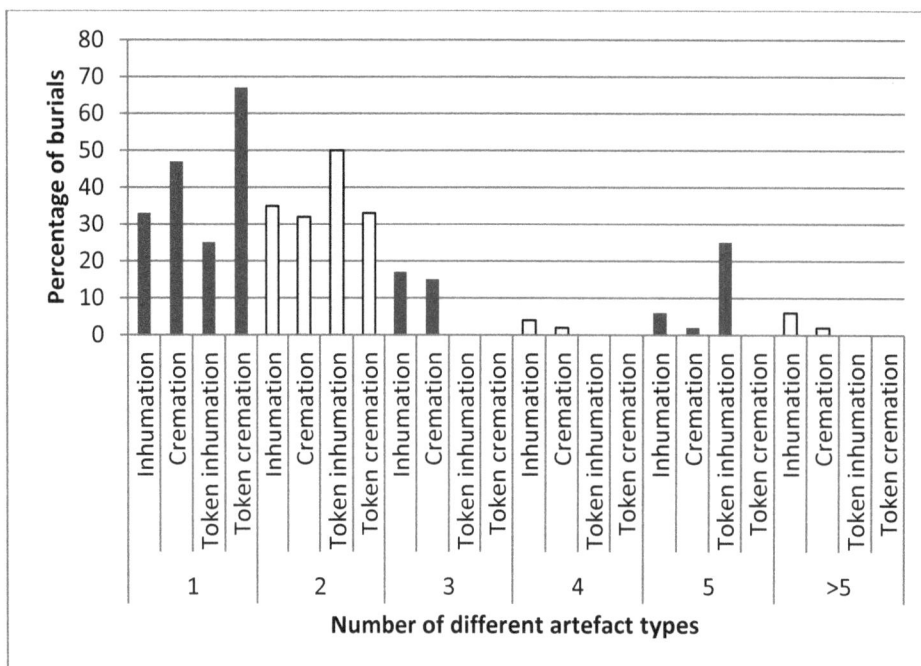

Figure A3.5: Number of different artefacts in burials by burial method.

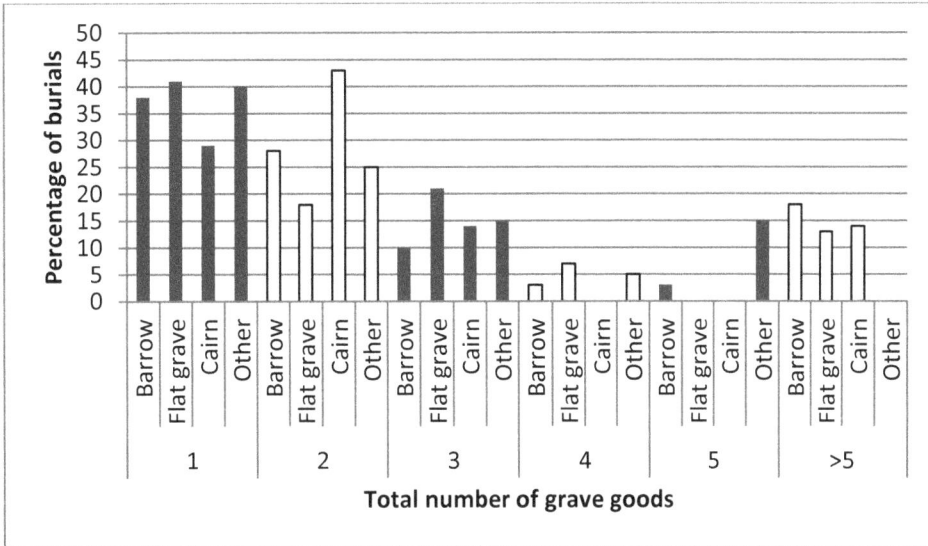

Figure A3.6: Total number of grave goods by burial form.

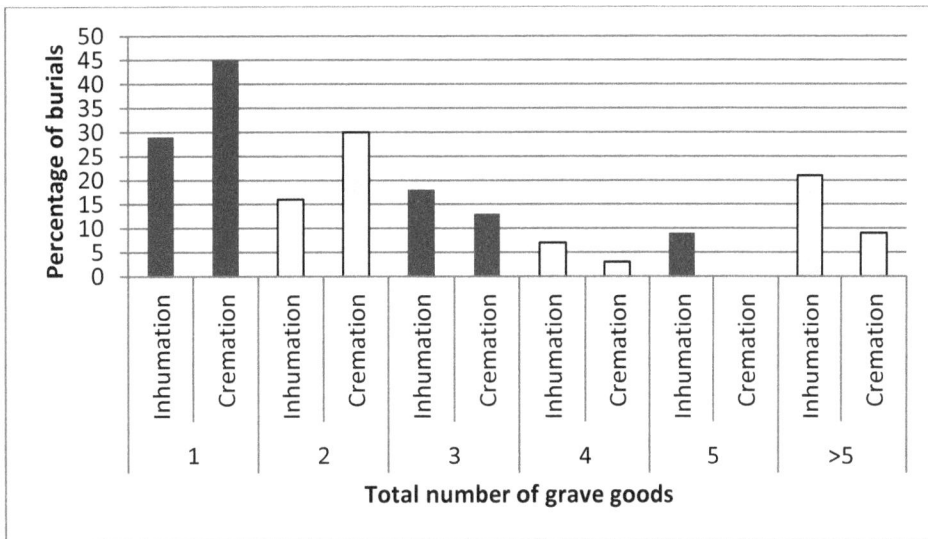

Figure A3.7: Total number of grave goods by burial method.

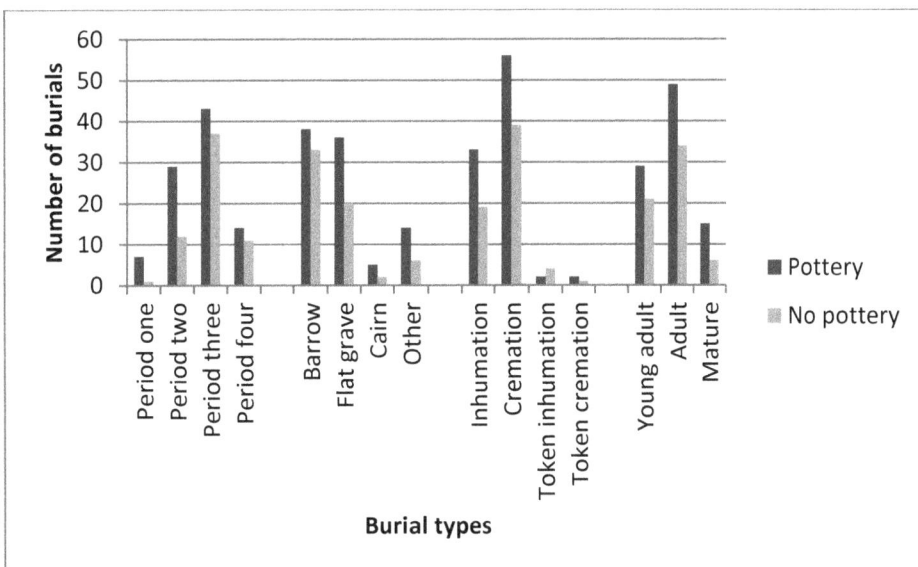

Figure A3.8: Number of burials with and without pottery of the different burials types.

Unlike the number of different types of grave good, the total number of items in burials is not distributed equally across the different methods (Figure A3.7). This is because female inhumation burials are provisioned with the lower totals of grave goods (one or two items) less than expected, but more with the highest numbers (five or greater than five). The opposite is the case with the cremations. This may partly be because more inhumations are buried with large numbers of beads than cremations, though not to a significant extent and thus cannot fully explain it.

A3.4. Grave good types

Pottery

When looking at the number of burials with and without pottery across periods, burial forms, burial methods and ages the distribution is equal (Figure A3.8).

The only place that there is a noticeable divergence from the pattern is with token inhumation burials, where there are fewer burials than would be expected with pottery and more without.

Alongside looking at the number of burials with and without pottery, the distribution of the different pottery types among the burial forms, methods and ages of the deceased was also considered. Pottery type was not considered in relation to periods as many of the barrows were dated using the pottery and thus it would create a circular argument. When considering the age of the deceased and the pottery type the null hypothesis that the distribution would be equal was accepted (Figure A3.9). This means that the provision of different types of pottery did not depend upon the age that the person died.

However, though not at a significant level, young adults are the least likely to be provisioned with sherds of pottery or incomplete vessels and adults are also slightly less likely to be provisioned with Beakers.

Although distribution of pottery types among the different age categories is equal, the distribution of the pottery types by burial form is not (Figure A3.10). Beakers, although featuring in barrows at the expected frequency, appear far more often in flat graves than expected, and less in cairns and other forms. Food Vessels, however, are placed in burials in other forms more often than they would if distributed equally. Collared Urns are most likely to be in barrow burials, but not in flat graves or cairns. Miniature Vessels are also most likely to be found in burials in barrows, though they appear in cairn burials more often than expected. On the other hand, Cordoned Urns are least likely to feature in barrow burials but are much more likely to be placed in flat graves.

Like the burial forms, the distribution of pottery types between burial methods is also not equal (Figure A3.11). The disposal method chosen for the female corpses impacts upon the pottery type chosen for the burial. Beakers, in this dataset, are only associated with inhumation burials, especially whole inhumations. In contrast, Collared Urns are on the whole found with whole cremations. A similar pattern occurs with the Cordoned Urns. Sherds, however, are mainly found with token cremation deposits; perhaps mirroring their fragmentary nature. In contrast, Food Vessels and Miniature Urns are distributed among the different methods equally. However, this pattern may be partially as a result of the changing burial methods through time.

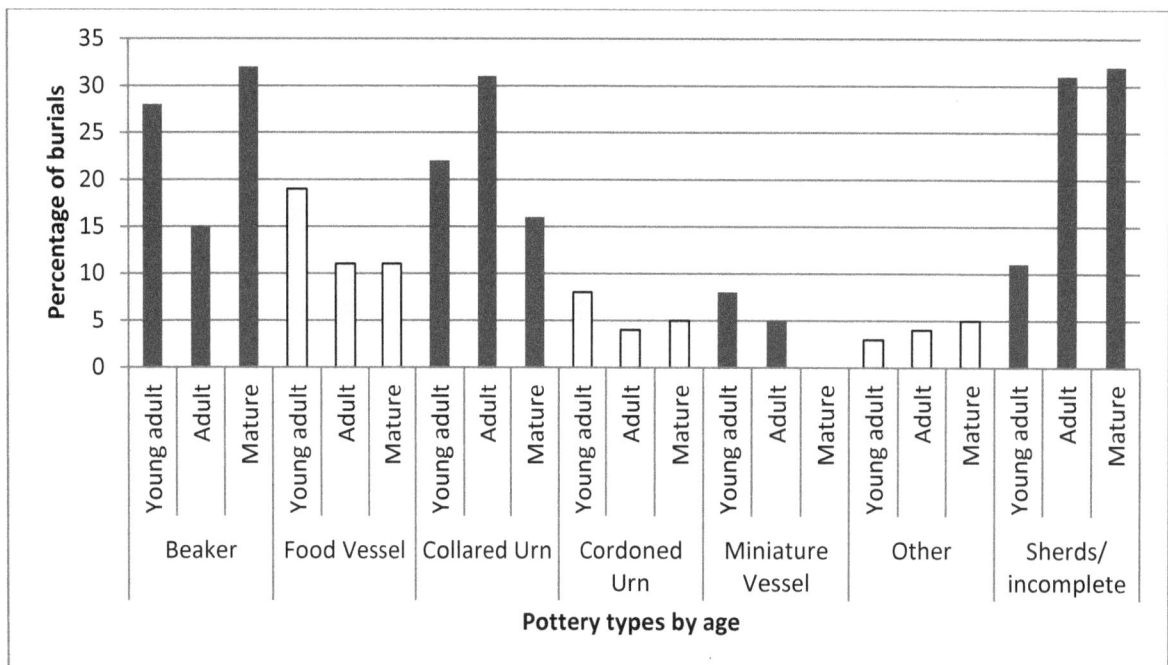

Figure A3.9: Distribution of pottery types in burials by ages.

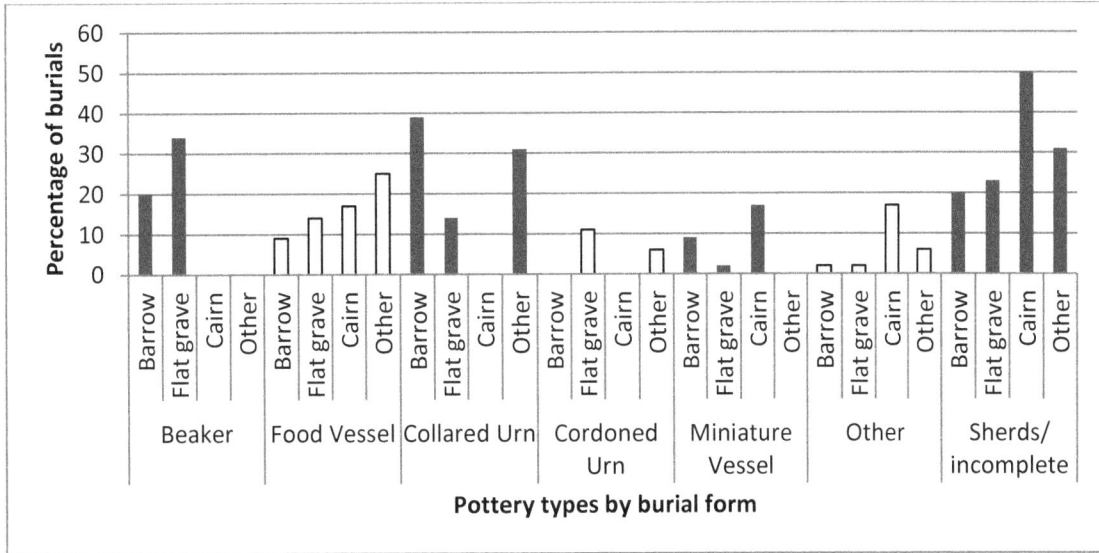

Figure A3.10: Distribution of pottery types by burial forms.

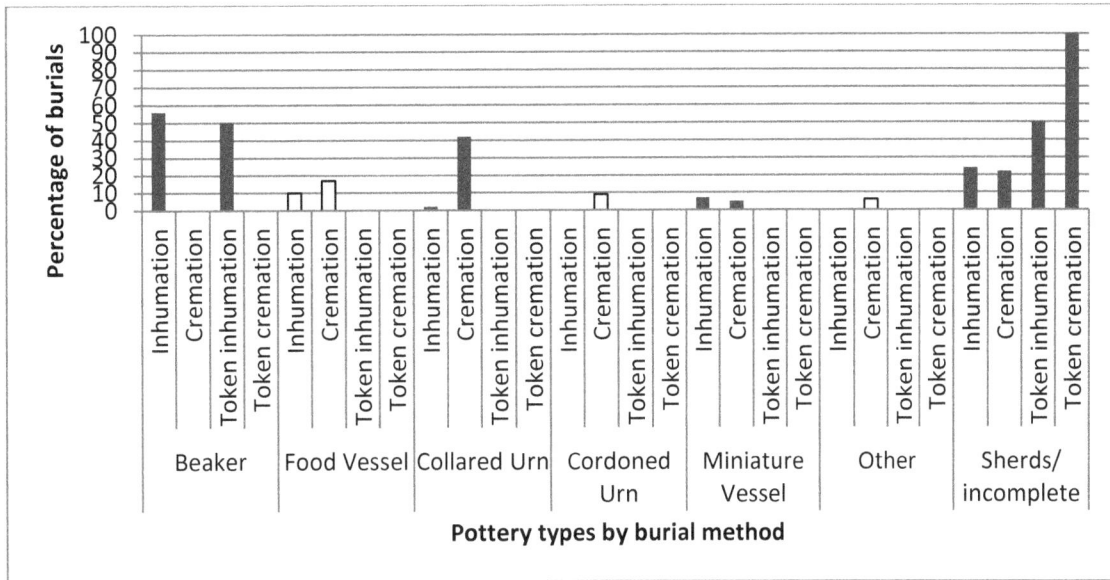

Figure A3.11: Distribution of pottery types by burial method.

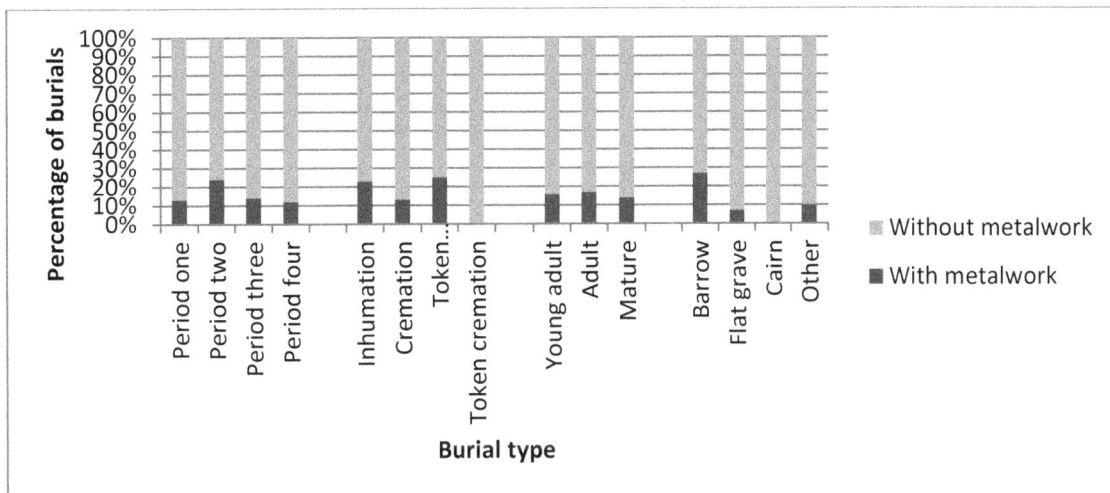

Figure A3.12: Percentage of burials with metalwork grave goods by different burial types.

Metalwork

When looking at the burials with and without metalwork grave goods it is clear that in the case of the different periods, separate burial methods and age categories the numbers are distributed equally (Figure A3.12). However, it appears that Period Two has the burials with the most amounts of metalwork grave goods and also that inhumations are slightly more likely to be buried with metalwork items.

However, the distribution of burials with and without metalwork grave goods is not equal between the different burial forms. This is because barrows have far more burials with metalwork artefacts than expected and flat graves and cairns fewer. Therefore, it appears that it is not the deceased's age, the period in which she was buried or the burial method chosen, but rather the form the burial took which impacted upon the likelihood of being provisioned with a metal grave good.

This research also looked at whether the factors of the burial itself made a difference to the type of metalwork accompanying the burials; figure A3.13 compares the period of the burial, the form and method and also the age of the deceased.

In each of these cases there was an equal distribution, demonstrating that none of these factors significantly

influenced the provision of metalwork in female burials. This research considered whether this distribution was a factor of the low occurrence of some of these items and so grouped the objects according to properties; awls were termed functional; cones, beads and "earrings" were decorative; daggers and axes were classed as weapons as they could be arguably both decorative and functional (demonstrated for axes by the axe tool marks at Seahenge; Brennand and Taylor 2003; or the Irish trackways; Raftery 1996); and rods became "unknown". However, this still made no difference to the results and distributions were still equal.

These metal objects were crafted from a choice of three metals; copper, bronze and gold. This research looked at whether the different burials types had an impact upon the metal the items were made from. However, once again the distribution was equal across the various factors considered (Figure A3.14).

All the above evidence suggests that the provision of the different metal artefacts placed in female graves during the Chalcolithic and Early Bronze Age is not dependent upon factors such as the period of the burial, the form the burial took, the method of burial used or the age of the deceased; at least not to a significant extent.

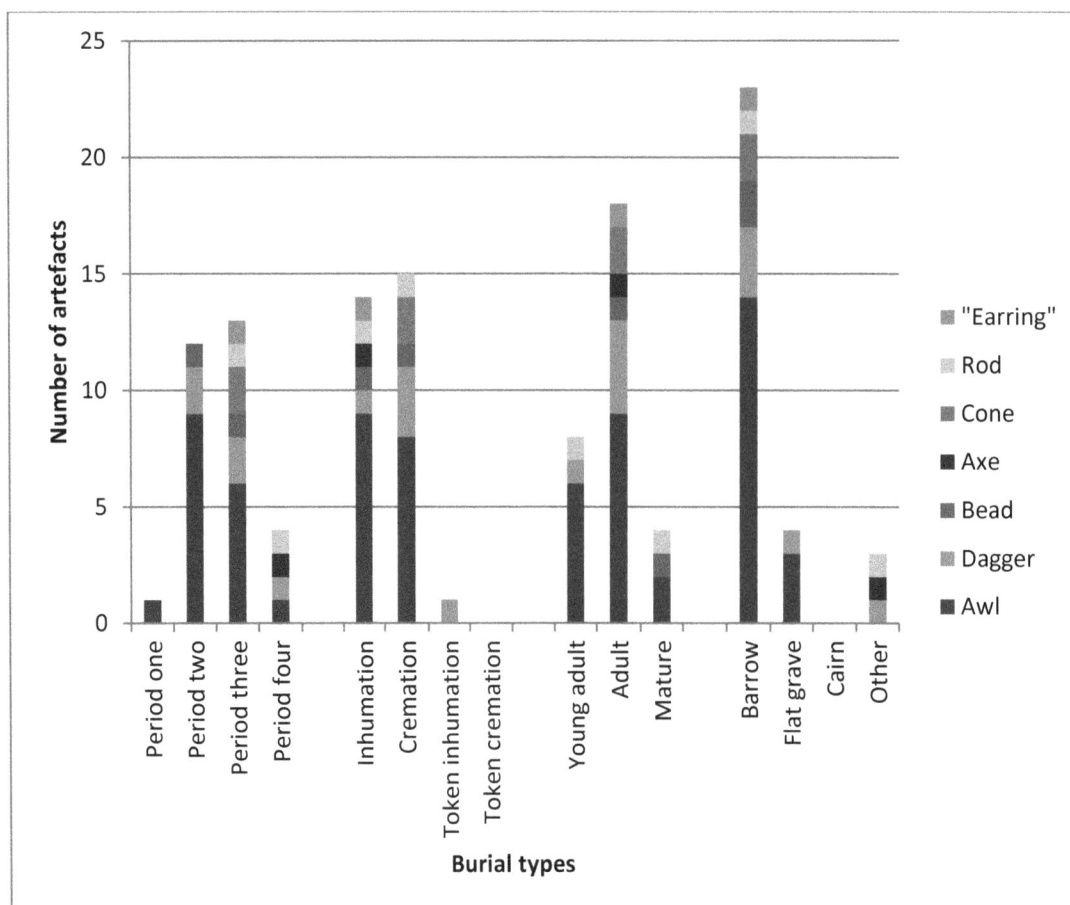

Figure A3.13: Number of the different metalwork items by burial types.

80

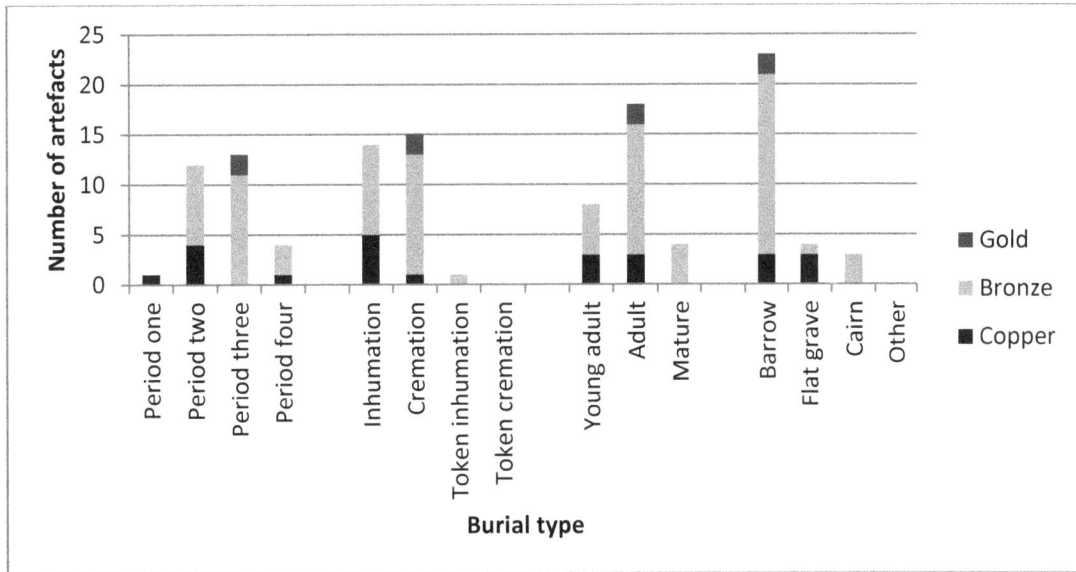

Figure A3.14: Number of artefacts of different metals by burial types.

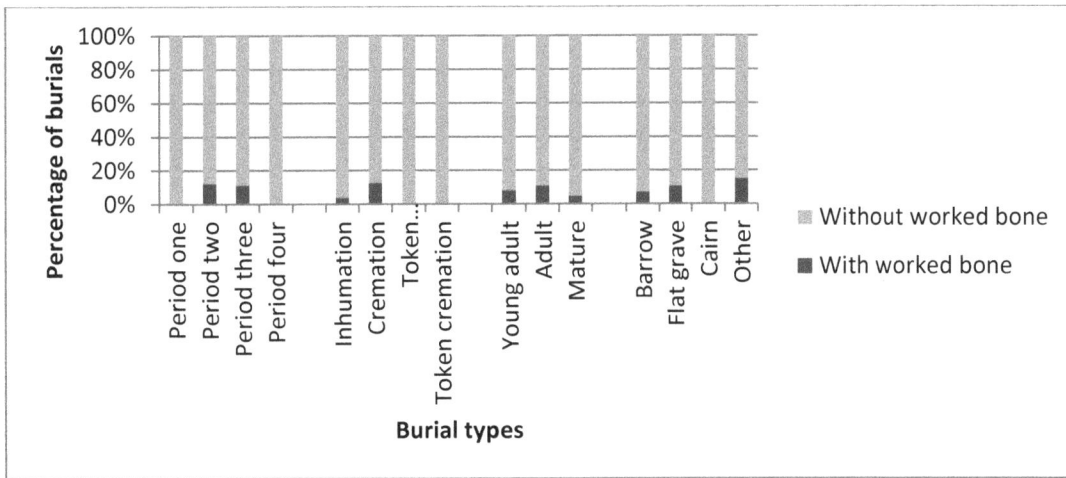

Figure A3.15: Percentage of burials with worked bone by different burial types.

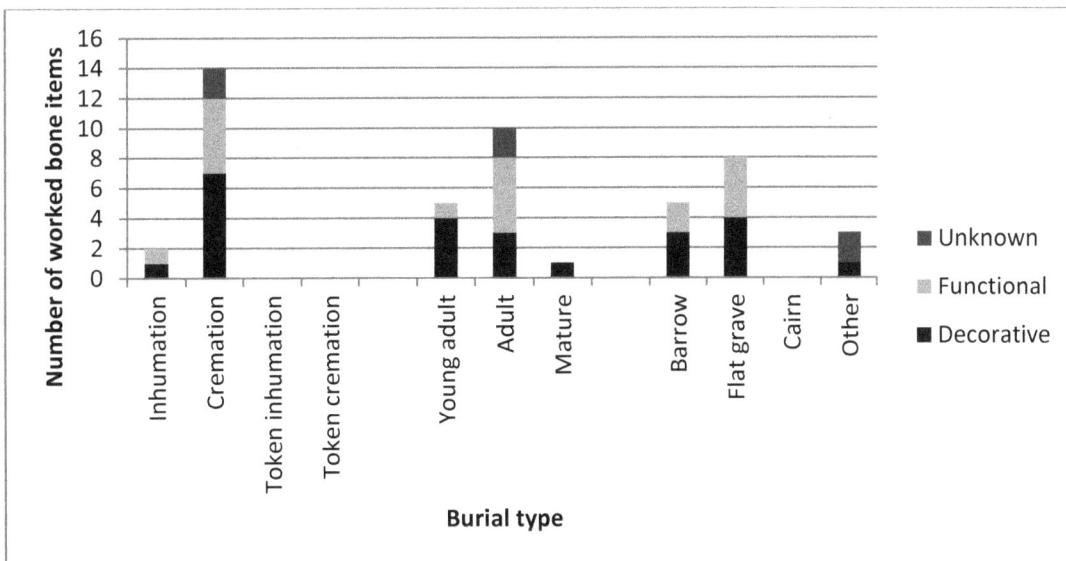

Figure A3.16: Number of worked bone item types by different burial types.

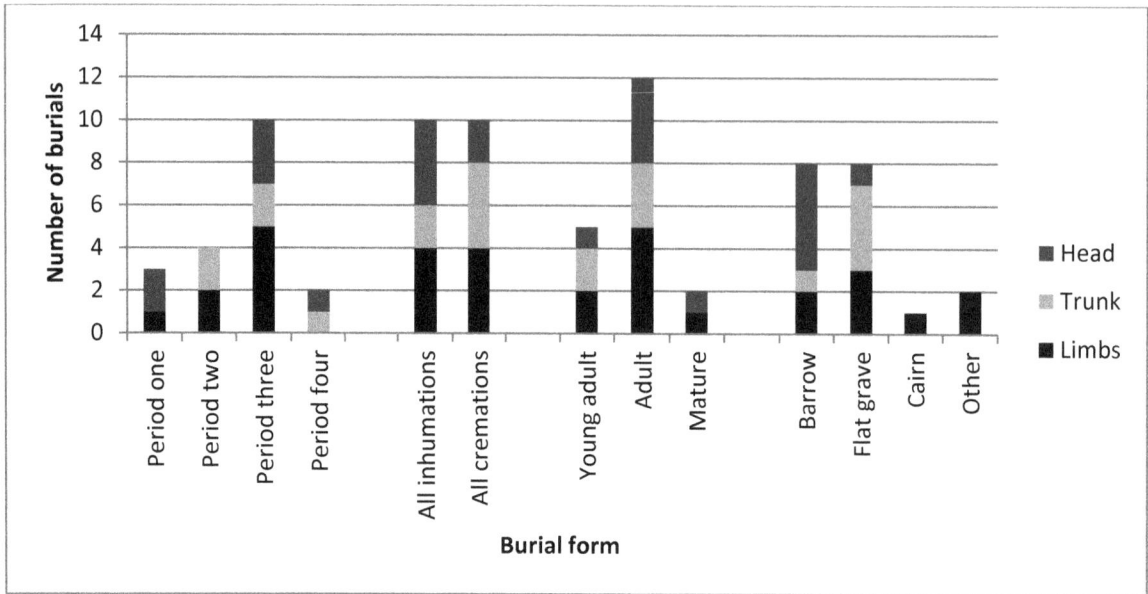

Figure A3.17: Distribution of animal parts by burial types.

Worked bone

Once again, when looking at the number of burials with grave goods of worked bones and the number with grave goods, the distribution is equal (Figure A3.15).

Burial form, burial method and age at death have equal distributions of worked bone artefact types (Figure A3.16). Functional items include the pins and spatulas, decorative items include beads and the polished tusk. There is one point to make regarding provision by age. Though not statistically significant, young adults seem to be more likely to be provisioned with decorative items, whereas adults seem to have more functional items.

Unworked animal bone

The distribution of animal parts by period, burial form, burial method and age of the deceased is equal (Figure A3.17). Therefore, the part of the animal chosen for burial does not depend upon any of these factors.

This pattern is also evident when looking at the species of animals represented in the burials by period, burial form and burial method (Figure A3.18).

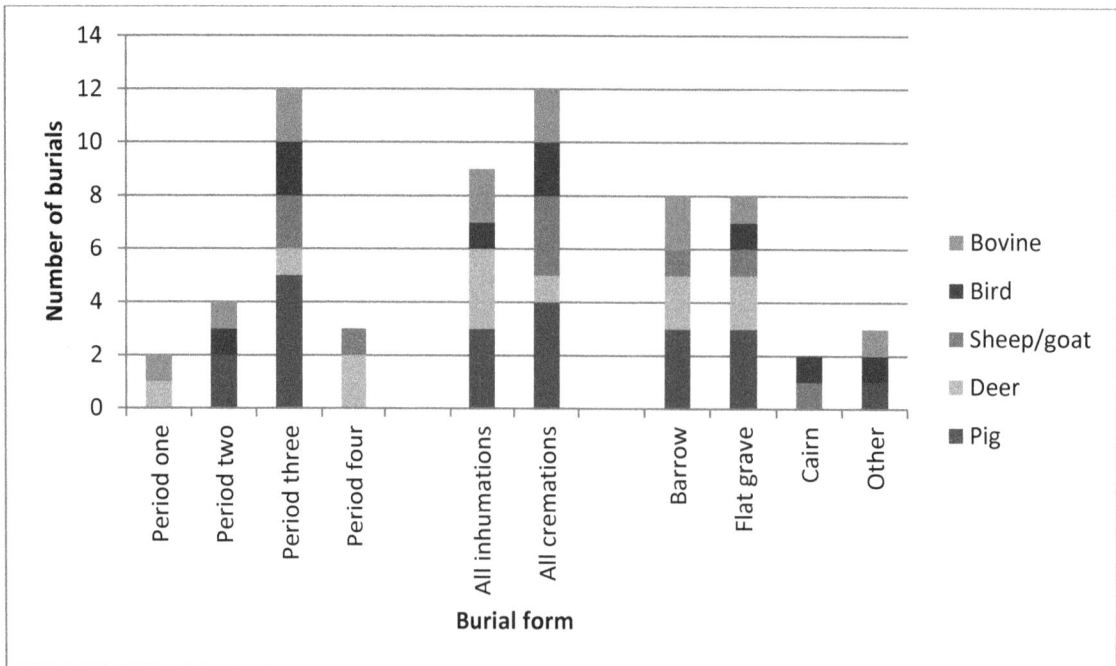

Figure A3.18: Distribution of animal species by burial types.

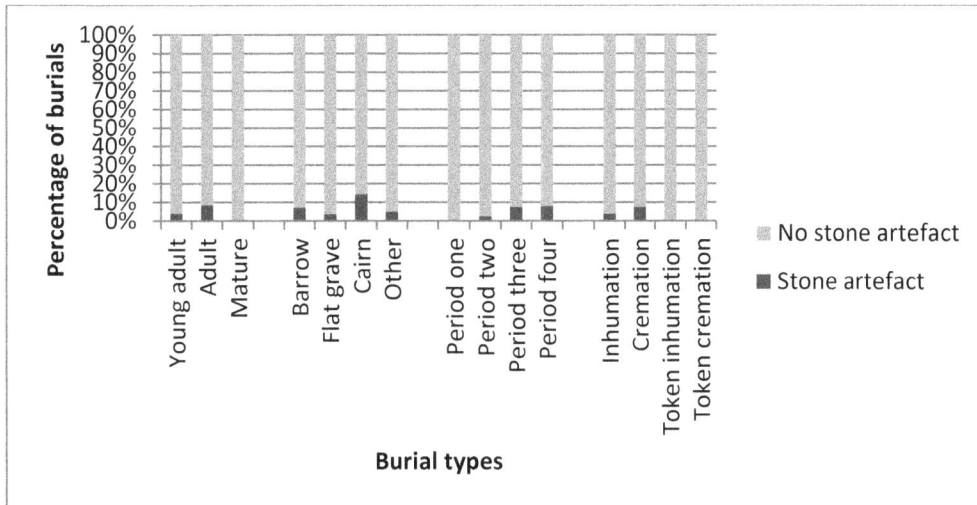

Figure A3.19: Percentage of burials with and without stone artefacts across burial types.

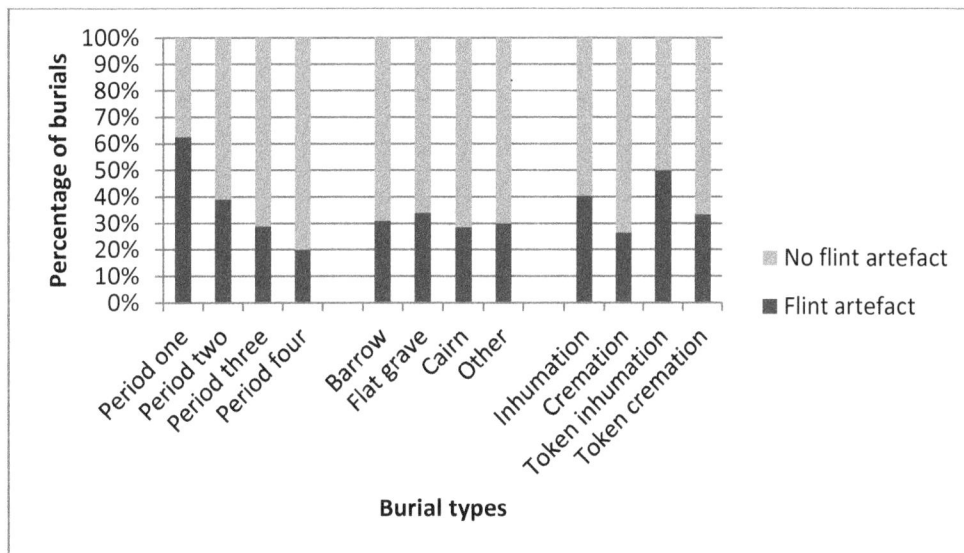

Figure A3.20: Percentage of burials with or without flint artefacts by burial types.

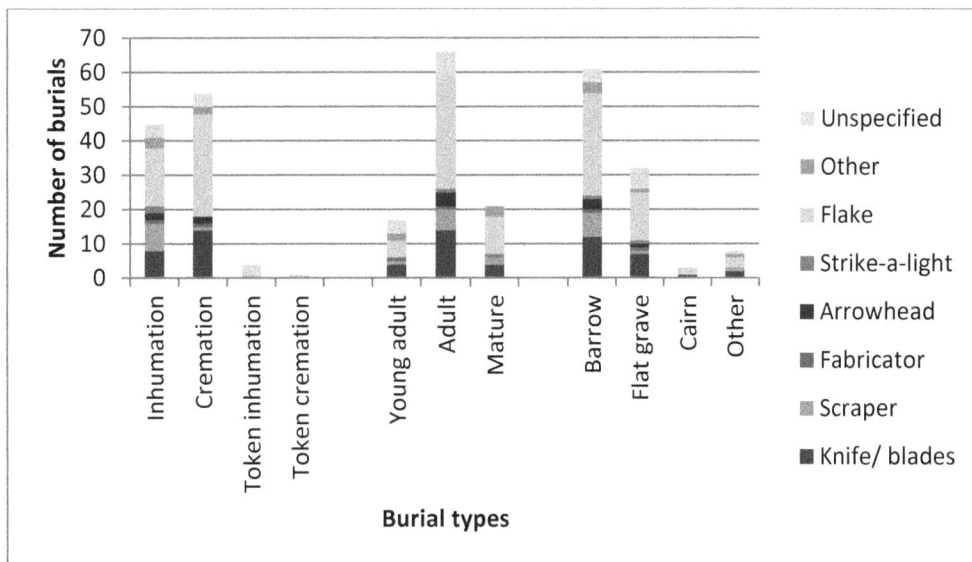

Figure A3.21: Number of different flint artefacts by burial types.

Stone

The distribution of the number of burials with grave goods which either have or do not have stone artefacts appears to be equal. This is the case for period distribution, burial form, burial methods and also age at death (Figure A3.19). Therefore, the provision of a stone grave good is not dependent upon any of these factors. However, one slight pattern does emerge from the data in which all the functional/ weapon items belong to the adult age category.

Flint

The number of grave good burials with and without flint items is equal across the different burial forms, the different periods and burial methods (Figure A3.20). However, Period One appears to have more burials with flint items than would be expected. This suggests that the provision of flint items as grave goods decreases through time.

Due to the large number of flint artefacts in the dataset, the distribution of the various types of flint artefact were examined (Figure A3.21). The distribution for the burial forms is almost exactly as you would expect if the distribution was equal. However, for the burial methods there are a several anomalies worth highlighting. Inhumation burials have far more scrapers than expected and also more strike-a-lights; cremations, however, demonstrate the opposite pattern. In addition, token inhumations have far more unspecified flint objects than expected. It is also noticeable that adults have far more flint objects than the other age groups. This is reflected by the fact that on average an adult will have 2.54 flint items, whereas a mature individual will have 1.75 and a young adult 1.55. Therefore, adults seem to be provisioned with more flint objects in the burials.

Other

The distribution of "other" items is equal across the different periods, the burial forms and also the age of the deceased (Figure A3.22). However, it does appear that Period Two is the period where are female is most likely to be buried with one of these artefacts, though not to a significant extent.

However, the distribution of burials with "other" artefacts is not equal across burial methods, the null hypothesis was rejected at $\alpha0.005$ significance considering only the inhumations and cremations (7.88; $\chi^2=8.37$). This is because inhumation burials are much more likely to be associated with one of these "other" items than cremation deposits are (Figure A3.23).

It was then asked whether the distribution of the different artefact categories (decorative, functional, etc.) was equal across the burial forms (Figure A3.24). However, though not statistically significant, trends were still evident. For the age categories it appears that adults are associated with tools more than is expected in equal distribution, whereas for young adults the opposite is true. Young adults also seem to have more of the "unknown" category (bone stains and charcoal) than expected.

The most trends, however, are found when looking at the artefact category distribution across burial forms (Figure A3.25). There seems to be a contrast in the provision of artefacts between the barrow burials and flat graves. Barrows have more decorative items than expected, and more in the way of grave furniture, but have less offerings and also "unknown" items. The opposite is true for flat graves which have more offerings and "unknown" items, but fewer decorative items and grave furniture than expected. Cairns also have more decorative items than anticipated in an equal distribution.

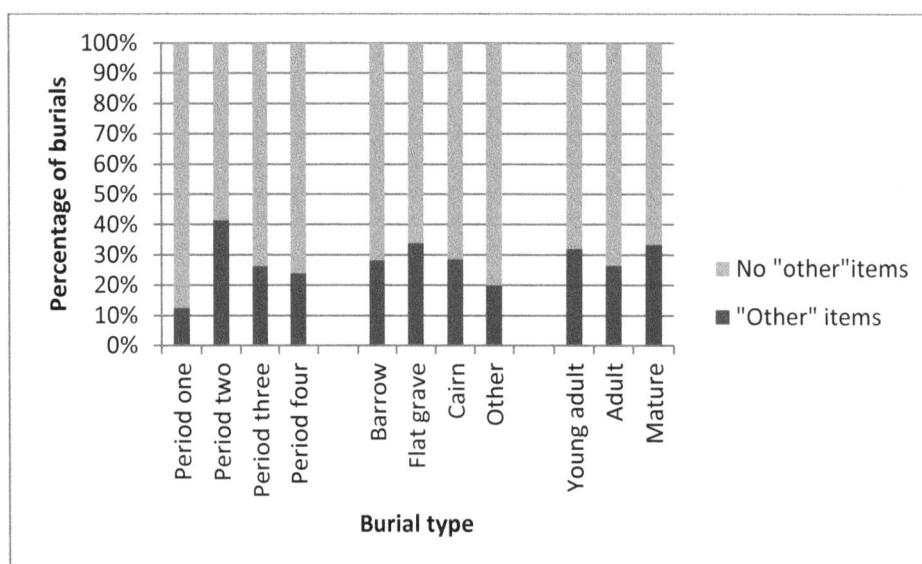

Figure A3.22: Percentage of burials with "other" artefacts by burial types.

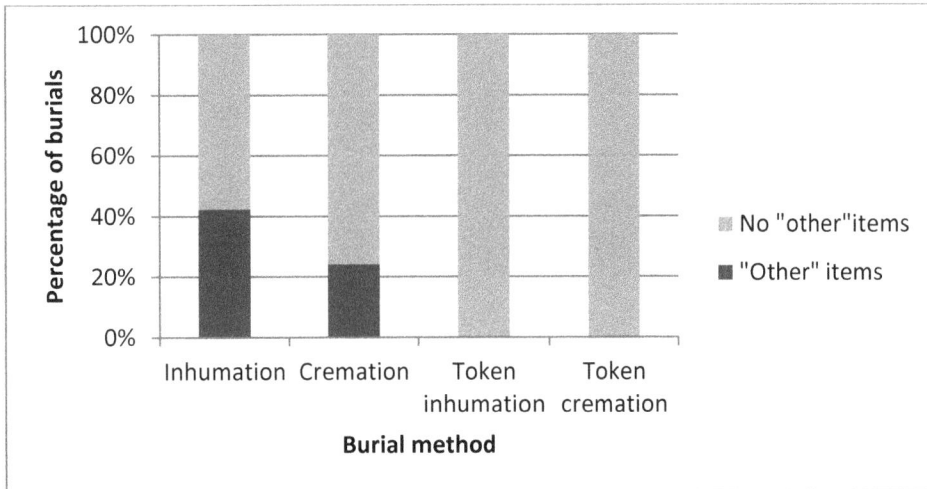

Figure A3.23: Percentage of burials with "other" artefacts by burial method.

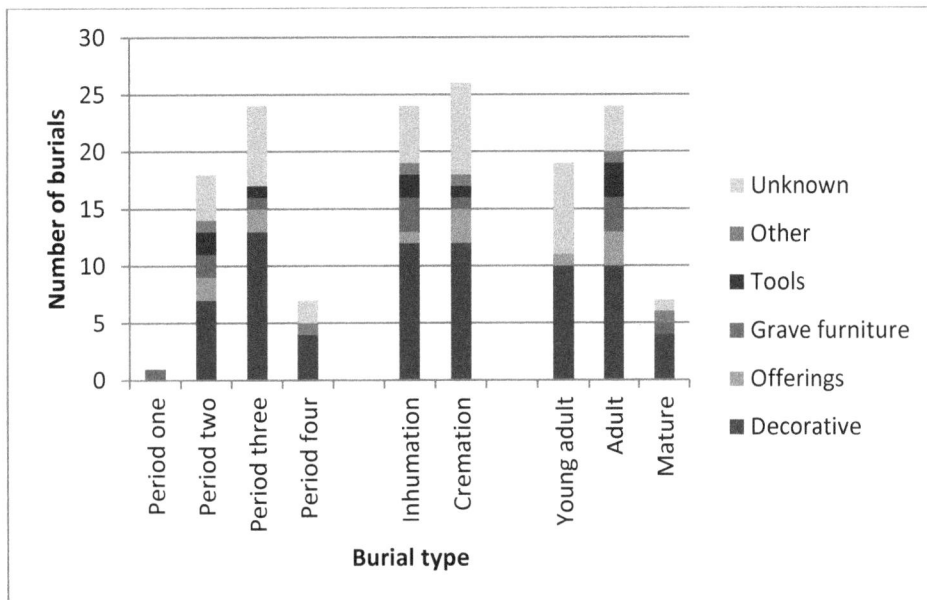

Figure A3.24: Number of "other" artefact categories by burial type.

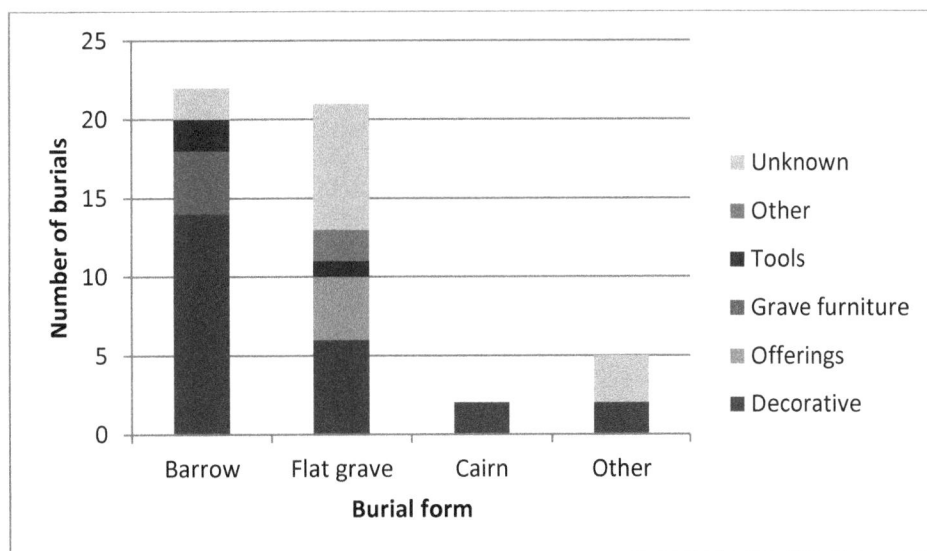

Table A3.25: Number of "other" artefact categories by burial form.

Since the materials represented in this "other" category are as diverse as the form of the artefacts, they were also subjected to analysis (Table A3.19).

Category	Substance	Number of items	Number of burials
"Rare"/ exotic	Jet and jet-like	768	14
	Amber	103	7
	Faience	34	7
"Natural"	Wood	10	8
	Chalk	1	1
	Flowers	2	2
	Leather	1	1
	Shell	2	2
	Human bone	1	1
	Cereal	2	2
Metal	Staining	12	12
Clay	Pottery/ceramic	3	3
Unknown		1	1

Table A3.19: Numbers of different material types of "other" artefacts.

In order for the numbers to be more manageable (rather than include the high numbers for jet, amber and faience), the number of *burials* with a specific material type was considered, rather than the number of artefacts (this removes the issue of beads). The materials were then divided into four categories; "rare"/exotics for the jet, jet-like substances, amber and faience; "natural" to encompass wood, chalk, shell, cereal etc; metal for the staining and iron nodules; and clay for the pottery/ceramic substance (i.e. transformed natural).

Once again, the different material types were distributed equally across all different burial types (Figure A3.26). This demonstrates that the period of burial, burial form and age of the deceased does not impact upon the material considered suitable for including in a burial.

However, although both inhumations and cremations (Figure A3.27) had the expected number of burials with exotic artefacts, inhumation burials had more burials with natural items than expected, but less with metal or clay. The opposite was the case for cremations. This can be partially explained by survival rates of items through the flames of cremations, where many natural items placed on the pyre would probably be destroyed (i.e. wood), and the higher rate of metal could be explained by metal items being placed on the pyre with the body, a stain transferring to the bone, and then either being removed from the ashes for recycling or being entirely destroyed in the process. However, this does not fully explain this pattern since cremation burials do have some items of natural material.

A3.5. Associated artefacts

As mentioned in Chapter Three, analysis was conducted into determining whether females were buried with any commonly associated artefacts. This applies to both types of item, such as whether pottery and flints items commonly occur together and also to actual artefacts, such as Food Vessels and flint knives. The following is a discussion of the results.

The female grave goods were examined as to material types and it was recorded which were frequently associated with each other (Figure A3.28). The numbers of artefacts of the different types were not counted individually, what mattered was their occurrence together.

If a burial contained an item of pottery then it was most likely to also contain at least one item of flint, as 34% of burials with pottery had a flint artefact. However, they were also likely to have artefacts of "other" forms (at 28%), but also have nothing (30%). When female burials contained metal items, 44% of the burials also had an item of pottery, flint or "other" form. The remaining artefact forms were most likely to contain an item of pottery (from 50% of burials with worked bone to 65% of burials with flint). This is also the case for burials with just the one type of item; that it is most likely to be an item of pottery (42%).

Though overall this pattern is not statistically significant, there are a few anomalies which need to be highlighted. It has already been mentioned that pottery items are more likely to be associated with flint and "other" artefacts, but they also occur more often than expected with un-worked bone. Though metal items do occur frequently with pottery ones, this is at the expected level; however they do occur in higher than expected numbers with flint and "other" items. Stone and worked bone items followed the expected patterns of associations with other forms. Unworked bone was associated with pottery more often than expected, and was also often the only type of grave good in a burial. In addition, unworked bone also occurred less with metal items than anticipated in an equal distribution. It has already been mentioned how flint and "other" items were associated with pottery and metal items more than expected, however, flint was also found with "other" items more than anticipated and both were rarely the only type of grave good in a burial.

There were also some associations of individual artefacts, rather than just the overall types, within this dataset. 29% of Beakers (not including Beaker sherds) were buried with flint flakes, and 24% with nothing else. Though not as frequent, metal awls and flint scrapers were each found in 19% of burials with Beakers. If the artefacts were divided into the groups used before in this analysis (decoration, tools, offerings etc.), it appears that 48% of Beakers are buried with at least one tool, which is a very large amount, and 19% are buried with a decorative item.

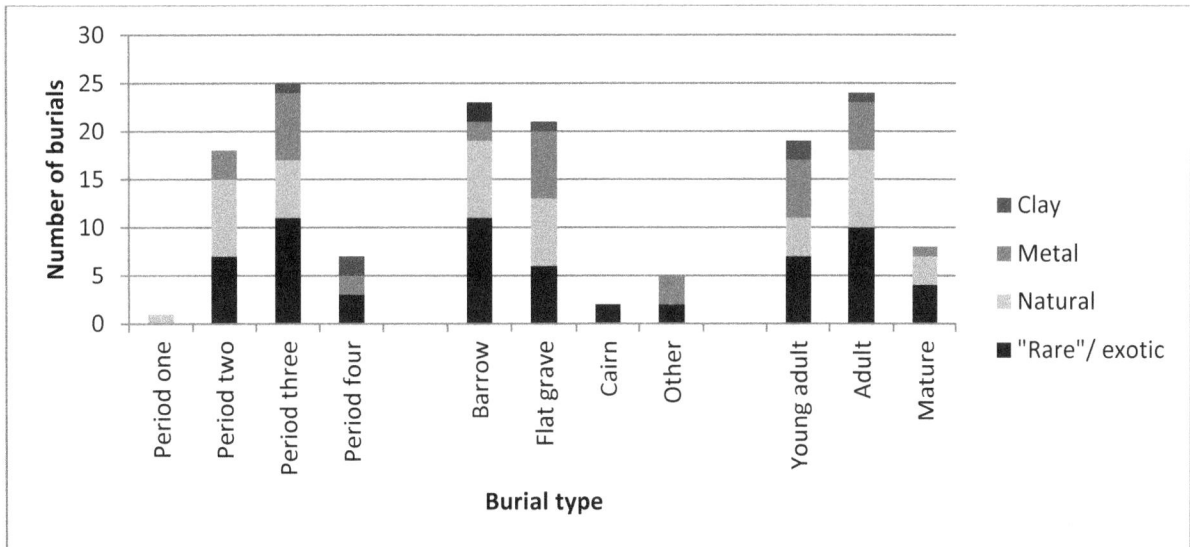

Figure A3.26: Number of material types by burial form.

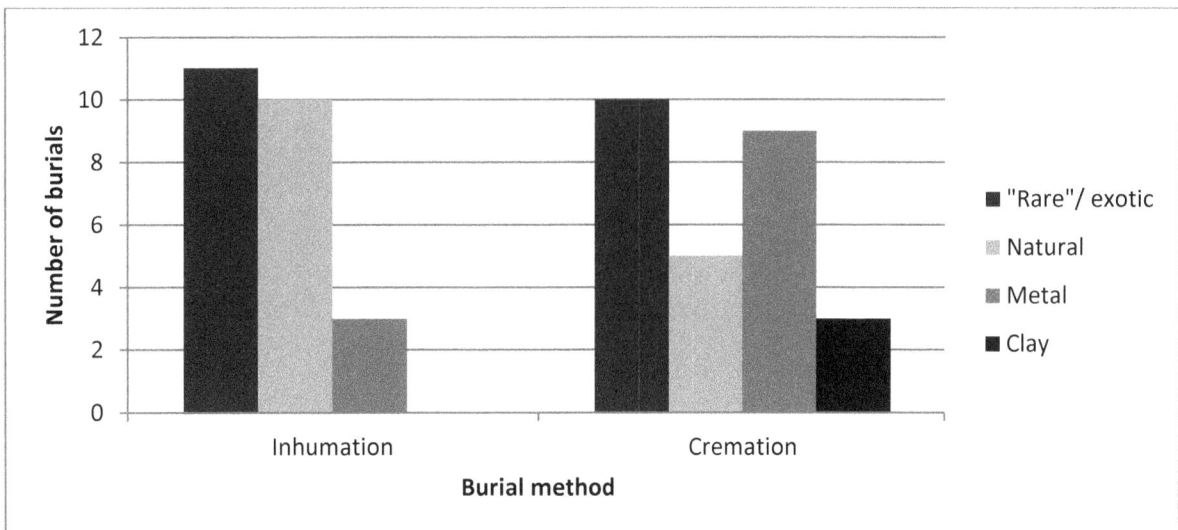

Figure A3.27: Number of material types by burial method.

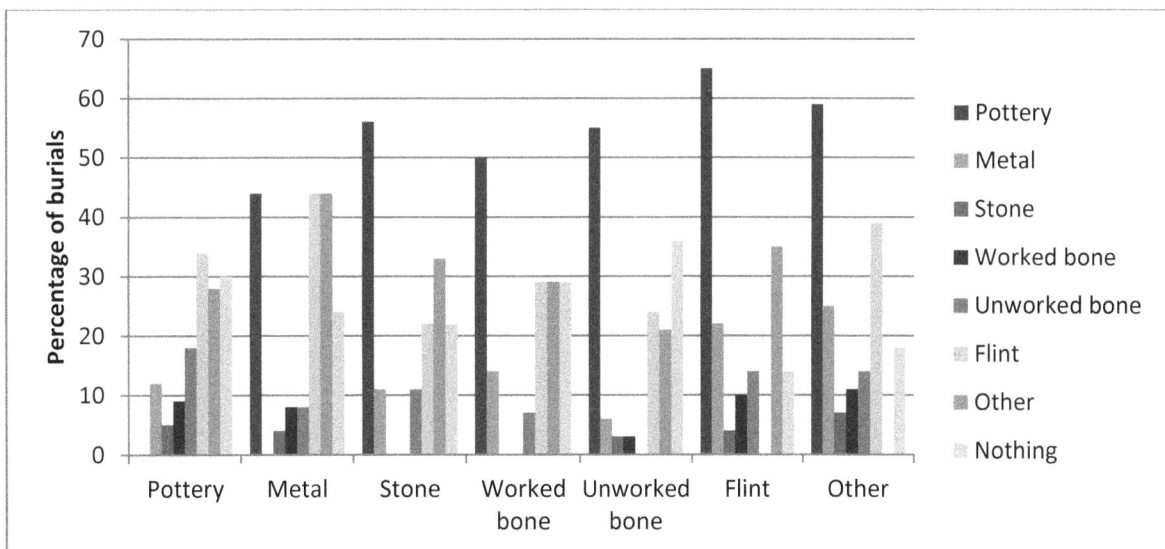

Figure A3.28: The percentage of burials containing different types of artefacts by artefact type.

Food Vessels are most frequently associated with flint knives or blades, with a total of 33% of burials containing Food Vessels also containing one of the items. However, slightly more burials (40%) contain just the Food Vessel. Of individual items Collared Urns are most frequently associated with nothing else (29%), followed by unworked bone in 25% of the burials. When looking at artefact groups it appears that Collared Urns are most frequently found in burials with tools, with 36% of burials containing at least one. 21% of Collared Urns are also associated with decorative items in the form of beads and studs.

Of the six burials with Cordoned Urns 67% are associated with bones with staining from contact with metal item and 33% with faience beads. The percentage of decorative items increases to 67% when including beads of other material and also a pendant.

Miniature vessels do not follow the same trends as the other pottery types in that the most common item they are associated with are in fact other pottery vessels, rather than any other artefact. However, when looking at artefact groups it emerges that 67% of Miniature Vessels are buried with either a tool or decorative item, or indeed both, and that in no cases are they buried alone.

Beads (of any number or material) in a female burial are most likely to be accompanied by no other items (29%). Awls are the most common (21%) individual artefact. When looking at artefact groups the most common items with beads are tools or pottery, which each feature in 38% of burials with beads. It is interesting to note that only 13% of burials with beads actually contain other items which could be considered decorative, such as buttons. When considering necklaces or strings of beads

which were probably associated together for body adornment (≥ 4 beads) the proportion of burials containing pottery remains the same. However, the number with tools increases (to 46%), as does the number with additional decorative items (to 23%). In fact, all the bead burials with additional decorative items are from these "necklace" burials.

The three different weapon forms were grouped together for the purposes of this analysis, which included bronze daggers/ knives; bronze axes and barbed-and-tanged arrowheads. The most numerous associations were with no other item (25%) rather than any individual item. However, when looking at the groups of artefacts the weapons are most commonly associated with tools (50%), followed by other weapons (25% - an additional arrowhead and an axe with a dagger), and sherds of pottery (25%). However, what was noticeable was that the range of items interred in these burials with weapons was small in comparison to other artefacts; the eight burials only had 11 different items types between them.

Flint knives or blades, on the other hand, were associated with a greater range of items. The most common items found in burials with flint knives or blades are Food Vessels and flint flakes (each found in 28% of the burials). The high prevalence of Food Vessels is echoed by the fact that 53% of burials with flint blades or knives are also buried with an item of pottery. Their association with tools is the next most common, accounting for 41% of the burials; finally decorative items are also fairly numerous (in 24% of burials). What is interesting is that flint blades or knives are always associated with other objects; they never occur in a burial by themselves in this dataset.

Figure A3.29: Placement of awls in relation to the body of the deceased. Each individual symbol represents one burial with the artefact in that position.

A3.6. Positions

Awls also do not seem to have any concentration in placement in relation to the body. Of the six awls whose placements could be studied, each was in a unique location (Figure A3.29). When dividing awls between front and back placement there seems to be a slight preference for in front of the body (in contrast to Beakers and flint artefacts). A position by the legs is also slightly preferred, with 50% of the awls found in this position.

Beads, on the other hand, do have a preferred placement; around the neck and head area (Figure A3.29), suggesting that they were worn as necklaces when interred with inhumations. There are three exceptions to this pattern; a group of four located at the wrist, which can be envisioned as a bracelet, and two beads, one at the waist and one at the lower back, which may not have been worn at all, instead they were placed in the grave as individual items.

Figure A3.30: Placement of beads and bead sets in relation to the body of the deceased. Each individual symbol represents one burial with the artefact(s) in that position.

BIBLIOGRAPHY

ABRAMSON, P. 1996. Excavations along the Caythorpe gas pipeline, North Humberside, *Yorkshire Archaeological Journal* 68: 1 – 88.

ALLEN, D. 1981. The excavation of a Beaker burial monument at Ravenstone, Buckinghamshire in 1978, *Archaeological Journal* 138: 72 – 117.

ALLEN, M.J., GARDINER, J. AND SHERIDAN, A. (EDS.) 2012. *Is There a British Chalcolithic? People, place and polity in the late 3rd millennium.* Oxford: Oxbow Books, Prehistoric Society research Paper No. 4.

ALLEN, T.G. AND KAMASH, Z. 2008. *Saved from the grave. Neolithic to Saxon discoveries at Spring Road Municipal Cemetery.* Thames Valley Landscape Monographs no. 28. Oxford: Oxford Archaeology Unit.

APPADURAI, A. 1986. *The Social Life of Things: Commodities in a cultural perspective.* Cambridge: Cambridge University Press.

APSIMON, A.M. 1973. The excavation of a Bronze Age barrow and a menhir at Ystrad-Hynod, Llanidloes (Mont), 1965-66, *Archaeologia Cambrensis* 122: 35 – 54.

ASHBEE, P. 1960. *The Bronze Age round barrow in Britain.* London: Phoenix House.

ASHBEE, P. 1985. The excavation of Amesbury Barrows 58, 61a, 61, 72, *Wiltshire Archaeological and Natural History Magazine* 79: 39 – 91.

ASHBEE, P. 1986. The excavation of Milton Lilbourne Barrows 1-5, *Wiltshire Archaeological and Natural History Magazine* 80: 23 – 96.

ASKEW, P. 2006. *The prehistoric, Roman and medieval landscape at Northumberland Bottom, Gravesend, Kent.* Channel Tunnel Rail Link Integrated Site Report Series (edited by P. Booth).

BABIĆ, S. 2005. Status identity and archaeology, in M. Díaz Andreu, S. Lucy, S. Babić and D. N. Edwards (eds.), *The archaeology of identity. Approaches to gender, age, status, ethnicity and religion*: 67-85. London: Routledge.

BAILEY, C.J. 1980. Excavation of three round barrows in the parish of Kingston Russell, *Dorset Natural History and Archaeology Society Proceedings* 102: 19 – 32.

BAKER, M. 2000. Gender: enabling perspective or politically correct term? An analysis of how gender and material culture are viewed by 1990s academia, in M. Donald and L. Hurcombe (eds.), *Gender and material culture in archaeological perspective*. 56-68. Basingstoke: Macmillan Press Ltd.

BANKS, I. 1995. The excavation of three cairns at Stoney-burn Farm, Crawford, Lanarkshire, 1991, *Proceedings of the Society of Antiquaries of Scotland* 125: 289 – 343.

BARBER, M. 2003. *Bronze and the Bronze Age. Metalwork and society in Britain c. 2500-800 BC.* Stroud: Tempus

BARCLAY, A., GRAY, M. AND LAMBRICK, G. 1995. *Excavations at the Devil's Quoits, Stanton Harcourt, Oxfordshire, 1972-73 and 1988.* Oxford: Thames Valley Landscapes: the Windrush Valley, volume 3. Oxford Archaeology Unit.

BARCLAY, A. AND HALPIN, C. 1999. *Excavations at Barrow Hills, Radley, Oxfordshire, volume 1: The Neolithic and Bronze Age monument complex.* Oxford Archaeology Unit. Thames Valley Landscapes Volume 11. Oxford: Oxbow Books.

BARCLAY, G. 1983. Sites of the third millennium BC to the first millennium AD at North Mains, Strathallan, Perthshire, *Proceedings of the Society of Antiquaries of Scotland* 113: 122 – 281.

BARCLAY, G. AND RUSSELL-WHITE, C.J. 1993. Excavations in the ceremonial complex of the fourth to second millennium BC at Balfarg/ Balbirnie, Glenrothes, Fife, *Proceedings of the Society of Antiquaries of Scotland* 123: 43 – 210.

BARNATT, J. 1994. Excavation of a Bronze Age unenclosed cemetery, Cairns and field boundaries at Eaglestone Flat, Curbar, Derbyshire, 1984, 1989 – 90, *Proceedings of the Prehistoric Society* 60: 287 – 370

BARNATT, J. 1996. Excavations of a barrow at Roystone Grange, Ballidon, Derbyshire, 1993, *Derbyshire Archaeology Journal* 116: 12 – 26.

BATEMAN, T. 1848. *Vestiges of the Antiquaries of Derbyshire.* London: John Russell Smith.

BATEMAN, T. 1861. *Ten Years Digging.* London: George Allen and Sons.

BENNET, P., CLARKE, P., HICKS, A., RADY, J. AND RIDDLER, I. 2008. *At the Great Crossroads. Prehistoric, Roman and medieval discoveries on the Isle of Thanet 1994-95.* Canterbury Archaeology Trust Occasional Paper No. 4. Oxford: Oxbow Books.

BEWLEY, R.H., LONGWORTH, I.H., BROWNE, S., HUNTLEY, J.P. AND VARNDELL, G. 1992. Excavation of a Bronze Age cemetery at Ewanrigg, Maryport, Cumbria, *Proceedings of the Prehistoric Society* 58: 325 – 354.

BEYRIES, S. AND ROTS, V. 2005. The contribution of ethno-archaeological macro- and microscopic wear traces to the understanding of archaeological hide-working processes, in L. Longo and N. Skakun (eds.), *"Prehistoric Technology" 40 years later: Functional Studies and the Russian Legacy*. 21-28. Oxford: BAR Publishing.

BIDDULPH, E. AND WELSH, K. 2011. *Cirencester before Corrinium. Excavations at Kingshill North, Cirencester, Gloustershire.* Thames Valley Landscapes Monograph 34. Oxford: Oxford University School of Archaeology and Oxford Archaeology.

BINFORD, L. 1972. Mortuary practices: their study and their potential, in L. R. Binford (ed.), *An archaeological perspective*: 208-243. London: Seminar Press.

BINFORD, L. R. 1981. Behavioural Archaeology and the "Pompeii Premise *Journal of Anthropological Research*: 37: 195-208.

BOSTON, C., BOWATER, C., BOYLE, A. AND HOLMES, A. 2003. Excavation of a Bronze Age barrow at the proposed Centre for Gene Function, South Parks Road, Oxford, 2002, *Oxoniensia* 68: 179 – 200.

BRADLEY, R. 2007. *The Prehistory of Britain and Ireland.* Cambridge: Cambridge University Press.

BRADLEY, R. 2011. *Stages and Screens.* Edinburgh: Society of the Antiquaries of Scotland.

BRASSIL, K.S., OWEN, W.G. AND BRITNELL, W.J. 1991. Prehistoric and early medieval cemeteries at Tandderwen, near Denbigh, Clwyd, *Archaeological Journal* 148: 46 – 97.

BRENNAND, M. AND TAYLOR, M. 2003. The survey and excavation of a Bronze Age timber circle at Holme-next-the-sea, Norfolk 1989-9, *Proceedings of the Prehistoric Society* 69: 1 – 314.

BRICKLEY, M.B. 2007. A case of disposal of a body through burning and recent advances in the study of burned human remains, in M. B. Brickley and R. Ferllini (eds.), *Forensic Anthropology: Case studies from Europe.* 69 – 85. Springfield, Illinois: Charles C Thomas Ltd.

BRIGGS, C.S. 1997. A Neolithic and Early Bronze Age settlement and burial complex at Llanilar, Ceredigan, *Archaeologia Cambrensis* 146: 13 – 59.

BRINDLEY, A.L. 2007. *The dating of Food Vessels and Urns in Ireland.* Bronze Age Studies 7. Galaway: Department of Archaeology, National University of Ireland.

BRITNELL, W. 1982. The excavation of two round barrows at Trelystan, Powys, *Proceedings of the Prehistoric Society* 48: 133 – 201.

BRODIE, N. 1997. New perspectives on the Bell Beaker culture. *Oxford Journal of Archaeology.* 16(3): 297-314.

BRONK RAMSEY, C. 2009. Bayesian analysis of radiocarbon dates. *Radiocarbon* 51(1): 337-360.

BRÜCK, J. 2004. Material metaphors. The relational construction of identity in Early Bronze Age burials in Ireland and Britain. *Journal of Social Archaeology.* 4(3): 307-333.

BRÜCK, J. 2009. Women, death and social change in the British Bronze Age. *Norwegian Archaeological Review* 42(1): 1-23.

BRUZEK, J. 2002. A method for visual determination of sex, using the human hip bone, *American Journal of Physical Anthropology.* 117: 157-168.

BULL, R. 2006. *The prehistoric landscape at Whitehill Road Barrow, Longfield and New Barn, Kent.* Channel Tunnel Rail Link Integrated Site Report Series (edited by A. Barclay).

BURGESS, C. 1972. Goatscrag: A Bronze Age rock shelter cemetery in north Northumberland. With notes on other rock shelters and crag lines in the region, *Archaeologia Aeliana 4th Series* 1: 15 – 69.

BURGESS, C. & SHENNAN, S. J. 1976. The Beaker phenomenon. Some suggestions, 1: General comments and the British evidence, 2: Some comments on the European evidence, in C. Burgess & R. Miket (eds.) *Settlement and Economy in the Third and Second Millennia BC.* 309–331. Oxford: British Archaeological Reports British Series 33.

BUTLER, J. 2006 [1990]. *Gender Trouble: feminism and the subversion of identity.* Abingdon, Oxon: Routledge Classics.

BYERS, S.N. 2008. *Introduction to Forensic Anthropology. 3rd edition.* London: Pearson.

CAHILL, M. AND SIKORA, M. (EDS.) 2012. *Breaking Ground, Finding Graves – Reports on the excavations of burials by the National Museum of Ireland, 1927 – 2006. 2 Volumes.* Dublin: Wordwell.

CASE, H. 1977. The Beaker culture in Britain and Ireland, in R. Mercer (ed.) *Beakers in Britain and Europe.* 71-101. Oxford: British Archaeological Reports Supplementary Series 26.

CALDWELL, W.E. AND MOLOY, H.C. 1932. Sexual variation in the pelvis, *Science* New Series 76: 37-40.

CHAFFEY, G. AND BROOK, E. 2012. Domesticity in the Neolithic: Excavations at Kingsmead Quarry, Horton, Berkshire, in H. Anderson-Whymark and J. Thomas (eds.) *Regional Perspectives on Neolithic Pit Deposition: Beyond the mundane.* 200-215. Oxford: Oxbow Books.

CHAPMAN, A. 2007. A Bronze Age Barrow cemetery and later boundaries, pit alignments and enclosures at Gayhurst Quarry, Newport Pagnell, Buckinghamshire, *Records of Buckinghamshire* 47.2: 81 – 211.

CHAPMAN, R. In press. The living and the dead in later Prehistoric Iberia, in L. Nilsson Stutz and S. Tarlow (eds.), *The Oxford handbook of the archaeology of death and burial.* Oxford: Oxford University Press.

CLARKE, C. AND HAMILTON, J. 1999. Excavation of a cist burial on Doons Law, Leetside Farm, Whitsome, Berwickshire, *Proceedings of the Society of Antiquaries of Scotland* 129: 189 – 201.

CLARKE, D.V., COWIE, T. G. AND FOXTON, A. 1985. *Symbols of Power at the Time of Stonehenge.* Edinburgh: National Museum of Antiquities of Scotland/ HMSO.

CLARK, D.L. 1970. *Beaker pottery of Great Britain and Ireland.* Cambridge: Cambridge University Press.

CLOSE-BROOKS, J. 1972-4. Short cists at Buckstone Road, Fairmilehead, Edinburgh, *Proceedings of the Society of Antiquaries of Scotland* 105: 281 – 284.

CLOSE-BROOKS, J., NORGATE, M. AND GRAHAM RITCHIE, J.N. 1971-2. A Bronze Age cemetery at Aberdour Road, Dunfermline, Fife, *Proceedings of the Society of Antiquaries of Scotland* 104: 121 – 136.

CONKEY, M. & SPECTOR, J. 1984. Archaeology and the study of gender, in M. Schiffer (ed.), *Advances in archaeological method and theory* 7: 1-38. London: Academic Press.

CRAWFORD, I. 1976-7. A corbelled Bronze Age burial chamber and beaker evidence from the Rosinish Machair, Benbecular, *Proceedings of the Society of Antiquaries of Scotland* 108. 94 – 107.

CRUSE, R.J. AND HARRISON, A.C. 1983. Excavation at Hill Road, Wouldham, *Archaeologia Cantiana* 99: 81 – 108.

CRUSE, R.J. 2007. Dating the cremation in a biconical urn at the Early Bronze Age barrow, Hill Road, Wouldham, *Archaeologia Cantiana* 127: 163 – 173.

DE'ATH, R. Unpublished. *Early Iron Age metalworking and Iron Age/ Early Romano-British settlement evidence along the Barton Stacey to Lockerley gas pipeline.* Salisbury: Wessex Archaeology.

DENT, J.S. 1979. Bronze Age burials from Wetwang Slack, *Yorkshire Archaeological Journal* 51: 23 – 39.

DERRY, D.E. 1909. Note on the innominate bone as a factor in the determination of sex, *Journal of Anatomy and Physiology.* 43: 266-276.

DERRY, D.E. 1927. On the sexual and racial characteristics of the human ilium, *Journal of Anatomy.* 58: 71-83.

DIAZ ANDREU, M. & LUCY, S. 2005. Introduction, in M. Díaz Andreu, S. Lucy , S. Babić and D. N. Edwards (eds.), *The archaeology of identity. Approaches to gender, age, status, ethnicity and religion*: 1-12. London: Routledge.

DODWELL, N. 2010. Human Bone, in C. Evans and J. Tabor (eds.) *The Over Narrows: archaeological investigations in Hanson's Needingworth Quarry. The Low Grounds Barrows (Part IV, 2008).* 48 – 53. Cambridge: Cambridge Archaeological Unit Report 940.

DONALDSON, P. 1977. The excavation of a multiple round barrow at Barnack, Cambridgeshire 1974-76. *Antiquaries Journal* 57: 197 – 231.

DOWNES, J. 1994. Excavation of a Bronze Age burial at Mousland, Stromness, Orkney, *Proceedings of the Society of Antiquaries of Scotland* 124: 141 – 154.

DUFFY, P. 2005. The excavation of a mound and three cist burials at Ferndale, Rendall, Orkney, *Scottish Archaeology Internet Reports* 16.

DWIGHT, T. 1894. The range and significance of variation in the human skeleton, *Boston Medical and Surgical Journal.* 131.5: 97-101.

EGGING DINWIDDY, K. AND BRADLEY, P. 2011. *Prehistoric activity and a Romano-British settlement at Poundbury Farm, Dorchester, Dorset.* Salisbury: Wessex Archaeology.

ELLIS, C. 2004. *A prehistoric ritual complex at Eynesbury, Cambridgeshire: excavation of a multi-period site in the Great Ouse Valley, 2000 – 2001.* East Anglian Archaeology Occasional Papers 17. Salisbury: The Trust for Wessex Archaeology Ltd.

ELLIS, C. AND POWELL, A. 2008. *An Iron Age settlement outside Battlesbury Hillfort, Warminster and sites along the Southern Range Road.* Salisbury: Wessex Archaeology Report 22.

EVANS, C., WITH BRUDENELL, M., PATTEN, R. AND REGAN, R. 2013a. *Process and History: Prehistoric Fen-edge Communities at Colne Fen, Earith (The Archaeology of the Lower Ouse Valley, Volume I).* Cambridge: Cambridge Archaeological Unit.

EVANS, C., WITH TABOR, J. AND VANDER LINDEN, M. 2013b. *Twice-crossed River: Prehistoric and Palaeoenvironmental Investigations at Barleycroft Farm/ Over, Cambridgeshire (The*

Archaeology of the Lower Ouse Valley, Volume III). Cambridge: Cambridge Archaeological Unit.

EVANS, C. AND KNIGHT, M. 1998. *The Butcher's Rise ring-ditches, excavations at Barleycroft Farm, Cambridgeshire.* Cambridge: Cambridge Archaeology Report 283.

EVANS, C. AND TABOR, J. 2010a. *The Over Narrows: archaeological investigations in Hanson's Needingworth Quarry. The Low Grounds Barrows (Part IV, 2008).* Cambridge: Cambridge Archaeological Unit Report 940.

EVANS, C. AND TABOR, J. 2010b. *The Over Narrows (part V): archaeological investigations in Hanson's Needingworth Quarry. The O'Connell Ridge East – The site II barrow.* Cambridge Archaeological Unit Report 967.

FAUSTO-STERLING, A. 1993. The five sexes: why male and female are not enough, *The Sciences.* March/April: 20-24.

FITZPATRICK, A.P. 2002. 'The Amesbury Archer': a well-furnished Early Bronze Age burial in southern England. *Antiquity* 76.293: 629-630.

FLETCHER, M. AND LOCK, G.R. 2005. *Digging Numbers. Elementary statistics for archaeologists. Second Edition.* Oxford: Oxford University School of Archaeology.

FORD, S., BRADLEY, R., HAWKES, J. AND FISHER, P. 1984. Flint-working in the metal age, *Oxford Journal of Archaeology* 3.2: 157 – 173.

FOWLER, C. 2004. *The archaeology of personhood.* London: Routledge.

FRENCH, C. 1994. *Excavation of the Deeping St. Nicholas Barrow complex, south Lincolnshire.* Lincolnshire Archaeology and Heritage Report Series no. 1. Lincolnshire: Heritage Trust of Lincolnshire.

FRENCH, C., LEWIS, H., ALLEN, M.J., GREEN, M., SCAIFER, R. AND GARDINER, J. 2007. *Prehistoric landscape development and human impact in the upper Allen valley, Cranbourne Chase, Dorset.* Cambridge: McDonald Institute Monographs.

FRENCH, C. AND PRYOR, F. 2005. *Archaeology and environment of the Etton landscape.* East Anglian Archaeology 109. Peterborough: Fenland Archaeological Trust.

GARDINER, J., ALLEN, M.J., POWELL, A., HARDING, P., LAWSON, A.J., LOADER, E., MCKINLEY, J., SHERIDAN, A. AND STEVENS, C. 2007. A matter of life and death: Late Neolithic, Beaker and Early Bronze Age settlement and cemeteries at Thomas Hardye School, Dorchester. *Proceedings of the Dorset Natural History and Archaeology Society* 128: 17 – 52.

GARWOOD, P. 1991. Ritual tradition and the reconstruction of society, in P. Garwood, D. Jennings, R. Skeats and J. Toms (eds.) *Sacred and Profane.* 10-32. Oxford: Oxbow Books. Monograph no. 32.

GARWOOD, P. 2007. Before the hills in order stood: chronology, time and history in the interpretation of Early Bronze Age round barrows, in J. Last (ed.), *Beyond the grave: new perspectives on barrows.* 30-52. Oxford: Oxbow Books.

GERLOFF, S. 1975. *The Early Bronze Age daggers in Great Britain and a reconsideration of the Wessex Culture.* Munich: Beck.

GERLOFF, S. 2007. Reinecke's ABC and the chronology of the British Bronze Age, in C. Burgess, P. Topping and F. Lynch (eds.), *Beyond Stonehenge. Essays on the Bronze Age in honour of Colin Burgess.* 117-161. Oxford: Oxbow Books.

GIBBS, L. 1989. *Sex, gender and material culture patterning in later Neolithic and earlier Bronze Age England.* University of Cambridge: Unpublished PhD dissertation.

GIBSON, A. 1993. The excavation of two cairns and associated features at Carneddau, Carno, Powys, 1989-90, *Archaeological Journal* 150: 1 – 45.

GIBSON, A. 2007. A Beaker veneer? Some evidence from the burial record, in M. Larsson and M. Parker Pearson (eds.), *From Stonehenge to the Baltic: Living with cultural diversity in the Third Millennium BC* . 47 – 64. Oxford: BAR International Series 1692.

GIBSON, A.M. AND MCCORMICK, A. 1985. Archaeology at Grendon Quarry, Northamptonshire. Part 1: Neolithic and Bronze Age sites excavated in 1974-75, *Northamptonshire Archaeology* 20: 23 – 66.

GIBSON, D. AND KNIGHT, M. 2006. *Bradley Fen excavations, Whittlesey, Cambridgeshire 2001-2004.* Cambridge: Cambridge Archaeology Unit Report 733.

GILCHRIST, R. 2000. Archaeological biographies: realizing human lifecycles, -courses and –histories. *World Archaeology* 31: 325-328.

GILLESPIE, S. D. 2001. Personhood, agency, and mortuary ritual: a case study from the ancient Maya, *Journal of Anthropological Archaeology.* 20: 73-112.

GINGELL, C. 1988. Twelve Wiltshire round barrows. Excavations in 1959 and 1961 by F. de M and H.L. Vatcher, *Wiltshire Archaeological and Natural History Magazine* 82: 19 – 76.

GOODENOUGH, W. H. 1965. Rethinking "status" and "role". Toward a general model of the cultural organization of social relationships, in M. Banton (ed.), *The relevance of models for social anthropology*: 1-24. ASA Monograph 1. New York: Praegar.

GÖTHERSTRÖM, A., LIDIN, K., AHLSTRÖM, T. KÄLLERSJÖ, M. AND BROWN, T.A. 1997. Osteology, DNA and sex identification: morphological and molecular sex identifications of five Neolithic individuals from Ajvide, Gotland, *International Journal of Osteoarchaeology*. 7: 71-81.

GOWLAND, R. 2006. Ageing the past: examining age identity from funerary evidence, in R. Gowland and C. Knüsel (eds.) *Social archaeology of funerary remains*. Oxford: Oxbow Books. 143-154.

GREEN, C., LYNCH, F. AND WHITE, H. 1982. 'The excavation of two round barrows on Launceston Down, Dorset (Long Critchel 5 and 7)', *Dorset Natural History Society and Archaeological Society Proceedings* 104: 39 - 58.

GREEN, C. AND ROLLO-SMITH, S. 1984. The excavation of 18 round barrows near Shrewton, Wiltshire, *Proceedings of the Prehistoric Society* 50: 255 – 318.

GREEN, H.S. 1974. Early Bronze Age burial, territory and population in Milton Keynes, Buckinghamshire, and the Great Ouse Valley, *Archaeological Journal* 131: 75 – 139.

GREIG, M.K., GREIG, C., SHEPHERD, A.N. AND SHEPHERD, I.A.G. 1989. A beaker cist from Chapelden, Tore of Troup, Aberdour, Banff and Buchan District, with a note on the orientation of beaker burial in north-east Scotland. *Proceedings of the Society of Antiquaries of Scotland* 119: 73-81.

HALL, D. AND WOODWARD, P.J. 1977. Radwell excavations, 1974 – 1975: the Bronze Age ring ditches, *Bedfordshire Archaeological Journal* 12: 1 – 16.

HARDING, J. AND HEALY, F. 2007. *The Raunds Area Project. A Neolithic and Bronze Age landscape in Northamptonshire*. Swindon: English Heritage.

HARRISON, R.J. 1980. *The Beaker folk: Copper Age archaeology in Western Europe*. London: Thames and Hudson.

HART, P. AND MOODY, G. 2008. Two Beaker burials recently discovered on the Isle of Thanet, *Archaeologia Cantiana* 128: 165 – 177.

HEALY, F. 2012. Chronology, corpses, ceramics, copper and lithics, in M.J. Allen, J. Gardiner and A. Sheridan (eds.) *Is There a British Chalcolithic? People, place and polity in the late 3rd millennium*. 144-163. Oxford: Oxbow Books, Prehistoric Society research Paper No. 4.

HERBERT, E.W. 1984. *Red gold of Africa. Copper in precolonial history and culture*. Wisconsin: University of Wisconsin Press.

HOARE, R.C. 1812. *Ancient Wiltshire, volume i*. London: William Miller.

HODDER, I. 1980. Social structure and cemeteries: a critical appraisal, in P. Rahtz, T. Dickinson and L. Watts (eds.), *Anglo-Saxon cemeteries 1979*. 161-169. Oxford: British Archaeological Reports, British Series 82.

HRDLIČKA, A. 1920. *Anthropometry*, Philadelphia: Wister Institute of Anatomy and Biology.

HUNT, A.M., SHOTLIFF, A. AND WOODHOUSE, J. 1986. A Bronze Age barrow cemetery and Iron Age enclosure at Holt. *Transactions of the Worcestershire Archaeological Society, 3rd Series* 10: 7 – 46.

İŞCAN, M.Y. 2005. Forensic anthropology of sex and body size, *Forensic Science International*. 147:107-112.

JACOBS, S-E. AND CROMWELL, J. 1992. Visions and revisions of reality, *Journal of Homosexuality*. 23.4: 43-70.

JOBEY, G. AND NEWMAN, T.G. 1975. A collared urn cremation on Howich Heugh, Northumberland, *Archaeologia Aeliana 5th Series* 3: 1 – 16.

JOHNSTON, D.E. 1980. The excavation of a bell-barrow at Sutton Veny, Wilts, *Wiltshire Archaeological and Natural History Magazine* 72/73: 29 – 50.

KEEN, J.A. 1950. A study of the difference between male and female skulls, *American Journal of Physical Anthropology*. 8: 65-79.

KING, D.G. 1966. The Lanhill Long Barrow, Wiltshire, England: An essay in reconstruction, *Proceedings of the Prehistoric Society* 32: 73 – 85.

KING, J. M. 2004. Grave-goods as gifts in Early Saxon burials (ca. AD 450-600), *Journal of Social Archaeology*. 4.2: 214-238.

KINNES, I. 1978. A Beaker burial on Ringstead Downs, Old Hunstanton, in P. Wade-Martins (ed.), *Norfolk*. 19 – 22. East Anglian Archaeology 8. Norfolk: The Norfolk Archaeology Unit.

KINNES, I. 1979. *Round Barrows and Ring Ditches in the British Neolithic*. London: British Museum.

KINNES, I., GIBSON, A., AMBERS, J., BOWMAN, S., LEESE, M. and BOAST, R. 1991. Radiocarbon dating and British Beakers: The British Museum programme. *Scottish Archaeological Review*. 8: 35-68.

KJELLSTRÖM, A. 2004. Evaluation of sex assessment using weighted traits on incomplete skeletal remains, *International Journal of Osteoarchaeology.* 14: 360-373.

LAMDIN-WHYMARK, H. 2003. The worked flint and burnt stone, in C. Boston, C. Bowater, A Boyle and A Holmes. Excavation of a Bronze Age barrow at the proposed Centre for Gene Function, South Parks Road, Oxford, 2002, *Oxoniensia* 68: 179 – 200.

LANTING, J D AND VAN DER WAALS, J D 1972 British Beakers as seen from the continent, *Helinium.* 12: 3–31.

LAQUEUR, T. 1990. *Making sex. Body and gender from the Greeks to Freud.* London: Harvard University Press.

LAWSON, J.A., HENDERSON, D. AND SHERIDAN, A. 2002. An Early Bronze Age short-cist burial at Abbey Mains Farm, Hoddington, East Lothian, *Proceedings of the Society of Antiquaries of Scotland* 132: 193 – 204.

LELONG, O. AND POLLARD, T. 1998. Excavation of a Bronze Age ring cairn at Cloburn Quarry, Cairngryffe Hill, Lanarkshire, *Proceedings of the Society of Antiquaries of Scotland* 128: 105 – 142.

LOVEDAY, R. AND BARCLAY, A. 2010. "One of the most interesting barrows ever examined" – Liffs Low revisited, In J. Leary, T. Darvill and D. Field (eds.), *Round Barrows and Monumentality in the British Neolithic and Beyond:* 108-129.Oxford: Oxbow Books.

LUCAS, G. 1996. Of death and debt. A history of the body in Neolithic and Early Bronze Age Yorkshire. *Journal of European Archaeology.* 4: 99-118.

LUCY, S. 1997. Housewives, warriors and slaves? Sex and gender in Anglo-Saxon burials, in J. Moore and E. Scott (eds.), *Invisible people and processes: writing gender and childhood into European Archaeology:* 150-168. London: Leicester University Press.

LYNCH, F. AND MUSSON, C. 2001. A prehistoric and early medieval complex at Llandegai, near Bangor, North Wales, *Archaeologia Cambrensis* 150: 17 – 142.

MACGREGOR, G. 1998. The excavation of a cordoned urn at Benderloch, Arggyll, *Proceedings of the Society of Antiquaries of Scotland* 128: 143 – 159.

MACLAGAN WEDDERBUM, L.M. 1974-75. A short cist at Darnaway, Forres, *Proceedings of the Society of Antiquaries of Scotland* 106: 191 – 194.

MARSDEN, B.M. 1970. The excavation of the Bee Low round cairn, Youlgreave, Derbyshire. *Antiquaries Journal* 50.2: 186-215.

MARTIN, E.A. 1975-76. The excavation of two tumuli on Waterhall Farm, Chipppenham, Cambridgeshire, 1973. *Proceedings of the Cambridge Antiquarian Society* 66: 1 – 21.

MARTIN, E.A. 1976. The excavation of a tumulus at Barrow Bottom, Risby, 1975, in S.E. West (ed.), *Suffolk.* East Anglian Archaeology 3. 43 – 62. Ipswich: Suffolk County Planning Department.

MARTIN, E.A. AND DENSTON, C.B. 1986. A Bronze Age multiple burial at Exning, *Proceedings of the Suffolk Institute of Archaeology and History* 36.2: 131 – 134.

MAYS, S. AND COX, M. 2000. Sex determination in skeletal remains, in M. Cox and S. Mays (eds.), *Human Osteology in Archaeology and Forensic Sciences.* 117-130. London: Greenwich Medical Media Ltd.

MCKINLEY, J. 1994. A pyre and grave goods in British cremation burials; have we missed something? *Antiquity* 68: 132 – 134.

MCKINLEY, J. 1997. Bronze Age 'barrows' and funerary rites and rituals of cremation, *Proceedings of the Prehistoric Society* 63: 129 – 145.

MERCER, R.J. 2007. By other means? The development of warfare in the British Isles 3000-500 BC, in T. Pollard and I. Banks (eds.) *War and sacrifice: Studies in the archaeology of conflict.* 119-151. Netherlands: Brill.

MERCER, R.J. AND MIDGLEY, M.S. 1997. The Early Bronze Age cairn at Sketewan, Balnaguard, Perth and Kinross, *Proceedings of the Society of Antiquaries of Scotland* 127: 281 – 338.

MESKELL, L. 1999. *Archaeologies of social life. Age, sex, class et cetera, in Ancient Egypt.* Oxford: Blackwell.

MIZOGUCHI, K. 1992. A historiography of a linear barrow cemetery: a structuralist's point of view. *Archaeological Review from Cambridge* 11.1: 39-49.

MIZOGUCHI, K. 1993. Time in the reproduction of mortuary practices. *World Archaeology* 25.2: 223 – 235.

MIZOGUCHI, K. 1995. The 'materiality' of Wessex Beakers. *Scottish Archaeological Review.* 9/10: 175-185.

NEEDHAM, S. 1996. Chronology and periodisation in the British Bronze Age, in K. Randsborg (ed.). *Absolute Chronology: Archaeological Europe 2500 – 500 BC.* *Acta Archaeologica* 67: 121-140.

NEEDHAM, S. 1999. Radley and the development of early metalwork in Britain, in A. Barclay and C. Halpin. 1999. *Excavations at Barrow Hills, Radley, Oxfordshire, Vol. 1. The Neolithic and Bronze Age monument complex.* Thames Valley Landscapes Vol. 11. 186 – 192. Oxford: Oxbow.

NEEDHAM, S. 2005. Transforming Beaker culture in north west Europe; Processes of fusion and fission. *Proceedings of the Prehistoric Society.* 71: 171-217.

NEEDHAM, S. 2011. *Enriching the female persona.* Lecture given at the Rhind Lectures, 30/04/2011, 3.30pm. Accessed: http://www.screencast.com/t/P6PnEC6vCc 10/07/2011, 12.35pm.

NEEDHAM, S., PARKER PEARSON, M., TYLER, A., RICHARDS, M. AND JAY, M. 2010. A first 'Wessex 1' date from Wessex. *Antiquity* 84: 363-373.

NEWMAN, T.G. AND MIKET, R.F. 1973. A dagger-grave at Allerwash, Newbrough, Northumberland, *Archaeologia Aeliana, 5th Series* 1: 87 – 95.

NILSON STUTZ, L. 2003. *Embodied rituals and ritualized bodies.* Lund: Acta Archaeologia Lundensia.

NORDBLADH, J. & YATES, T. 1990. This perfect body, this virgin text: between sex and gender in archaeology, in I. Bapty & T. Yates (eds.), *Archaeology after structuralism*: 222-237. London: Routledge.

OLIVIER, A.C.H. 1987. Excavation of a Bronze Age funerary cairn at Manor Farm, near Borwick, North Lancashire, *Proceedings of the Prehistoric Society* 53: 129 – 186.

PACITTO, A. 1972. Rudstone barrow LXII: The 1968 excavation, PACITTO, A. 1972. Rudstone barrow LXII: The 1968 excavation, *Yorkshire Archaeological Journal* 44: 1 – 22.

PADER, E-J. 1982. *Symbolism, social relations and the interpretation of mortuary remains.* Oxford. British Archaeological Report, International Series 130.

PARKER PEARSON, M. 1993. The powerful dead: archaeological relationships between the living and the dead, *Cambridge Archaeological Journal.* 3.2: 203-229.

PEARSON, K. 1899. Mathematical contributions to the theory of evolution. V. On the reconstruction of the stature of prehistoric races, *Philosophical Transactions of the Royal Society London.* 192: 169-244.

PEEBLES, C. S. 1971. Moundville and surrounding sites: some structural considerations of mortuary practices II, in J. A. Brown (eds.), *Approaches to the social dimensions of mortuary practices*: 68-91. Memoirs of the Society for American Archaeology, vol 25.

PETERSEN, F. 1972. Traditions of multiple burial in Later Neolithic and Early Bronze Age, *The Archaeology Journal* 129: 22 - 55.

PETERSEN, F., SHEPHERD, I.A.G. AND TUCKWELL, A.N. 1972-74. A short cist at Horsbrugh Castle Farm, Peeblesshire, *Proceedings of the Society of Antiquaries of Scotland* 105: 43 – 62.

PHILLIPS, M. 2009. *Four millennia of human activity along the A505 Baldock Bypass, Hertfordshire.* East Anglian Archaeology Monograph 128. Bedford: Albion Archaeology.

PIERPOINT, S. 1980. *Social Patterns in Yorkshire Prehistory.* Oxford: British Archaeological Reports British Series 74.

PIGGOTT, S. 1962. *The West Kennet long barrow, excavations 1955-56.* London: Her Majesty's Stationery Office.

POWLESLAND, D. 1986. Excavations at Heslerton, North Yorkshire 1978 – 82. *Archaeological Journal* 143: 53 – 173.

PRYOR, F. 1974. Two Bronze Age burials near Pilsgate, Lincolnshire, *Proceedings of the Cambridge Antiquarian Society* 65: 1 – 12.

RAFTERY, B. 1996. *Trackway excavations in the Mount Dillon Bogs, Co. Longford, 1985-1991.* Irish Archaeological Wetland Unit Transactions volume 3. Dublin: Crannóg Publication.

RALSTON, I. 1996. Four short cists from north-east Scotland and Easter Ross, *Proceedings of the Society of Antiquaries of Scotland* 126: 121 – 155.

RANDSBORG, K. 1973. Wealth and social structure as reflected in bronze age burial – a quantitative approach, in C. Renfrew (ed.), *The Explanation of Cultural Change: Models in prehistory*: 565-570. London: Duckworth.

RAUTMAN, A.E. & TALALAY, L.E. 2000. Introduction: diverse approaches to the study of gender in archaeology, in A. E. Rautman (ed.), *Reading the body: representations and remains in the archaeological record*: 1-12. Philadelphia: University of Pennsylvania Press.

REGAN, R., EVANS, C. AND WEBLEY, L. 2004. *The Camp Ground Excavations, Colne Fen, Earith. Assessment Report, Volume 1.* Cambridge: Cambridge Archaeological Unit Report 654.

RICE, P.M. 1991. Women and prehistoric pottery production, in D. Walde and N. D. Willows (eds.), *The archaeology of gender.* Proceedings of the 22nd annual conference of the Archaeological Association of the University of Calgary: 436 – 443. Canada: The University of Calgary Archaeological Association.

RICHARDS, J. 1986-90. Death and the past environment. The results of work on barrows on the Berkshire Downs, *Berkshire Archaeological Society* 73: 1 – 42.

RIDDLER, I. AND TREVARTHEN, M. 2006. *The prehistoric, Roman and Anglo-Saxon funerary landscape at Saltwood Tunnel, Kent.* Channel Tunnel Rail Link Intergrated Site Report Series (edited by J. Mckinley).

RIDE, D.J. 2001. The excavation of a cremation cemetery of the Bronze Age and a flint cairn at Easton Down, Allington, Wiltshire, 1983 – 1995, *Wiltshire Archaeological and Natural History Magazine* 94: 161 – 176.

RITCHIE, J.N.G. 1971-72. Excavation of a chambered cairn at Dalineum, Lorn, Argyll, *Proceedings of the Society of Antiquaries of Scotland* 104: 48 – 62.

RITCHIE, J.N.G. 1974. Excavation of the stone circle and cairn at Balbirnie, Fife, *Archaeological Journal* 131: 1 – 32.

RITCHIE, J.N.G. 1987. A cist from Kentraw, Islay, *Proceedings of the Society of Antiquaries of Scotland* 117: 41 – 45.

RITCHIE, J.N.G. AND RITCHIE, A. 1974. Excavation of a barrow at Queenafjold, Twatt, Orkney, *Proceedings of the Society of Antiquaries of Scotland* 105: 33 – 40.

ROGERS, A.J. 2013. The afterlife of monuments in the English Peak District: The evidence of Early Bronze Age burials. *Oxford Journal of Archaeology* 32(1): 39-51.

RUSSEL-WHITE, C.J., LOWE, C.E. AND MCCULLAGH, R.P.J. 1992. Excavations at three Early Bronze Age burial monuments in Scotland. *Proceedings of the Prehistoric Society* 58: 285 – 323.

SAFONT, S., MALGOSA, A. AND SUBIRÀ, M.E. 2000. Sex assessment based on long bone circumference, *American Journal of Physical Anthropology.* 113: 317-328.

SALANOVA, L. 1998. Le statut des assemblages campaniformes en contexte funéraire: la notion de « bien de prestige », *Bulletin de la Société Préhistorique Français* 95(3) : 315-326.

SAUNDERS, S.R AND YANG, D. 1999. Sex determination: XX or XY from the human skeleton, in S.I. Fairgreve (ed.), *Forensic osteological analysis.* 36-59. Springfield, Illinois: Charles C. Thomas.

SAXE, A. 1970. *Social dimensions of mortuary practices.* Unpublished PhD thesis. Ann Arbor, Michigan: University Mirofilms International, The University of Michigan.

SCHULTZ, A.H. 1930. The skeleton of the trunk and limbs of higher primates, *Human Biology.* 2.3: 303-438.

SHENNAN, S. 1997. *Quantifying Archaeology.* 2nd Edition. Iowa: University of Iowa Press.

SHEPHERD, A. 2012. Stepping out together: men, women, and their Beakers in time and space, in M.J. Allen, J. Gardiner and A. Sheridan (eds.) *Is There a British Chalcolithic? People, place and polity in the late 3rd millennium.* 257-280. Oxford: Oxbow Books, Prehistoric Society research Paper No. 4.

SHEPHERD, I.A.G. 1981. Bronze Age jet working in north Britain, in J. Kenworthy (ed.), *Early technology in north Britain. Scottish Archaeological Forum 11.* 43 – 51. Edinburgh: Edinburgh University Press.

SHEPHERD, I.A.G. 2009. The V-bored buttons of Great Britain and Ireland, *Proceedings of the Prehistoric Society* 75: 335 – 369.

SHEPHERD, I.A.G. AND COWIE, T.G. 1976-77. An enlarged food vessel urn burial and associated artefacts from Kiltry Knock, Alvah, Banff and Buchan, *Proceedings of the Society of Antiquaries of Scotland* 108: 114 – 123.

SHEPHERD, I.A.G. AND SHEPHERD, A.N. 2001. A cordoned urn burial with faience from 102 Findhorn, Moray, *Proceedings of the Society of Antiquaries of Scotland* 131: 101 – 128.

SHERIDAN, A. 2003a. New dates for Scottish Bronze Age cinerary urns: results from the National Museums of Scotland Dating cremated bones project, in A. Gibson (ed.), *Prehistoric Pottery: people, pattern and purpose.* 201-226. Oxford: British Archaeological Reports International Series 1156.

SHERIDAN, A. 2003b. Supernatural power dressing. *British Archaeology* 70: 18-23.

SHERIDAN, A. 2004. Scottish Food Vessel chronology revisited, in A. Gibson and A. Sheridan (eds.), *From sickles to circles. Britain and Ireland at the time of Stonehenge.* 243-267. Stroud: Tempus.

SHERIDAN, A. 2006. Inchmarnock, Northport, cist 3. *Discovery and Excavation in Scotland* 7: 39-40.

SHERIDAN, A. 2007a. Dating the Scottish Bronze Age: 'There is clearly much that the material can tell us', in C. Burgess, P. Topping and F. Lynch (eds.), *Beyond Stonehenge. Essays on the Bronze Age in honour of Colin Burgess.* 162-185. Oxford: Oxbow Books.

SHERIDAN, A. 2007b. Scottish Beaker dates: the good, the bad and the ugly, in M. Laarson (ed.), *From Stonehenge to the Baltic.* 91-123. Oxford: British Archaeological Reports Supplementary Series S1692.

SHERIDAN, A. AND DAVIS, M. 2002. Investigating jet and jet-like artefacts from prehistoric Scotland: the National Museums of Scotland project. *Antiquity* 76: 812 – 25.

SIMPSON, D. AND COLES, J. 1990. Excavations at Grandtully, Perthshire, *Proceedings of the Society of Antiquaries of Scotland* 120: 33 - 44.

SMITH, I.F. 1991. Round barrows Wilsford cum Lake G51-G54: Excavations by Ernest Greenfield in 1958, *Wiltshire Archaeological and Natural History Magazine* 84: 11 – 39.

SOFAER DEREVENSKI, J. 2002. Engendering context. Context as gendered practice in the Early Bronze Age of the Upper Thames Valley. *European Journal of Archaeology* 5(2): 191-211.

SOFAER, J. 2006. Gender, bioarchaeology and human ontogeny, in R. Gowland and C. Knüsel (eds.) *Social Archaeology of funerary remains*. 155-167. Oxford: Oxbow Books.

SØRENSEN, M.L.S. 1997. Reading dress: the construction of social categories and identities in Bronze Age Europe. *Journal of European Archaeology* 5.1: 93-114.

SØRENSEN, M.L.S. 2010. Bronze Age bodiness – maps and coordinates, in K. Rebay-Salisbury, M.L.S. Sørensen and J. Hughes (eds.), *Body parts and bodies whole. Changing relations and meanings*. 54 – 63. Oxford: Oxbow Books.

STEEN, S.L. AND LANE, R.W. 1998. Evaluation of habitual activities among two Alaskan Eskimo populations based on musculoskeletal stress markers, *International Journal of Osteoarchaeology*. 8: 341-353.

TABOR, J. AND EVANS, C. 2010. *The Over Narrows (part v). Archaeological investigation in Hanson's Needingworth Quarry. The O'Connell Ridge East – The Site II Barrow*. Cambridge: Cambridge Archaeological Report 967.

TAYLOR, A. AND WOODWARD, P.J. 1985. A Bronze Age barrow cemetery at Roxton, Beds, *Archaeological Journal* 142: 73 - 149.

THIEME, F.P. AND SCHULL, W.J. 1957. Sex determination from the skeleton, *Human Biology*. 29.3: 242-273.

THOMAS, J. 2007. Three Bronze Age round barrows at Cossington: a history of use and re-use. *Transactions of the Leicestershire Archaeology and History Society* 81. 35-64.

THOMSON, A. 1899. The sexual differences of the foetal pelvis, *Journal of Anatomy and Physiology*. 33: 359-380.

THORPE, I.J.N. 2006. Fighting and feuding in Neolithic and Bronze Age Britain and Ireland, in T. Otto, H. Thrane, and H. Vandkilde (eds.) *Warfare and society: archaeological and anthropological perspectives*. 141-165. Denmark: Aarhus University Press.

TILLEY, C. 1991. Interpreting material culture, in I. Hodder (ed.), *The meaning of things*: 185-194. London: Routledge.

VANDKILDE, H. 2006. Warriors and warrior institutions in Copper Age Europe, in T. Otto, H. Thrane, and H. Vandkilde (eds.) *Warfare and society: archaeological and anthropological perspectives*. 393-422. Denmark: Aarhus University Press.

VAN GENNEP, A. 1960 [1909]. *The rites of passage*, translated by M.B. Vizedom and G.L. Caffee. Chicago: University of Chicago Press.

VATCHER, F. DE M. AND VATCHER, H.L. 1976. The excavation of a round barrow near Poor's Heath, Risby, Suffolk, *Proceedings of the Prehistoric Society* 42: 263 – 292.

VERDERY, K. 1999. *The Political lives of dead bodies. Reburial and postsocial change*. Chichester, West Sussex: Columbia University Press.

WALKER, P.L. 2005. Greater sciatic notch morphology: sex, age and population differences, *American Journal of Physical Anthropology*. 127: 385-391.

WALKER, P.L. 2008. Sexing skulls using discriminant function analysis of visually assessed traits, *American Journal of Physical Anthropology*. 136: 39-50.

WATKINS, T. 1982. The excavation of an Early Bronze Age cemetery at Barns Farm, Dalgety, Fife, *Proceedings of the Society of Antiquaries of Scotland* 112: 48 – 141.

WATTS, M. AND QUNNELL, H. 2001. A Bronze Age cemetery at Elburton, Plymouth, *Proceedings of the Devon Archaeological Society* 59: 11 – 43.

WEISS, E. 2010. Cranial muscle markers: a preliminary examination of size, sex and age effects, *HOMO – Journal of Comparative Human Biology*. 61: 48-58.

WELFARE, H. 1976-77. A beaker cist at Newbiggingmill Quarry, Lanarkshire, *Proceedings of the Society of Antiquaries of Scotland*: 108: 73 – 79.

WESSEX ARCHAEOLOGY 2005. *Boscombe Down phase V excavations, Amesbury, Wiltshire, 2004. Post-excavation assessment and report and proposals for analysis and final publication*. Salisbury: Wessex Archaeology Report 56240.02.

WESSEX ARCHAEOLOGY 2008. *Lower Camp, Boscombe Down, Amesbury, Wiltshire. Assessment of the results of a watching brief undertaken during the upgrading*. Salisbury: Wessex Archaeology Report 53535.01.

WESSEX ARCHAEOLOGY 2008. *Land to the north of Poundbury Farm, Poundbury, Dorchester, Dorset. Post-excavation assessment report and updated product design for analysis and publication.* Salisbury: Wessex Archaeology Report 60024.01.

WEST, S. 1990. *West Stow, Suffolk: The prehistoric and Romano-British occupations.* East Anglian Archaeology 48. Bury St. Edmonds: Suffolk County Planning Department.

WHELAN, M. K. 1991a. Gender and historical archaeology: eastern Dakota patterns in the 19th century, *Historical Archaeology* 25.4: 17-32.

WHELAN, M. K. 1991b. Gender and archaeology: mortuary studies and the search for the origins of gender differentiation, in D. Walde and N. D. Willows (eds.), *The archaeology of gender.* Proceedings of the 22nd annual conference of the Archaeological Association of the University of Calgary: 358-365. Canada: The University of Calgary Archaeological Association.

WILD, C. A Bronze Age cremation cemetery at Allithwaite, Cumbria, *Transactions of the Cumberland and Westmorland Antiquarian and Archaeological Society 3rd Series* 3: 23 – 50.

WILLIAM, J.H. AND HOWARD-DAVIES, C. 2004. Excavations on a Bronze Age cairn at Hardendale Nap, Shap, Cumbria, *Archaeological Journal* 161: 11 – 53.

WOODWARD, A. 2000. *British Barrows: A matter of life and death.* Stroud: Tempus.

WOODWARD, A. 2002. Beads and beakers: heirlooms and relics in the British Early Bronze Age. *Antiquity.* 76: 1040-1047.

WOODWARD, A., HUNTER, J., IXER, R., ROE, F., POTTS, P.J., WEBB, P.C., WATSON, J.S. AND JONES, M.C. 2006. Beaker Age bracers in England: sources, functions and use. *Antiquity* 80: 530-543

WOODWARD, A.B. AND WOODWARD, P.J. 1996. The topography of some barrow cemeteries in Bronze Age Wessex. *Proceedings of the Prehistoric Society*: 62: 275-291.

www.ingramcontent.com/pod-product-compliance
Lightning Source LLC
Chambersburg PA
CBHW061008030426

42334CB00033B/3404